Trails & Treks of Missouri & Northern Arkansas

By
Kelly Frey
&
Steve Baron

Prayer of the Woods

"I am the heat of your hearth on the cold winter nights,
the friendly shade screening you from the summer sun,
and my fruits are refreshing draughts
quenching your thirst as you journey on.
I am the beam that holds your house,
the board of your table, the bed on which you lie,
and the timber that builds your boat.
I am the handle of your hoe, the door of your homestead,
and the wood of your cradle.
I am the bread of kindness and the flower of beauty.
Ye who pass by, listen to my prayer. Harm me not."

—Author unknown

Published by Show–Me Outdoors.

ISBN 0–9649525–9–9

Book design & production by O'Neal Design, St. Louis, Missouri.

Trails & Treks of Missouri & Northern Arkansas printed and bound in
the United States of America.

On the cover:
Klepzig Mill, Missouri
Kings Bluff Falls, Arkansas
Hawksbill Crag, Arkansas

Table of Contents

Legend

———————————— Road—Main

———————————— Road—Rural

———————————— Trail

— — — — — — — Alternate Trail / Trail Shortcut*

•••••••••••••••••••••••••• Overlook

———————————— Creek

〰〰〰〰〰 River

Lake

TH Trailhead

P Parking

C Camping

* Areas with more than 2 trails may have trail designations
  other than the solid and dashed lines shown here.

Trails at a Glance—Missouri

SOUTHERN MISSOURI

	Trail	Miles	Rating	Trail Notes	Page
1.	Big Oak Tree State Park Boardwalk Trail Bottomlands Trail	1.25 1.5	Easy Easy	Stroll through Missouri's "ancient forest" where you can stand at the base of a 140' tree, or wrap your arms around a trunk that is over 17' in circumference!	8
2.	Blair Creek	20.6	Easy	A backpacker's trail for sure! Get a taste of the Ozark Trail.	11
3.	Busiek State Park	7–15	Mod.–Diff.	Radical elevation changes for this nearby Branson trail create fabulous views within a surprisingly remote atmosphere.	15
4.	Coyote Trail	3	Easy	Feels so much like *Dances With Wolves* that all you're missing is Kevin Kostner!	18
5.	Crane Lake	4.5	Moderate	Ideal family trail or day hike get-a-way.	20
6.	Devil's Backbone McGarr Bridge Trail Backbone Trail	6	Moderate	After discovering the unique features of this trail, take a side trip to nearby Rockbridge for a fantastic meal of fresh salt-baked trout!	23
7.	Grand Gulf Northwest Rim Trail Chasm Trail	1 .25	Easy Easy–Mod.	This "Little Grand Canyon" of the Ozarks is a must see!	26

Trails at a Glance—Missouri

SOUTHERN MISSOURI

v

Trails at a Glance—Missouri

SOUTHERN MISSOURI

Trail	Miles	Rating	Trail Notes	Page
15. McCormick Lake	4.2	Mod.–Diff.	This trail holds fabulous bluff top vistas of the Eleven Point River with camping options on either end.	48
16. Noblett Loop	8	Easy–Mod.	The gentle terrain of this trail becomes somewhat challenging as infrequent usage keeps paths faint.	50
17. North Fork Loop	12	Moderate	Not heavily used, this loop can be hiked on it's own or connected with the longer backpacking trail—Ridge Runner.	53
18. Paddy Creek Wilderness Slabtown Bluff Trail Paddy Creek Trail Big Piney Trail	1.75 1 17	Moderate	Pack your overnight gear and spend time on this 17 mile loop that displays everything from freshwater springs designing steep creeks, to rocky blufflines providing spectacular vistas.	55
19. Piney Creek Wilderness	3–13	Mod.–Diff.	Rugged and remote, this trail can be difficult to follow. Bring a topo map and compass!	58
20. Raccoon Hollow	5	Easy	Pack a lunch and hike to the bluffline at this trail's end for an overlooking view of the North Fork River.	60

Trails at a Glance—Missouri

SOUTHERN MISSOURI

Trail	Miles	Rating	Trail Notes	Page
21. Ridge Runner Trail	22	Mod.–Diff.	Running between the North Fork River and Noblett Lake, this backpacking trail holds fabulous scenery spots scattered within terrain traditional to the Ozarks.	62
22. Ritter Springs	1–2	Easy	Easy hiking within a network that offers varied lengths and pleasant scenery—a great outing for the family.	65
23. Roaring River Firetower Trail Eagles Nest Trail Devil's Kitchen Trail Pibern Trail River Trai Deer Trail	3.5 2.3 1.5 1.5 .7 .2	Moderate Moderate Moderate Moderate Easy East	This park housing the pleasant winding stream of Roaring River offers everything from fabulous day hiking to fly fishing, as well as weekend cabin rentals and spots for family recreation.	66
24. Rocky Falls	2–9	Easy–Difficult	This spectacular cascading waterfall can be a simple family picnic or a base camp for some fabulous side trips.	69
25. Sam A. Baker State Park Mudlick Mountain Trail Shut-Inns Trail	12 1.5	Difficult Easy	From the vistas of Mudlick Mountain to the shut-ins of Big Creek, this park is perfect for families, hikers, and backpackers.	72

Trails at a Glance—Missouri

SOUTHERN MISSOURI

Trail	Miles	Rating	Trail Notes	Page
26. Springfield Nature Center Trails	5–6	Easy	Highpoint vistas, rocky creeks, glades and a lake—all this packed within minutes of the Springfield metro area!	75
27. Victory Horse Trail	18	Moderate	An Ozark Trail section winding through mild terrain hikers should be sure to carry water with them.	78
28. Wappapello Lake	15	Mod.–Diff.	Beautiful lakeside hiking that exchanges "up-close" shoreline glimpses for expansive views along the elevated ridgetops.	81
29. White River Bluffs Trail	1.6	Easy	After hiking this scenic little trail, take a quick tour of the trout hatchery, or spend some time fishing.	85
30. Whites Creek Trail	21	Mod.–Diff.	A fabulous backpacking loop with a perfect campsite mid-way through right alongside the Eleven Point River.	87

CENTRAL MISSOURI

Trail	Miles	Rating	Trail Notes	Page
31. Bell Mountain	9	Mod.–Diff.	Little usage and gorgeous scenery make this a fabulous destination for a quiet day's hike—might bring a map and compass though.	90

Trails at a Glance—Missouri

CENTRAL MISSOURI				
Trail	Miles	Rating	Trail Notes	Page
32. Berryman Trail	24	Mod.–Diff.	A definite overnight, unless you're up for a long day of mountain biking.	93
33. Cedar Creek	9	Moderate	This giant trail network offers optional hiking lengths through a variety of terrain packed with hidden and spectacular highlights.	96
34. Coakley Hollow	2	Easy	Geological fascinations, lakeside views, natural springs and rocky glades are all packed in this pleasant little trail.	100
35. Grand Glaize Trail	2.5	Easy	Rolling through the hardwoods and winding between hollows, this is a fabulous fall hike.	102
36. Ha Ha Tonka State Park			A favorite state park of this author, come prepared for an awesome day of exploration within this feature packed corner of Lake of the Ozarks.	104
Dell Rim Trail	.5	Easy–Mod.		
Castlebluff Trail	.5	Easy–Mod.		
Colosseum Trail	.5	Easy–Mod.		
Island Trail	.75	Easy–Mod.		
Turkey Den Hollow	.75	Easy–Mod.		
Devil's Kitchen Trail	1	Easy–Mod.		
Quarry Trail	1.5	Easy–Mod.		
Spring Trail	1.5	Easy–Mod.		

Trails at a Glance—Missouri

CENTRAL MISSOURI

Trail	Miles	Rating	Trail Notes	Page
37. Hawn State Park Whispering Trail Pickle Creek Trail	4–10	Moderate	Taken as a day hike or overnight, this trail is sure to thrill you with tremendous geology and continuous trail highlights.	107
38. Johnson's Shut-Ins	2.5	Easy	Reserve spots for overnight camping well in advance—it's very popular, but don't miss it.	110
39. Kaintuck Trail	3–15	Mod.–Diff.	A massive natural bridge is only one of this trail's many beauties and highlights.	112
40. Lake of Ozarks Woodland Trail Trail of 4 Winds Fawn Ridge Trail Squaw's Revenge Trail Lakeview Bend Trail	6 6 2.5 2.0 1	Easy Easy Easy Easy Easy	With a beautiful campground located along the shoreline of Lake of the Ozarks most pristine spot, this park and it's trails reside in a fabulous setting.	117
41. Mina Sauk Falls Trail	3	Easy	Springtime is the time to see the masterpiece of this trail—Missouri's tallest waterfall.	122
42. Ozark Trail	200+	Difficult	The largest trail network in Missouri, this trail, broken down into sections, winds through many hidden treasures.	125

Trails at a Glance—Missouri

CENTRAL MISSOURI

Trail	Miles	Rating	Trail Notes	Page
43. Pickle Springs	2	Easy	If you are anywhere near this part of the state, don't miss a chance to experience this tiny hidden jewel of Missouri.	127
44. Rockbridge State Park Rockbridge Trail Springbrook Trail Sinkhole Trail	 .5 2.4 1.5	 Easy Easy–Mod. Easy	Amazing geology packed within a fabulous wilderness setting, yet easily accessible for all types of hikers.	129
45. Rockpile Mountain	8–11	Mod.–Diff.	Mild in terrain but without markers, this hike centered around viewing a simple "pile of rocks" is pretty cool.	133
46. Rocky Top Trail	3	Moderate	The best trail in Lake of the Ozarks State Park!	136
47. St. Francois State Park Pike Run Trail Mooner's Hollow Trail Swimming Deer Trail Missouri Trail	 11 3 2.7 .5	 Moderate Moderate Moderate Easy	This park is another display of this side of the state's tremendous wealth in wilderness scenery. If hiking Pike Run, bring water!	138
48. Silver Mines Trail	1–3	Easy	Running alongside the St. Francois River, you're sure to enjoy the scenery and maybe catch a kayaker or two in action.	140

Trails at a Glance—Missouri

Trails at a Glance—Missouri

	Trail	Miles	Rating	Trail Notes	Page
NORTHERN MISSOURI					
54.	Graham Cave	1–3	Easy	Rich in history and unique in structure, Graham Cave is ideal for family outings, or a relaxing afternoon outdoors.	160
55.	Green Rock Trail	10	Moderate	Linking two of St. Louis's best wilderness areas, this trek is sure to be a hiking favorite.	162
56.	Lewis and Clark Trail	5.3–8.2	Moderate	Bordering the Katy Trail, you could combine a small hike with an afternoon bike ride.	165
57.	Lone Spring Trail	3–6	Easy–Mod.	Winding through the shallow hollows of a pristine forest, this is a pleasant and easy afternoon stroll.	167
58.	Rockwoods			This fabulous wilderness reserve, once a St. Louis secret, has been discovered as an awesome hiking and walking area. No dogs allowed however, so unfortunately the four-legged friend stays at home.	169
	Lime Kiln Loop	3.25	Moderate		
	Rock Quarry Trail	2.25	Moderate		
	Trail Among the Trees	1.5	Moderate		
	Turkey Ridge	2	Moderate		
59.	Washington State Park			Don't miss the Indian rock carvings (petroglyphs) that are a historic highlight of this beautiful state park.	172
	1,000 Steps Trail	1.5	Easy		
	Opossum Track Trail	3	Easy		
	Rockywood Trail	10	Moderate		

Trails at a Glance—Missouri / Arkansas

NORTHERN MISSOURI

Trail	Miles	Rating	Trail Notes	Page
60. Weston Bend State Park	.5–3	Easy	Check out the quaint and historic town of Weston during your visit to this park.	174
61. White Bison Trail (Lone Elk Park)	4	Easy	An excellent picnic place and educational outing for kids as well as a beautiful hike.	176

NORTHERN ARKANSAS

Trail	Miles	Rating	Trail Notes	Page
62. Alum Cove Trail	1	Easy	Centered around this area's largest natural bridge, Alum Cove is a creation masterpiece.	180
63. Buffalo River Trail (Boxley to Ponca)	11	Mod.–Diff.	Running the ridge of the Buffalo's upper section, this trail is packed with tremendous views, and houses plenty of trail highlights.	182

Trails at a Glance—Arkansas

NORTHERN ARKANSAS

Trail	Miles	Rating	Trail Notes	Page
64. Buffalo River Trail	10	Difficult	Hiking this trail will cause you to question whether you really are in the Midwest.	185
65. Cow Creek Trail	12	Difficult	This trail rises to some incredible highpoints through some challenging climbs, but also contains the serenity of a Buffalo River gravel bar that makes for a splendid campsite.	189
66. Cecil Creek Loop	7.4	Mod.–Diff.	Criss-crossing Cecil Creek in the lower portions, offering spectacular views on the upper, and highlighting a few old homesteads in between, this trail is rich in variety.	192
67. Centerpoint Trail	8	Mod.–Diff.	Numerous highlights packed within the unmatched wilderness of Arkansas, make the uphill challenges on your way out well worth the effort.	197
68. Glory Hole	2	Easy	With water formations being the main attraction, this hike is a definite must after a good, solid rain!	199

Trails at a Glance—Arkansas

NORTHERN ARKANSAS

Trail	Miles	Rating	Trail Notes	Page
69. Hawksbill Crag	3	Easy	The drive to the trailhead is an adventure in itself and the trail's destination could pass for a magazine cover!	202
70. Hemmed-In Hollow	.5–8.5	Difficult	One of Arkansas's famed highlights and a definite showpiece for the Buffalo River area—don't miss it!	204
71. Hide-Out Hollow	2	Easy	A perfect setting for "Cowboys and Indians" this remote spot encircled by one giant bluffline possesses scenic highlights as well as secret discoveries.	206
72. Indian Rockhouse	5	Mod.–Diff.	Another trail packed with Arkansas wonders, this trail is slightly easier and more accessible with other family type options available as well.	208
73. Kings Bluff	2	Easy	A massive bluffline and winding creek come together to bring a waterfall standing second only to Hemmed-In Hollow.	211
74. Lost Valley	3.5	Easy–Mod.	A tremendous short trail leading into an "enchanted" like forest!	214

Trails at a Glance—Arkansas

NORTHERN ARKANSAS

Trail	Miles	Rating	Trail Notes	Page
75. Pedestal Rocks	2.6	Easy	The spectacular scenery and unique rock formations combine to produce an unmatched bluffline.	217
76. Pigeon Roost Trail	8.4	Easy–Mod.	Backing up alongside beautiful Beaver Lake, this trail offers fabulous day hiking or provides campsites available for overnights.	220
77. Round Top Mountain	4	Moderate	Another hidden jewel for the Arkansas mountains, this little trail is a picturesque place—striking in scenery and unrivaled in blufftop views.	222
78. Shores Lake Trail	8–14.5	Mod.–Diff.	Easy if hiked from White Rock Mountain down and quite the challenge in reverse, this trail is packed both ways with awesome stuff!	225
79. White Rock Mountain	2	Easy	Reserve a rustic cabin and make a weekend out of this indescribable place—one of this author's favorite spots ever!	228

Author's Foreword & Acknowledgements

The same intense love for the outdoors that sparked the interest and idea behind publishing our first book, *Trails of Missouri*, has led to the compilation of this new collection of trails centered not only within Missouri's wilderness, but Northern Arkansas's as well. Sharing the same dream of publishing trail notes and adventures, Steve and I have worked hard together in putting this collection of Missouri and Northern Arkansas highlights into book form. Our hiking endeavors and desire to write about them however, would not have been accomplished had it not been for the motivation, direction and "on trail" support of a few key individuals. First and foremost, we extend an enormous thanks and appreciation to our third hiking partner, Ruth Baron, whose help in logistical arrangements, preparation, and fabulous photography skills, has made this publication a reality.

Aside from the hiking help of Ruth, Steve and I also want to mention others who have taken part by accompanying us on a wilderness adventure, or assisting in compiling stacks of raw data. My sister Tracy Frey, my father Ted Frey and my friend Dwight Gold have all shared trail miles with me at some point in this book, and their company has been much appreciated. My mother, Billie Frey has been the faithful proofreader and grammar consultant, as well as continual teacher in the area of creative writing. A special thanks also goes out to Larry Jacobs, who played a crucial role in saving and recovering much of our recorded, field-researched information from a devastating computer virus. And finally, our word-processed work, along with hand-drawn maps, and spontaneous ideas have all been beautifully pieced together and organized into what you see on these pages, by Steven O'Neal at his graphic design company, O'Neal Design.

On a broader note, Steve and I would both like to thank the many individuals within the Mark Twain National Forest, Conservation Department and Department of Natural Resources for their expertise, suggestions and help in formulating trail information within their respective districts.

Trinity and Katy — our faithful four-legged backpackers

Introduction

The selection of trails for this guide was made in efforts to provide a solid variety of trails in length, difficulty, highlights and location. Each trail write-up is accompanied by a map, and provides content concerning location, length and general information for the hike.

A specific difficulty level is not given for each trail simply because the level of trail difficulty is very much dependent on one's general fitness and hiking experience. If you are inexperienced, just getting into hiking and backpacking, or not in the best physical shape, plan to take a little extra time for your hike. Some of the trails in this book hold some rather surprising changes in elevation and steep climbs that will be noted under the "comments" section of each trail, but most Missouri trails can be hiked by anyone, provided adequate time is allotted relative to one's ability and/or experience. As you start to hike more regularly, you will begin to get an idea of your pace and how much can be covered in one hour, or in one day, at the particular pace that's right for you. As a general guide, three miles an hour, with a pack on, and over varied terrain, is a fairly steady pace. Two miles an hour is probably more realistic, and less than that if terrain is extremely rugged or frequent stops are needed.

The majority of Missouri trails contain markers or blazes identifying direction of travel and eliminating confusion that results from trail junctions or creek crossings. A few Missouri trails however, do lack adequate provisions for trail identification due to insufficient markings along the trail's route. Some of the wilderness preserve areas are especially prone to this, and therefore should be hiked with a map and compass in efforts to ensure that you remain accurate in maintaining the desired course. As mentioned above, each of the trails outlined in this guide are accompanied by a basic map outlining the trail's general route, length and direction. These maps however, will provide more specific information when combined with the corresponding topographic map suggested for each trail.

Throughout this guide you will also notice certain areas specified as a BTV (Breath Taking View). These BTV areas serve to highlight a chosen area or point of interest as especially scenic, interesting or unique to Missouri, and the specified trail.

WHAT TO BRING

Having just encountered the newfound excitement of selecting and preparing for your day hike or backpacking trip, you sit down to ponder what items are necessary to bring. Below is a list of suggested items that are either essential, or helpful in aiding you on your trip.
- Hiking boots (preferably all leather and/or waterproof if backpacking)
- Socks (wool and/or synthetic blend, rather than cotton)
- Sock liners (polypropylene or Capilene)
- Lightweight, fast-drying shorts or pants
- Non-cotton shirt that wicks, rather than absorbs moisture and sweat
- Fleece or wool top for cooler weather or cool evenings

- This book and topographic maps
- Compass
- First-Aid Kit
- Water and water treatment mechanism
- Bandanna
- Outdoor knife
- Food and/or snack items high in energy
- Matches and/or lighter
- Raingear
- Insect repellent
- Camera
- Flashlight or headlamp
- Whistle
- Water sandals for wet crossings
- Hat
- Cooking stove and accessories if overnight
- Tent, rainfly, and tarp if overnight
- Sleeping bag and pad if overnight
- Dry change of clothes and socks if overnight
- Trowel and toilet paper
- Backpack, daypack or fanny pack

PRESERVING THE AREA

As hiking and backpacking become more popular, and backcountry areas become more accessible, special care needs to be taken in preserving the wilderness that creates the occasion to hike or backpack to begin with. Areas along the trail can be dangerously fragile in places and are easily damaged through carelessness, even if unintentional. In efforts to maintain the purity of nature's beauty, some suggestions are given below.

- Hike only on the trail. Cutting corners, hiking alongside the trail, or shortcutting up embankments can create erosion problems as well as deaden vegetation unnecessarily, thus detracting from the areas beauty.
- Camp in designated or already established areas whenever possible. Impact is high for overnight stays, damaging the area from tents, fire rings and human presence. If you spend the night out in the woods, you should be able to leave "without a trace." This means leaving no fire rings, no trash, and no damaged vegetation. Basically, no one should be able to tell that camp was ever made at your overnight spot.
- Protect and preserve the water. It is so easy to abuse our area's streams by dumping into them our leftover dinner, scraps from a dirty pot, or soap from cleaning your plate. Left-over food should be packed out with the trash, pots and pans can be cleaned with a pine cone or leaves first, and dishes can be "camper clean" without soap. If soap is an absolute must, use the biodegradable brands sparingly, but no soap at all is the best option for keeping our water clean, fresh and pure.

- Practice proper outdoor bathroom procedures. The outdoor toilet is not everyone's favorite subject but it cannot be avoided if one is out for longer than a day. A selective spot for bathroom duties should be at least 200 feet from the trail, and 200 feet from any water source. A small hole (also known as the "BIFF"—Bathroom In Forest Floor) needs to be dug and filled in when finished. If toilet paper is used, it should be burned and/or buried.

STATE PARKS, NATIONAL FORESTS, AND WILDERNESS AREAS

Missouri is fortunate to hold a sizeable amount of wilderness land under the combined protection of state parks, national forests, and wilderness areas.

Missouri's state park system is a fabulous collection of preserved areas diverse in landscape, geology, and natural wonders. From the Black River rapids carving out chutes through exposed rock, thus creating Johnson's Shut-Ins, to the towering stone wall remnants of Ha Ha Tonka, Missouri holds claim to some of the most extraordinary and unrivaled features of the Midwest. Managed by the Department of Natural Resources, the mission statement regarding the goal and philosophy in protecting state park land is "to preserve and interpret the state's most outstanding natural and cultural features, and to provide recreation". Although a bit more developed than wilderness areas, the state parks are built recreationally on the resources and features already present and naturally characteristic for that area. Unlike national forest and wilderness areas, hunting is also illegal within state park boundaries, making these regions an excellent haven for outdoor recreation during the weeks of open hunting season.

In addition to state parks, Missouri also features national forest areas, the prized jewel of which is the 1.5 million acres of Mark Twain National Forest preserved in sections spreading throughout southern Missouri. Originally created in the 1930's to preserve waterways, and re-establish forestlands where timber had been heavily harvested, national forest land currently offers timber and mining management, as well as recreational opportunities. Unlike state parks, national forests are protected and managed federally, with land being purchased from either states or individuals. Regulated logging, mining and hunting are allowed within the national forest domain, along with miles of trails accessible to hikers, mountain bikers, and equestrians.

It is within the boundaries of these federally protected, national forest areas, that wilderness areas reside. Wilderness areas are tracts of land designated by Congress to remain in a pristine state, thereby preserving undisturbed plots of federal land. With the goal in mind of maintaining the wilderness in its natural state, each wilderness area is protected from timber and mining management. Motorized equipment, and road construction of any sort, are totally prohibited. Currently, eight wilderness areas belong to Missouri, providing reservoirs for wildlife to inhabit, unique vegetative species to flourish, and forest stands to reside untouched. Due to the objective of preserving the undisturbed, pure nature of these wilderness tracts, trails leading through these areas are generally unmarked and require the use of topographic maps and compass to orient direction. Camping is allowed within wilderness area boundaries, but should be low-impact, primitive camping, located at least 100 feet from the trail.

WATER—IS IT SAFE?

As a general rule, no creek water is safe to drink without first being purified through a water filter, treated with a chemical such as iodine tablets, or simply boiled. Even the purest, clearest spring water could contain small amounts of bacteria, chemicals or viruses that cause illness if ingested without first being purified out. With the inconvenience and extra fuel requirements necessary for boiling water, iodine tablets, along with water filtration systems, have become the most common means of purifying water prior to drinking. Both methods rid the water of dangerous bacteria causing the most common illnesses such as Giradia, but iodine tablets, being a chemical treatment rather than a filter, leave a slight stale taste to the water dampening your enjoyment of a cool drink from the stream. A water purifier on the other hand, filters water through a series of small, microscopic pores, that catch hold of the bacteria and chemicals, leaving your water not only free of critters, but fresh and tasteful to drink. Most purifiers on the market now offer the ability to remove viruses from the water as well, something iodine tablets can't do. Whatever the choice, make sure you treat all water before drinking.

SEASONAL HIKING

The familiar statement concerning Missouri weather states: "If you don't like the current weather conditions, then stick around a few minutes and it will change." Unpredictable and constantly changing, weather in the Ozarks will always have you guessing and might catch you out on the trail unprepared if you're not careful. Keeping in mind that true preparation requires packing in extra clothing or raingear items for the all too often unforecasted weather changes, this section provides quick reference to probable conditions according to the seasons.

December, along with January, February and March, constitute much of the winter season in Missouri and are excellent months for hiking. Possessing most trails all to yourself, winter hiking can create a remote sense of seclusion and allow for a wonderfully pleasant hike, provided you're equipped with the proper gear. Snow, ice or rain are all precipitation possibilities, and temperatures could potentially drop below zero for short periods, but for the most part, Missouri winters are fairly mild, creating brisk, sunny afternoons that are ideal for hiking and backpacking. Vistas, overlooks, and views that scan the horizon are also much more apparent during this period, adding yet another plus to gathering up your winter gear for a winter hike. Should the occasion find you hiking in the midst of a long steady cold snap, creek beds become a haven for frozen water formations that add the final touches of winter beauty to your hike.

Spring approaches in March, but officially resides within the months of April and May, yielding fabulous hiking and outdoor activities for Missouri. Night time temperatures can still be a bit chilly, but day time highs range from pleasantly brisk to optimum and ideal, making this season highly popular for

4

outdoor enthusiasts. Typically, these months might be characterized by ample to excess precipitation that will most assuredly require packing in a rain jacket and/or pants. Large amounts of rain, however, can create an ideal opportunity for hikers as it opens up beautiful waterfalls and other displays created by the swift moving creeks. Also characteristic of this spring season is the budding of trees and blooming of wild flowers. Missouri trails contain a wide diversity of wild flower types that, scattered amongst the fields and mingled within the trees, add tremendous contrast with their striking colors. Dogwoods, redbuds and azaleas are common to the Ozarks as well, and are laced between the oak and hickory trees to accent the hardwood forest.

Spring graduates into the summer months of June, July and August, and settles into the season least ideal for hiking in the Midwest. Early parts of June are fabulous due to the ending of spring rains and the intermission preceding humidity and insect introduction commonly seen in July. If hiking within these extremely hot and humid months of summer, be certain to drink plenty of water, expect numerous chiggers and ticks, and plan on a slower than normal pace to allow for frequent breaks.

After the "Missouri mugginess" created by summertime heat dissipates, fall introduces a new vigor for hitting the trail during September, October and November. Temperatures and humidity both fall into pleasant ranges, and the turning of leaves within the thousands of acres of Missouri hardwood forest creates a fabulous hiking backdrop. Yellow, red and orange leaves carpet the trail, brightening the forested surroundings, and the sighting of deer and turkey add finishing touches to the pleasure of spending time in the woods. Be cautioned here not to be caught in the evenings without warm enough clothing. Daytime temperatures are wonderfully pleasant, but with the setting of the sun, temperatures could drop rather sharply, creating occasions to easily get chilled.

Trail Locator—
Missouri

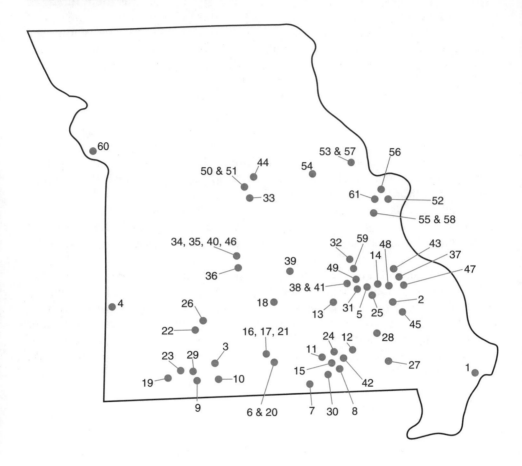

1. Big Oak Tree State Park
2. Blair Creek
3. Busiek State Park
4. Coyote Trail
5. Crane Lake
6. Devil's Backbone
7. Grand Gulf
8. Greer Springs
9. Henning State Forest
10. Hercules Glades
11. Klepzig Mill
12. Letter Look Trail
13. Loggers Lake
14. Marble Creek
15. McCormick Lake
16. Noblett Loop
17. North Fork Loop
18. Paddy Creek Wilderness
19. Piney Creek Wilderness
20. Raccoon Hollow
21. Ridge Runner Trail
22. Ritter Springs
23. Roaring River
24. Rocky Falls
25. Sam A. Baker State Park
26. Springfield Nature Center Trails
27. Victory Horse Trail
28. Wappapello Lake
29. White River Bluffs Trail
30. Whites Creek Trail
31. Bell Mountain

32. Berryman Trail
33. Cedar Creek
34. Coakley Hollow
35. Grand Glaize Trail
36. Ha Ha Tonka State Park
37. Hawn State Park
38. Johnson's Shut-Ins
39. Kaintuck Trail
40. Lake of Ozarks
41. Mina Sauk Falls Trail
42. Ozark Trail
43. Pickle SPrings
44. Rockbridge State Park
45. Rockpile Mountain
46. Rocky Top Trail
47. St. Francois State Park
48. Silver Mines Trail
49. Taum Sauk Trail
50. Three Creeks North
51. Three Creeks South
52. Chubb Trail
53. Cuivre River Trail
54. Graham Cave
55. Green Rock Trail
56. Lewis and Clark Trail
57. Lone Spring Trail
58. Rockwoods
59. Washington State Park
60. Weston Bend State Park
61. White Bison Trail
    (Lone Elk Park)

1. Big Oak Tree State Park

LOCATION: Located down by the bootheel, Big Oak Tree State Park is 11 miles south of East Prairie, Missouri. Take HWY 102 south from the junction of HWY 102 and YY. Signs will lead you directly to Big Oak Tree on your right.

LENGTH: Big Oak Tree has two trails that are 1.25 and 1.5 miles long.

COMMENTS: Big Oak Tree State Park is an absolutely incredible place that can best be described as a priceless piece of land, holding a collection of unrivaled trees, all matchless in age and stature. The over 1,000 acres of virgin bottomland forest that this park consists of, is home to several champion-sized trees that tell a story of survival throughout Missouri history. The timber and woodlands that once dominated terrain in the bootheel region, was slowly harvested by foresters in the 1800's in efforts to take advantage of the mineral-rich soil for agriculture. Rescued momentarily by the New Madrid earthquake that transformed much of the area into swampland, the remaining giant trees were protected from further clear-cutting until a system for drainage and levees was implemented. As the conversion from woodland to cropland continued once

The State Champion Bur Oak at Big Oak Tree State Park

8

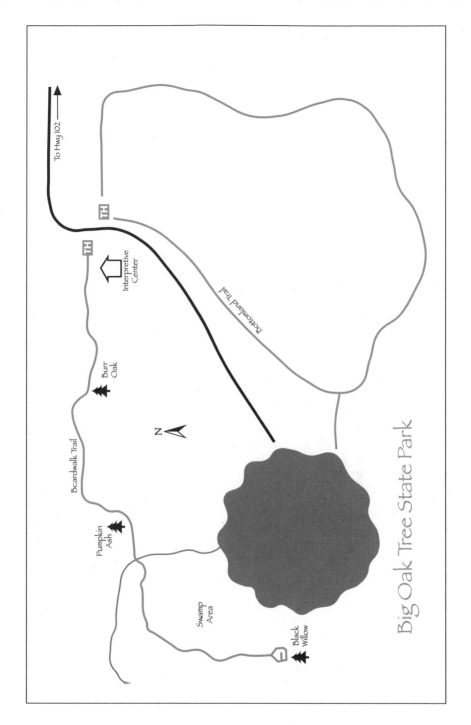

Big Oak Tree State Park

more, citizens of the region took notice of these magnificent lowland forests, and the detriment of their destruction. In the midst of the depression, business-men and area residents pooled their finances together to purchase one of the last tracts of land still possessing the extraordinary timber giants. Today that plot of land is known as Big Oak Tree State Park.

With several trees over 130 feet tall and an average canopy spread of 120 feet wide, Big Oak Tree is a virgin timber paradise, boasting of six state champion trees and two national champions. Living in the world of development and progress, trees of this stature, preserved within a forest of like peers, is truly an amazing, rare, and majestic sight. A stroll down the boardwalk that leads into the depths of this lowland forest, opens up a new appreciation for the outdoors and wilderness area that is taken so much for granted. If the opportunity arises to take you towards the bootheel, take time to visit this exceptional site.

TOPOGRAPHICAL MAPS: Bayouville

The Boardwalk Trail leads straight to the heart of this park's prized forest area, which is nestled within the swampland, and isolated from the surrounding agricultural farmland. Being completely boardwalked, this trail is of course easy to follow, and is also completely wheel-chair accessible. An interpretive center resides at the trail's beginning, which is excellent to tour through should you catch it open. Upon entering the forest via the boardwalk, you are instantly impressed by the collection of trees, that towering above you, stand amazingly straight and tall.

The first grand champion to greet you is the tremendous Burr Oak—a tree boasting of a 17'7" circumference, that extends skyward 142 feet claiming title as Missouri's largest tree. To think that at one time millions of Missouri acres once held trees of this potential, is quite astounding. As the boardwalk leads deeper into the forest, it winds through the swampland area displaying other champion trees that are each identifiable by a sign and marker. The national champion persimmon tree of 141 feet is viewed from this trail, as well as the pumpkin ash. The state champion black willow tree sets at the boardwalk's turn-around point, where two wooden benches also set for you to relax on. Now in the heart of the swampland area, if you're not completely overrun by mosquitoes, take some time to observe the waterfowl that also share this habitat.

Upon your return, which is a retracing of steps, take notice of some other more subtle signs of nature at work in this unique forestland. Mounds of dirt can be seen which have resulted from the fall of one of these towering giants pulling up pieces of the earth with its root system. Unfortunately several former champions have died in this park, including a sumac oak, 205" in circumference, and a smoke chestnut tree, 257" in circumference. Also of interest is the cypress tree root system which rises up out of the ground to act as an oxygen absorber and possibly a stabilizer, balancing out the massive tree's size. Keep your eyes open for many of these added little features, listen closely for the sounds of birds and wildlife, and enjoy your walk through Missouri's ancient forest!

2. Blair Creek

LOCATION: The trailhead for this hike can be found 3 miles down FS 2220, off P HWY, south of Bunker. From Bunker, travel 3 miles south down HWY 72, to P HWY on the south side. P HWY can also be accessed going north on HWY 72, 6 miles from Reynolds. Take P HWY south 2.5 miles to FS 2220, located on the left-hand side. FS 2220 extends 3 miles to the trailhead.

LENGTH: Blair Creek is a definite overnight excursion extending 20.6 miles in length.

COMMENTS: Another partial section of the Ozark Trail, this hiking segment stretches across an excellent variation and sampling of the wilderness scenery hidden within Missouri. It is the founding trail and original section of the Ozark Trail with a large portion of it extending across the privately owned Pioneer Forest. Because of this, some points along the way can be a bit foggy with markers being scarce. Otherwise, look for white diamonds or OT trail markers to determine your route.

One of the highlights of this trail is a very unique Missouri limnological feature known as "fen". A fen, which resembles a bog, yet slightly more elevated, is very unusual to this midwest area, holding some rare plant growth and vegetation, as well as uncommon microscopic creatures. Some literature describing the fen in greater detail is posted at the point where the trail and "fen" feature meet, so take a brief moment there to beef up on your science knowledge!

Throughout its entirety, the trail boasts of some gorgeous scenery, particularly from its southern section, as bluffs extend over the Current River to create a ridgetop for the trail to reside upon, as it peeks through trees to create multiple BTV's. During drier months water could be scarce so plan accordingly when outlining your trek. Overall the terrain for this trail is rough, but the variety of trees intermixed with scenic water formations and elevation changes, make this wilderness area a haven of beautiful sites to encounter and enjoy as you hike down the trail.

TOPOGRAPHICAL MAPS: Bunker

From the parking lot and start at FR 2220, the trail moves down through a cedar and hickory area leading to the crossing of Blair Creek at just under half a mile. After crossing the creek, the trail remains in the hollow for a bit and comes out onto a logging-type road that heads either up and to the right, or level and to the left. This is one of those "lack of adequate marking" spots. Stay to the left, following the logging road, and you will arrive at the trail's unique highlight of a Missouri fen. A fen resembles, and is very similar to a bog, yet

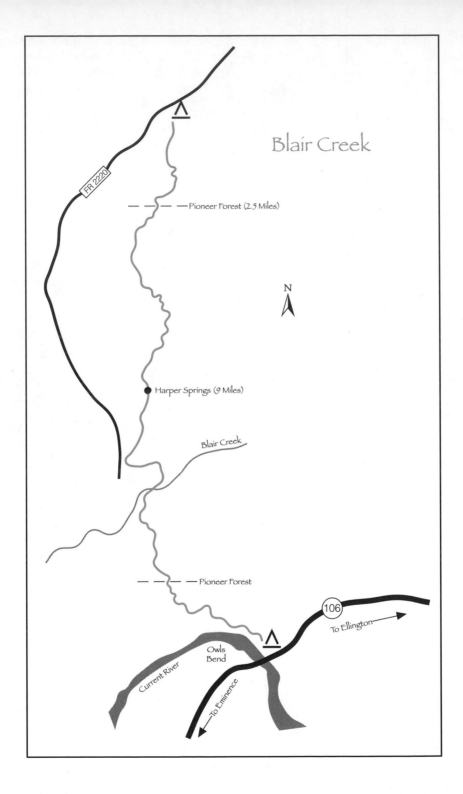

Blair Creek

FR 2220

— — — Pioneer Forest (2.5 Miles)

N

● Harper Springs (9 Miles)

Blair Creek

— — — Pioneer Forest

(106)
To Ellington

Owls
Bend

Current River

To Eminence

the fen's distinguishing characteristic is that while a bog has acidic still water, fens have non-acidic moving water. Unlike the bog, the minerals deposited into the fen from the moving water allow for growth of unusual vegetation; hence the presence of rare plants and organisms. It isn't necessarily a spectacular display of scenic beauty, but the very nature of its rarity is intriguing. Some posted information explains some details concerning its significance to this area, so take some time to appreciate and learn about this spot.

The trail skirts around this fen, across a creek, and begins to climb up by way of an old roadbed lined on either side with towering pines—a beautiful corridor and BTV. After passing through the pines, the trail moves alongside a creek on your left accompanied by a modest rock wall on your right. During the colder months, this bluffline transforms itself into a winter wonderland, acquiring a decor of long icicles and unusual ice formations. Along the creek, and then gradually ascending uphill, the trail moves toward the ridgetop where you will cross a logging road at 2.5 miles, entering into the privately owned Pioneer Forest. Across the road, the trail descends down into Barton Hollow, crossing a powerline path along the way. In Barton Hollow the trail comes up against a small creek which it follows slightly above, yet alongside, before eventually coming down and across it to outline the creek's opposite bank. The hollow here is beautiful, and with water in the creek a myriad of small waterfalls create an even prettier picture. Crossing the creek one last time, the trail begins its exit of Barton Hollow, initiating a gradual climb upward. Don't take this little climb lightly however, as it steepens before nearing the top at 3.5 miles where you flatten out to cross a road.

After crossing the road, the trail basically settles along a ridge for the next couple of miles, not changing much in elevation and offering gorgeous views to your right during periods of leaf-off. You will cross another logging road at 4.5, and afterwards pass by a huge boulder just off the trail to your left. This section along the ridge is laced with cedars and rocky glades—a beautiful stretch and excellent BTV. At approximately 6 miles, the trail dips down slightly into a hollow and comes back up to merge with a road which you will turn right on, following for the next mile. Situated on the ridge, this road offers views on either side with the hollows below—an excellent BTV during leaf-off. The road eventually leads down this ridge merging into Cedar Point, and at the bottom, the trail turns right to cross a creek at 7.5. There is a small clearing on the other side and once across, the trail heads uphill with views of the creek lingering below. Flattening out a bit in a cedar glade area, the trail crosses a creek and small logging road to end up alongside a bluffline. This small bluffline, although accenting the trail's beauty, becomes a bit overpowered by the larger more prominent rock face that resides just a bit further down. The trail remains content with hugging the ridgeside, continuing to offer BTV's while hovering over Blair Creek and the valley below. As the trail finally does move down off the ridge a bit, it crosses a logging road and heads down into the valley, following another road right, ¼ mile to Harper Springs which marks mile number 9.

After Harper Springs, the trail crosses a creek, and the road which you are on forks to the right heading up slightly. You will go through the cedar clearings followed by hardwood forest and at the top of this small climb, the trail crosses a logging road to head back down. At the bottom, you cross a creek, followed by a smaller creek with some interesting man made steps across it. The trail remains alongside the creek, making only minor changes in elevation while passing in and out of the alternate sections of cedar clearings and hardwood forest. If you watch closely you might catch a view of a large beaver dam at the 10.3 mile mark, on your left. At 11.5, you cross a logging road to head uphill until crossing another road that leads you to cross Blair Creek again (probably wet) at just over 12 miles.

For the next mile, the trail remains on the road until crossing a small creek, where it parts company with the road heading sharply left and back into the woods as the road veers right. At 13.5 the trail, residing a bit on the ridge, provides views to the left that look down into Holmes Hollow, location of a beautiful little unnamed spring and potential campsite. Just below this spring, the trail gently descends down, catching the aroma of fresh pine needles that lie scattered along the path, as it winds through a nice western-like stand of pines. The trail moves rather quickly through this pleasant area opening up into a spectacular panoramic BTV. Continue down the road, and the scenery will follow as views emerge in front of you now. Descending down through a cedar and hardwood mix, the trail crosses a creek at 17 miles. Although nearing the trail's end at this point, this creek area holds an excellent campsite on the left and offers a pleasant area for an overnight.

Cross the creek and the trail will wind back up to where it steadies out along the ridge momentarily, before heading back down to meet a small spring and yet another creek crossing at 18.5 miles. A roadbed then takes you to the right, directing your path for the next ¼ mile, before turning off to the left after another creek crossing. Off the road now, the trail crawls uphill offering views of the Current River that are like sneak previews of the fabulous scenery yet to come. Continuing this trek along the bluff, the trail moves away only briefly as it dips through a small hollow.

The final stretch is in front of you now, and in this last two mile section the trail has reserved the best for last, revealing the grand finale in the way of scenic views. BTV's continue alongside and to the right for much of the remaining length, eventually moving down from the ridge to meet with HWY 106. The sign here at 106 directs you across the bridge to continue the trail on the Current River's west side. This is a good choice if you are continuing your hike into the next section (Current River Section), but will bring you on the opposite side of the river from Owls Bend campground. If you are parked at Owls Bend, and wish to avoid swimming across the river to your car, the best route is to follow HWY 106 left for a short distance to the entrance of Owls Bend!

Hiking Tip — Pack Pins

If packing with an external frame pack, be sure and bring plenty of extra pack pins and retainers with you in case of needed repair while on the trail. These extras can be conveniently carried in the frame's extra holes that are normally used for size adjustment.

3. Busiek State Park

LOCATION: Busiek can be found approximately 22 miles south of Springfield, directly off Highway 65, on the east side.

LENGTH: The park has about 15 miles of trails scattered through 2,505 acres of forest. The trail outlined here is approximately 7 miles long.

COMMENTS: This area is surprisingly beautiful. During the spring months you will find it packed with numerous dogwood and redbud trees coloring the woodland landscape. The climbs bring you to some fabulous vista areas and there are even some creative water formations during the wet season. Hiking is rugged and the ascents are steep in places. The elevation climbs from 950' to about 1200' at the highest point. Water is plentiful, probably too much so during springtime, because it causes the entire trail to be wet. Be prepared for mud after a good rain! Trails are not marked but easy to follow.

TOPOGRAPHICAL MAPS: Day

The trail recommended for hiking, and that will be covered here, lies on the east side of the park, east of Highway 65. From the parking lot head south. You will actually begin the trail on the other side of the creek, and it will head south from there down a wide path that follows alongside the creek for a bit before entering into a cedar clearing. At this point you will see a path that leads uphill on your left. This is a short little climb that takes you up to Carter Cemetery, a unique little cemetery established in 1891, shared by a couple local families.

The main trail continues straight through a nice relatively flat area, mixed with cedars and dogwoods and a nice bluffline to your left. You will stay on this for one mile before crossing Woods Fork Creek again. There are about three different spots to cross here but to connect with the trail on the other side, the first crossing, to your right, is best. This will most likely be a wet crossing. Immediately after crossing, the trail will lead forward, and you will see a fork, that if taken left, will lead you alongside and back across the creek. Stay right, or straight ahead for the main trail. The trail remains fairly wide, passes through a field, and begins a slow, gradual climb upward in elevation. As it continues up, the trail passes a small wildlife pond on the left and shortly thereafter graduates to a small level clearing with an open expanse, giving hint to the scenery lying in wait ahead. There are the appearances of some camping areas here, and the trail splits to the left or right. To the right takes you up a small hill that dead ends at private property, so take the left route for the

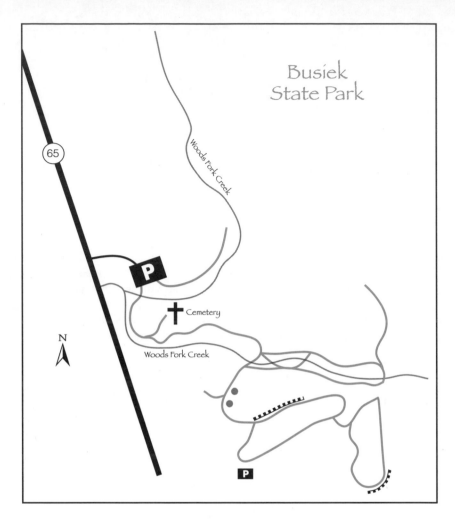

main trail which continues slightly downhill, passing by another pond on the left. Accompanied by the beginnings of a nice view that will be a big BTV at the top, the trail gradually moves towards the ridge above where the view comes into full bloom—a fabulous panoramic scene overlooking the Ozark highlands for miles.

Now on top, the trail empties onto a rocky plateau and glade like area, resembling that of Missouri's St. Francois Mountains. The trail splits here beginning a loop which you will hike by staying straight ahead cutting across the glade. At this point you have hiked about 1.75 miles. The trail continues slightly uphill and then back down. It crosses a small gully and then begins the trek up a steep incline that ends at a remote parking lot area, where the trail takes a sharp left back northeast to follow along the ridge. Starting down, a nice view opens up in front of you, narrowing a bit as you descend slightly. At 2.5 you reach another intersection that if taken left will loop back around to the rocky glade area. You will stay straight and shortly thereafter reach a second fork which takes you right and heads south. This is a the beginning of another little loop with hefty climb to the top taking you to 1200 feet. You know you're at the top when you see an old blue pickup truck door leaning against a tree on your left (We left our mark with the addition of an old leather glove in the door handle, which we found on the ground beneath it!). The trail doesn't stay on top very long before heading down an incline equal in steepness to what you just hiked up. The view on the way down is fabulous—a definite BTV.

At the bottom of this huge hill, you are greeted by a little creek and the trail heads to your left, or back west towards the completion of the mini loop. You will cross another part of the creek before reaching the fork that began the loop. Stay right, here, and then take another right to begin heading back on the larger loop. You have hiked about 4 miles. The trail proceeds up and along a ridge with a cedar glade appearance and some nice views on both sides. You come out of the cedar area to the large glade area with panoramic BTV and fork which is the completion of the larger loop. Take the trail back down to your right and it will eventually bring you back to the parking lot. With the completion of this loop you have hiked 5 miles and it will be a little under 2 miles back to the parking lot.

Flowers of a Dogwood Tree

4. Coyote Trail

Prairie State Park

LOCATION: Coyote Trail is located within Prairie State Park in Barton County. From Lamar, take HWY 160 west, about 16 miles to HWY NN. From NN, turn west again down Central Road, leading to Prairie State Park.

LENGTH: The Coyote Trail is a 3 mile long loop.

COMMENTS: This trail, as well as the entire Prairie State Park, proved to be a surprising favorite. Entering the park through the rugged timber-framed entrance, you are immediately immersed in thousands of acres of golden prairie land scattered with buffalo. It needs only the presence of a few tee-pees, a buckskin horse, and Kevin Kostner to confirm that you have just entered a scene from "Dances with Wolves". With waving reflections of various gold shaded colors, long grains come alive as the wind whips through this massive prairie land bringing a soft whistle through the air. Rare and unique, this preserved tract of rolling hills and tall grasses with brilliant colors, was once the common landscape for Western Missouri. Having lost 99.5% of all native prairie grassland, Missouri is fortunate to possess such a priceless preserve of 3,500 acres.

TOPOGRAPHICAL MAPS: Mindenmines

This park is excellent for day hiking, for a bit of Indian researching, and for family outings. Bison and elk can be seen in the park along with over 25 other species of plants and animals that are either rare or endangered. Fall and spring are definitely the times to visit this treasure piece, as springtime boasts of a tremendous wildlife display, and fall shines the bright golden grass colors. The visitor's center has excellent educational and informative material that would be especially entertaining for kids and families. Camping is also available within the shade of a nice little grove of trees close to the Coyote Trailhead, but facilities are primitive. Besides the Coyote Trail, Prairie State Park also offers two other trails, including a backpacking trail with an overnight site in the natural area.

The Coyote Trail begins off the road by the camping area. This trail holds a beautiful display of prairie vistas and wildlife viewing opportunities. In hiking this trail, electric fences are encountered that are put into place to contain the bison. At points of crossing, these fences are insulated, giving hikers the opportunity to crawl through to the next field safely! The trail is easy to follow as it weaves and winds through the landscapes of grasses. Marked in yellow, it loops in a counter-clockwise direction, with a white connector trail down the midsection to allow for a shorter hike if desired. At the trail's halfway point, on the southern end, it gently rolls down and comes to an intersection with the green trail, which is Gay Feather Trail. Taking the green route leads across Middle Drywood Creek to the Gay Feather Trail loop of 1.5 miles. If you wish to extend your hike a bit more even, take this spur on past the loop and over across the road to Drover's Trail. Drover's moves through the East Drywoods area for another 2.5 miles, and then on to the park's backpacking camp as well.

Staying on the main route of the Coyote Trail, proceed right at the green and yellow trail intersection and head across the rolling prairie terrain towards West Drywood Creek. The trail will loop back around to your starting point where you can crawl back through the bison fence and back to the trailhead.

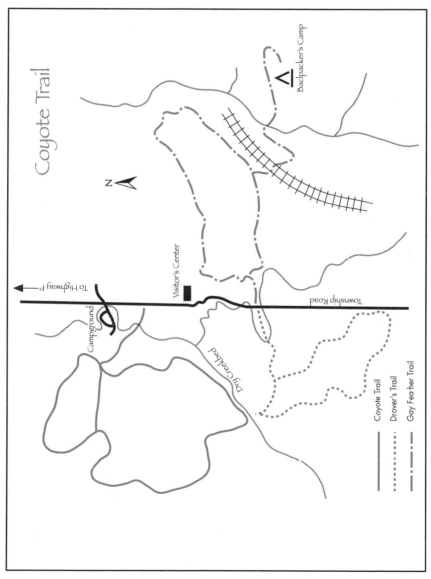

5. Crane Lake

LOCATION: Crane Lake turn-off is 3 miles down from the Marble Creek Campground on HWY E. Turn west down FR 124 (FH-69), a dirt road, and travel 4.5 miles. Turn south onto Crane Pond gravel road to the picnic area of Crane Lake. Crane Lake can also be accessed off HWY 49 south from Ironton. From HWY 49, turn east at Chloride onto FR 124 (FH-69) and then south onto Crane Pond Road.

LENGTH: The loop around Crane Lake is approximately 4.5 miles.

COMMENTS: A most ideal place to spend the day, Crane Lake not only offers this gorgeous 4.5 mile hike, but also serves as an excellent summer swimming spot or afternoon fishing place. The loop trail encircling the lake also dips down into the Crane Pond Creek area offering spectacular displays of rushing water as it carves out paths between multi-colored rocks. Views from atop the dam are equally as splendid, as is the shoreline path that the trail adopts along Crane Lake's waterline. Adjoining the trail's southern end is the Ozark Trail's Marble Creek section, an 8 mile stretch extending to Marble Creek campground located northeast of the Crane Lake area. Combining the two trails is a wonderful match-up, but keep in mind that Crane Lake is a day use area only, so any overnight camping needs to be either on the Ozark Trail portion of the hike, or at the Marble Creek Campground. Beautiful and relaxing with just the perfect length hike for an afternoon's exercise, a visit to Crane Lake provides all the outdoor ingredients for a full day's adventure.

TOPOGRAPHICAL MAPS: Lesterville

Beginning from Crane Lake, the trail splits to traverse along the shore on either side of the lake, encircling it with a 4 mile loop. Either route will lead to the Ozark Trail and Marble Creek, although the north side of the lake might offer a bit more scenery and will be the trail chosen for this walk through.

   The trail begins to the left as you face the lake and starts along the shoreline (past the restrooms) on even terrain. As you progress down the trail you will notice the rocky nature of the area and the pleasant mixture of hardwoods and pines. After looping around a very miniature cove of this lake, the trail begins veering deeper into the forest leaving behind any glimpses of the glassy serene water just viewed. Turning back towards the lake after winding through the wooded landscape, the trail leads to a large boulder on your left that marks the one mile point. At this point the lake is well into view again and the trail

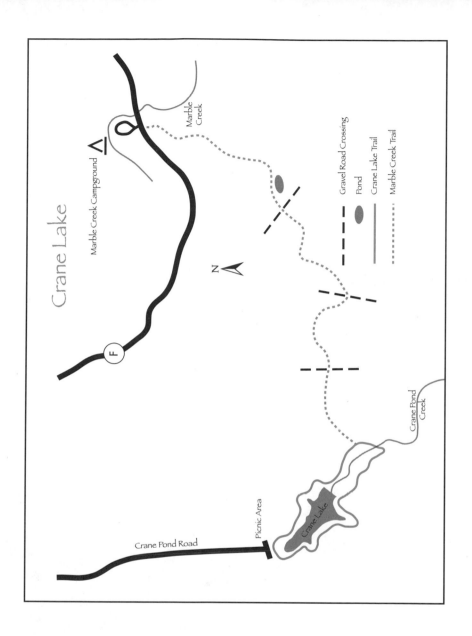

Crane Lake

Marble Creek Campground

Marble Creek

Gravel Road Crossing

Pond

Crane Lake Trail

Marble Creek Trail

N

F

Crane Pond Creek

Crane Lake

Picnic Area

Crane Pond Road

splits; right leading to the dam, and left uphill to a wonderful little rocky area and beautiful view overlooking the lake. Continue through this BTV and the panorama continues with bluffs protruding out from the trees straight across, and glimpses of the dam down and to the right. During seasons of rain, water spills over the dam and the sound of rushing water can be heard as the trail begins to descend down to the creek below. As you come off the plateau the trail winds down a rocky section lined with huge boulders on the left, and empties out into the creek that rushes water through a maze of boulders creating a beautiful water scene. Continuing to follow alongside the creek and heading downstream, the trail stays along the bank to provide further glimpses of the dazzling water formations before heading up to a level above the creek, and opening up into a field at the 2 mile mark.

Skirt around the right side of the field and the trail comes to a junction which is the joining point of the two trails of Crane Lake and Marble Creek. Turn right to continue the Crane Lake loop. The trail follows the lake around its opposite shore to traverse along Crane Pond Creek, which residing in the lowlands can hold some wet crossings and muddy terrain during springtime or wet season. Shortly after turning right from this intersection, the trail encounters the first of these wet areas as it crosses Crane Pond Creek. Although springtime rains might cause your crossing to be soggy, you will appreciate the incredible energy and beauty created by the water rushing between multi-colored rocks, and place the creek in competition with the lake for this trail's highlight.

Across the creek, stay left and head away from the wonderful rushing water sound to hike along an old roadbed that leads through a clearing area. Slowly climbing now, valley and creek are left behind as the trail moves up into the hardwoods. The creek is not forgotten however, as views from above give glimpses of this picturesque "water trail" still in full force below. Approaching the lake again at 3 miles, the trail forks offering a small spur to the right leading to the dam and more creek shut-in views. Left continues the trek down the main trail which loops around the finger like arm of the lake's northwest side, crossing a small tributary. Homeward bound now, the trail pretty much copies the contours of the lake's shoreline following it the remaining 1.5 miles back to the trailhead.

Crane Lake

6. Devil's Backbone

LOCATION: The Devil's Backbone area contains 2 trailheads.

McGarr Ridge Trail: This first trailhead allows access into the southern portion of the backbone and can be reached by turning south on Highway AP from CC, 1¼ miles east of Hammond's Camp. From AP turn west on Highway KK and look for a dirt road with accompanying sign on your right.

Backbone Trail: This second trailhead hits the north side and is four miles east of Highway 181 at Dora, on Highway CC.

LENGTH: McGarr Ridge Trail offers an 8.5 mile loop. The Backbone Trail loop connects in 6 miles.

COMMENTS: This is a beautiful area with some spectacular sites, but trails can be difficult to follow due to their interconnection with each other, as well as the lack of proper trail marking. Low lying trails can also be washed out from flooding, so hikers should take topo and compass with them.

Crooked Creek lies in a unique area with limestone rock outcroppings that create very scenic and pleasant surroundings. McGarr and Amber Springs are both highlights of this trail as well as the area's namesake, the "Backbone" itself. Water should not be difficult to come by on this trail due to the many springs, as well as the North Fork River.

TOPOGRAPHICAL MAPS: Cureall NW and Topaz

MCGARR RIDGE TRAIL

Starting from this trailhead at CC, the trail leads down a ridge for ½ mile until reaching a pond on the right, at which point the trail splits. Stay to the right, hiking along McGarr Ridge, which, situated 1000 feet above sea level, yields outstanding scenery glimpses of the hollow depths lying below. The trail forks again at ¾ of a mile with the option to the left leading down to McGarr Springs. Continue straight and at 1.5, the trail merges with another trail on the right that comes up from Blue Spring. Stay straight, and the trail begins to descend slowly for about 1 mile and then drops sharply into the river valley at 600ft. As you reach the bottom you will come out into an open field with the option to take a side trail to the right. This takes you to the North Fork River, a good water stop as well as an excellent camping area. If, instead of taking the jog down to the river you go left, then the trail continues for about a quarter of a mile before crossing Crooked Creek (You will see immediately the appropriateness of the name). After crossing Crooked Creek, the trail forks and you want to

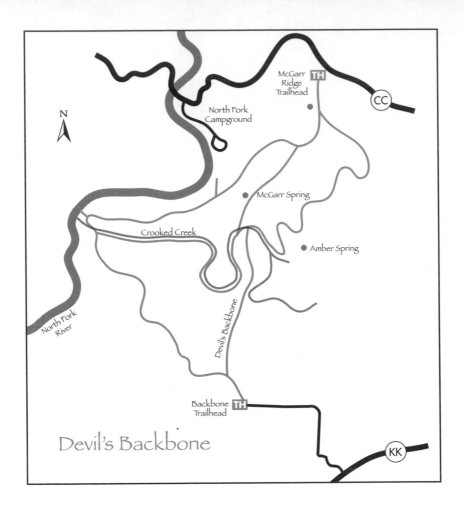

Devil's Backbone

stay left, following alongside the creek for about 2 miles. It is at this point that the trail is hard to follow because you actually hike in the creek bed for a bit before picking up the actual trail again as it zig-zags back and forth across either side. The creek and surrounding area are beautiful though, making this 2 mile section worth the extra effort. Towards the end of this stretch, there is a small trail that crosses the creek on the left and heads up McGarr Hollow about ½ mile to McGarr Spring which is a beautiful, scenic spot, and excellent overnight stop. If you go back down to the main trail where you turned off to the spring, and proceed straight for another ¼ a mile, you will reach another fork. The trail heading off to the right leads along the "backbone" for which this area earned its name, but exits out the south side of the wilderness at Highway KK. In efforts to loop back from your origination point, and complete the north section of the trail, proceed left heading back up towards CC. The route out is about 3 miles long and initially remains in the lower lying creek bed area winding up through Mary Hollow. As you approach the final mile, the trail will move steadily up in elevation to some higher points revealing scenic bluffs and rock outcroppings. Having reached the plateau, the trail moves up to a fork which is the origination of the large loop. Left here goes back up McGarr Ridge and right to Highway CC.

BACKBONE TRAIL

The trailhead from KK starts with crossing the road to the beginning of The Backbone Trail. At the half mile mark you will pass an old homestead as evidenced by the remaining rock walls, and soon after a fork in the trail. Proceed right along the trail, heading towards the trail's "backbone" for the next mile. This is a pleasant section weaving through the fresh smelling pines more characteristic of the West, but is especially beautiful upon reaching the actual backbone of the trail. The trail and ridge merge into one with slopes on either side gradually disappearing into the hollow depths below. As the trail leads across this continuing BTV, the surrounding scenery, combined with pine trees scattered along the backbone's rugged topography, introduces a new respect and appreciation for Missouri wilderness. The hike continues along the backbone for a bit before heading down about ½ mile to Crooked Creek. At this point you have two options. If you proceed to the right and follow the creek up a short distance, you can bushwhack southeast from the trail down to Amber Springs, one of the area's beautiful little springs that gains its name from the amber coloring to the water. We will, however, continue left back at the fork at Crooked Creek and hike a quarter of a mile to the next fork. At this intersection, right will take you ½ mile to McGarr Spring, another one of this area's natural springs and an ideal location for camping, or restful enjoyment. If instead of taking a right to McGarr Spring you proceed straight, the trail will take you alongside Crooked Creek for approximately 2 miles before splitting again. This two mile stretch can be a bit hard to follow, so keep your eyes open and pay attention to the trail. At the arrival of this next fork, there is the option to proceed right and hook up with the North Fork River as well as the trail leading up McGarr Ridge granting access to the area's north side. Take the trail left, up to Collins Ridge, to form a loop of the wilderness's southern half. From the creek bottom the trail moves up in elevation and joins an old logging road that passes by a few ponds along the way. At about 2 miles from the junction at Crooked Creek, you will come up on a trail that heads to the left. This is the trail you took to get up to the Backbone. Stay straight and you will be back at the trailhead in half a mile.

Hiking Tip — Tackling Inclines

When hiking up a steep hill loosen the shoulder straps and load lifters on your pack so that all weight is distributed onto your hips. Also, don't forget to shorten your trekking poles, as this will help establish a better rhythm when tackling a steep hill.

7. Grand Gulf State Park

LOCATION: Grand Gulf is located just west of Thayer in southern Missouri, almost at the Missouri/Arkansas border. From Thayer, take HWY W west straight to the parking lot at Grand Gulf.

LENGTH: Grand Gulf has a small ¼ mile loop trail as well as longer more primitive canyon trail that extends along Grand Gulf's rim that is just under one mile.

COMMENTS: The Department of Natural Resources describes Grand Gulf as "one of the most spectacular geologic areas in Missouri". Also tagged as the "Little Grand Canyon", Grand Gulf truly is a phenomenal site and should definitely be on the "hit list" of any avid hiker, geologist or outdoor enthusiast. From a geologic standpoint, Grand Gulf evolved from years of water percolating through dolomite rock fractures, that created caves and passageways beneath the earth's surface. Gradually these underground passageways multiplied, caves formulated and collapsed, causing passageways to divert further, thus creating new cave openings. The gulf is basically the result of one giant collapse of a mammoth sized cave. Three quarters of a mile long, and as high as 120 feet tall in some places, Grand Gulf earned the title of National Natural Landmark in 1984. Adding further to the striking features already incorporated into this mini-canyon, is the state renown natural bridge that extends over 200 feet long and has an opening 75 feet high. Bussell Branch Creek flows through the canyon and into a remaining intact portion of the actual cave responsible for Grand Gulf. Water from Bussell Branch feeds a lake that sets inside the cave and then reappears 7 miles farther down into Mammoth Springs Arkansas. Although not accessible any longer, this lake was at one time explored by a handful of geologists and found to be home to some very rare and unique aquatic species.

Trail wise, this area contains paths that are short in length but packed full of an obviously spectacular and outstanding display of creational beauty and awe. Portions of the overlook trails are boardwalked and handicapped accessible, providing access to wheelchairs and the disabled. The park is a day-use area only, with no camping allowed and gates closing upon sunset each evening.

TOPOGRAPHICAL MAPS: Koshkonong

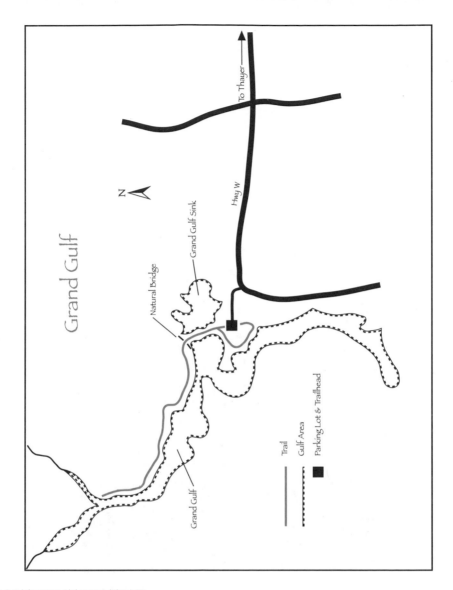

Grand Gulf

Natural Bridge

Grand Gulf Sink

Hwy W

To Thayer

N

Grand Gulf

Trail

Gulf Area

Parking Lot & Trailhead

NORTHWEST RIM TRAIL

Just to the right of the parking lot is the beginnings of the giant chasm, as well as the trailhead for the mini-loop trail extending around this area. A boardwalk path on the right leads to the Grand Junction Overlook. Leave the boardwalk and take the trail to your right and it will follow a ridgetop urging you down the NW Rim Trail. The ridge is narrow and the trail almost a bit on the dangerous side, so be careful with kids and watch your step. A spur to the left leads to an overlook of the fabulous natural bridge—75 feet high and 250 feet wide. Return to the main trail and continue on further alongside the gulf. Every step is a BTV, fabulous, amazing and awesome. As the trail skirts its way along the gulf, a passage known as "the narrows" can be seen. During wet weather, waterfalls originating from an intermittent stream cascade down the rockbed adding a scenic bonus to this already breathtaking chasm. The trail's end takes you down into the gorge area and offers some incredible photo shoot options. You can return by a re-tracing of your steps.

CHASM TRAIL

The Chasm Trail also begins from the parking lot but encircles the southern end of the gulf's renown chasm. Follow the trail past the boardwalk as if headed down the NW Rim Trail, deviating to the left at the next intersection. This trail option left actually leads up and over the outstanding natural bridge. Views of what you've been standing on are seen from the NW Rim Trail, which resides on the gulf's opposite side. Continue to follow the Chasm Trail around, catching views afforded by the boardwalk deck overlooks. At the trail' s most southern end, and at about the half-way point, opportunities to venture down into the chasm are provided via a series of steps descending down into the depths. If you're up for an added challenge to this small hike, spend some time exploring here. Your return to the parking lot extends from the top of these steps on around.

Grand Gulf State Park

8. Greer Springs Trail

LOCATION: The Greer Springs Trail is located off the HWY 19, at the bridge crossing over the Eleven Point River.

LENGTH: Greer Springs Trail is just under a mile, one-way.

COMMENTS: The Eleven Point river is packed with many small little springs, feeding in water that allows the river to flow almost year round, but outshining all of these is the beautiful Greer Spring. The second largest spring in the state, Greer pushes water out at over 300 cubic feet per second, pumping millions of gallons of water per day into the Eleven Point River residing 1.25 miles down. The massive amounts of water contributed by the spring nearly double the size of the Eleven Point below the HWY 19 bridge, making it floatable even in dry months. Rumor has it that at one time rafts used to run down the spring to the Eleven Point during high water times, until a drowning resulted ending this adventure. Now the spring, actually located on private property is accessible to the public via this trail, however, no permission is granted to float the spring.

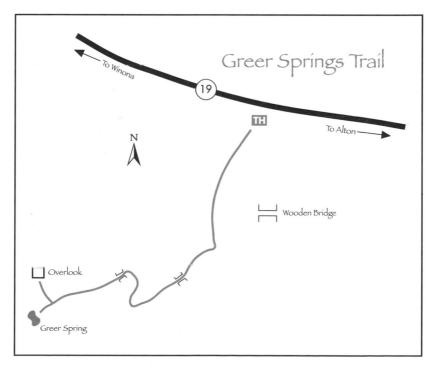

The hike is one of straight up and straight down, making the short trek a bit more challenging and requiring more time than a usual 2 mile out and back trip. The descent drops more than 250 feet in its mile or less stretch, crossing over rock spans, small wooden bridges and creek beds. The spring is gorgeous with its water plunging downward to the river, and is definitely worth seeing.

TOPOGRAPHICAL MAPS: Greer

Being short, straightforward and easy to follow, there's not much description needed to walk you through the trail. Equally as beautiful as the spring itself, the trail is a very pleasant hike. It begins at the parking lot directly across from the restrooms, dropping straight down from there. Dropping deep and heading down to the Eleven Point River Basin, the trail brings you to the famed spring in less than a mile. Arrival at the spring will be unquestioned as the natural water sieve is surrounded by ferns and other vegetation characteristic to the area.

Hiking Tip — DWR Coatings

Ever wonder about whether or not those wash-in water treatment coatings really work? Durable Water Repellency (DWR), gives a synthetic outer fabric its water-phobic quality. Over time, dirt, abrasion and laundering will hinder the DWR coating's ability to function properly. Rather than water beading up and running down the outer surface, water begins to saturate the outer fabric creating that "clammy" feel. In order to restore this DWR you can purchase wash-in treatments such as Nikwax TX-Direct. To get the most out of this product, here are a few wash-in tips:

- Pre-wash your garment so that the DWR will attach itself to the fabric only and not dirt or grease.
- Make sure you wash the garment right-side out, unless of course you want the DWR to coat the inside of the fabric, rather than the outside.
- If using a washing machine, add the DWR after it has filled completely with water, let it agitate a few moments, and then stop the washing process to allow the garment to soak before completing the rest of the cycle.

9. Henning Homestead Trail

LOCATION: The Henning Homestead Trail is located in the Ruth and Paul Henning State Forest northwest of Branson in Taney County. Take HWY 65 north from Branson to HWY 248 going west. Stay on 248, exiting off at 248/20 Road. Take 248/20, 3.2 miles north to Sycamore Church Road. The trailhead is 3.5 miles down, and on the left.

LENGTH: This is a 3.7 loop trail.

COMMENTS: Although not a part of the neighboring Shepherd of the Hills State Park, but rather a forestry area of its own, this little trail is more remote and less traveled, yet displays a gorgeous taste of the Ozark's outdoors and scenery. Henning State Forest is rich in steep terrain and wooded scenery, yet hidden within the thick of the timber, open glades lie interspersed, creating "bald areas" that give this White River Balds Natural Area its name. The single separating feature of this unique trail however, is not the scenery, but rather the historic nature that tells a story of Branson many years ago. The "balds" them-selves contribute historically to the Branson area as they were once the ren-

The Sycamore Log Church on the Henning Homestead Trail

dezvous point for post-Civil War groups that later became known as "baldknob-bers".

Packed within this short loop trail is a more detailed story of the past, as a handful of old homesteads and community remains stand like historic puzzle pieces giving hint to what the real picture was like years prior. Numbered in highlighted spots to identify significant remaining structures, the trail is pleas-ant, scenic and educational. Orange blazes on the trees mark the trail's path more or less, but pay attention a bit as the trail receives little use and is not fully distinguishable in all places. If you wish to pick up an interpreting guide, contact the Shepherd of the Hill Visitor's Center in Branson or contact them at 417-334-4865. With the tremendous amount of history packed within the con-fines of this preserved area, the self interpreting guide is recommended. It is also worth mentioning that caution should be taken when exploring this area to preserve the remains still standing, so that others too may learn a bit of this area's history.

Henning State Forest also has two other scenic and interesting trails that are worth checking out. They are located on the south side of the forest and are slightly shorter in length but meander through some of the "bald" areas as well as a few scenic BTV high spots. These trailheads can be reached directly of HWY 76 in Branson, just west of 76 and Shepherd of the Hills Expressway.

TOPOGRAPHICAL MAPS: Lakeview

The trail begins at the low-water bridge at Roark Creek located on the Sycamore Church Road. Crossing the bridge from the parking lot here, the trail heads off to the left and up a small incline to follow Fuller Creek. Because this trail is less hiked, it can be somewhat less distinguished in spots. Basically, it follows the orange blazes on the trees, and for the first portion, travels just alongside the creek. At less than half a mile in, you will cross Fuller Creek. This creek was at one time the main source of water for Cox, an old town founded in 1840. The remains of this establishment are still visible through portions of the old Stewart Store and Cox home. After crossing, take a left and the trail will follow through the bottomland area, meeting up with the beginnings of the homestead remains. Four large pines stand in position to be noticed, and just beyond them, an old 1920 pole barn. Backtrack from the pole barn a few steps, and wander up the path of the old logging road here. A few of the red cedars that you notice along this road are the remnants of what was at one time a thick cedar stand, but in 1945 was harvested by the American Eagle Pen-cil Co. Sad to think that these beautiful trees were sold for a penny a post back then!

Back to the trail. The road will curve around, and at 1.3 miles you will cross the remains of a fireplace from the Jone's house, built in the 1870's. Just beyond that, the Isaac's place once stood, and it was here, in 1849, that the "Baldknobbers" shot to death Sheriff Galba Branson—hence some Branson his-tory! Continue down the trail past some hand dug wells (hand-dug through limestone!), each less than 30 feet deep. Moving past these, the trail crosses a ravine and the beautiful scenic spot of a waterfall to which the trail travels right over the top of. Topping off at a glade like area, the trail merges right and at

2.5 miles you come across the new Cox place built in 1890. It is here that a self-explanatory loop trail resides, leading around the old homesteaded area.

Keep your exploration senses active as you "treasure hunt" down this historic trail. After coming out of the woods into the glade area, a foundation worth noting is one titled the old Garber place. A post office stood here at one time, and the remains of large handcut stonework along with some rather stately oak posts, surround the place. From the Garber place, the trail takes residence along an old road that was surely a transportation route at one time. It leads you to the Garber's nearest neighbor, the Sheltons, where an old well with a spring coming out of it still sets. After leaving this pleasant spring, at about 3.6 miles in, the trail passes by a rather unique set of 120 year old red oaks known as the twins, the evidence of their name being obvious. From here, as you come down off the ridge, be sure to stay on the trail as surrounding area is private property. Some steep steps lead you down the bluff and back to the origin of the trail.

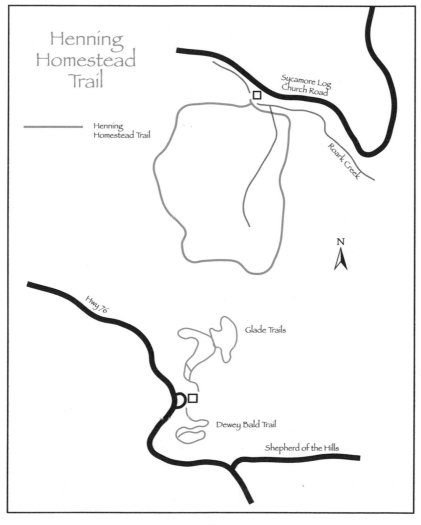

10. Hercules Glades

LOCATION: Hercules Glades is located in Taney County and is accessible via two trailheads: Hercules Firetower and Blair Ridge.

Firetower: The Tower trailhead can be reached by traveling south down Highway 125, 7 miles from the junction of Highway 125 and 76. The tower and accompanying parking lot are on your right.

Blair Ridge: Blair Ridge is found 2 miles down Blair Ridge Road located west off Highway 125 about a mile and a half south from the tower.

LENGTH: Hercules Glades holds a large network of trails allowing one to choose a nice relaxing day hike or opt for a more extensive overnight trip.

COMMENTS: The glades are a very unique feature for this area of the country, as common Missouri hardwood forest meets with the very fragile and more uncommon, desert grasses, to create the glade area. It is important to handle this area with care by staying on the trail and camping in designated areas only so as not to disturb the growth of these shallow rooted plants. Long Creek cuts a narrow trough through the center of Hercules, dissecting it into a north and south side and creating contrast in topography with the higher elevations of the upper and lower pilot knobs. During periods of rainfall, Long Creek and surrounding tributaries can show a fabulous display of waterfalls that color the area in spring. Dogwoods and redbuds are also rich in this area, further decorating the region when in full bloom. The entire wilderness area offers a lot to see, but trails are not marked and direction can be difficult to determine, so it is suggested that one carry topo map and compass.

TOPOGRAPHICAL MAPS: Hilda

FIRETOWER TRAILHEAD

Starting from the north side of the Firetower, the trail heads down into a thick forested area and past the remains of what was once an old homestead. In early spring this area has some exquisite dogwoods in bloom that mingle with the oak and hickory hardwood forest to create contrasting beauty and an almost picturesque scene. For the first mile you will traverse the hollow before coming to a intersection where there is a side trail off to your left. This is the first of a series of 4 trails that spur off the main trail and head to Long Creek which flows through the lower region of the glades, running almost the full length of the area.

This first side trail to the left follows a steep ridge for approximately one mile before bringing you to a trail intersection above the banks of Long Creek.

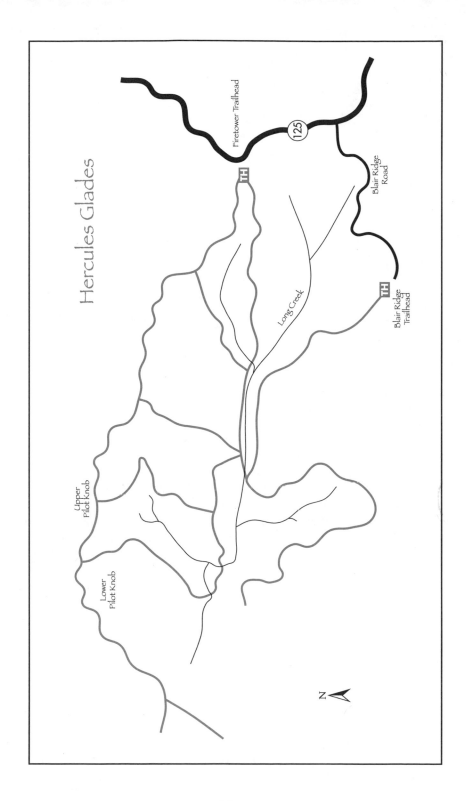

Hercules Glades

Firetower Trailhead

125

Blair Ridge
Road

Blair Ridge
Trailhead

Long Creek

Upper
Pilot Knob

Lower
Pilot Knob

N

Long Creek, Hercules Glades

Take a right here, following alongside the Long Creek for ⅛ of a mile, until reaching a place on your left that is a grooved embankment leading across the stream, and to the first campsite. If the water is low and you wish to camp, you can cross here to claim an ideal spot for the night with easy access to the creek. Stay to your right if continuing down the main trail, and ¼ of a mile down it crosses a spring fed stream flowing into Long Creek. Stay on the trail, following it alongside Long Creek and across an old logging road. From here, the trail will veer right and past the second campsite to your right, located about 150 yards down from the logging road. Past this campsite just a bit further, off the trail and on the right, lies Long Creek Falls; fabulous waterfall drops emptying into a deep, clear, water pool at its base creating a BTV. During dry season, when rainfall is not so abundant, water collects in a small pool at the base of barren rock ledges, exposed due to absence of the falls. Follow the trail a little further still and you will reach the final campsite, situated by another of the glade's scenic features, Devil's Den Falls. This scenic water formation, situated in the Devil's Den Hollow, displays a series of small drops of rushing water that results in the display of a beautiful set of cascading falls. The hike to this point has been about 3.5 miles and the most ideal return route is to backtrack the way that you came in.

Now back to the Firetower Trail. If you would have stayed on the main trail rather than taking the first left, you can opt for the second left down to Long Creek, which is two miles down the main trail from the firetower. This second left takes you down to Long Creek as well, with the trail junction at the creek bottom lying just to the east of Long Creek Falls and Devil's Den Falls. From this junction, the trail leading left will bring you to the first campsite as described in the above paragraph, which from this direction will be across the creek and on your right. By proceeding on past this campsite, you can continue hiking straight east and it will lead you to the firetower and beginning of the trail. If from the junction you proceed right, the trail follows the same path as described in the directions from the first spur. It crosses the spring fed stream flowing into Long Creek, follows alongside the creek and across the logging road, past the second campsite, and to Long Creek Falls. Following the trail a little further brings you, once again, to Devil's Den Falls.

If you follow the Firetower Trail up towards the third and fourth spurs you will come to a sign at the 4 mile mark that shows the road to upper and lower Pilot Knob, both of which are close to 1200 feet in elevation. These two spurs are good trail choices if you wish to explore the knobs or Devil's Den area. You can reach Long Creek from both of these side trails as well, but if the falls are your destination, then getting there by way of one of the first two spurs would be preferable. One of the unique features present along the path leading towards the knobs, is the famed "Elephant Walk", a peculiar set of depressions fossilized in the rock bottom streambed, resembling the tracks of primitive elephants. The tracks are hard to find, but are located at the stream crossing, encountered along Firetower Trail, approximately 3 miles from the tower, past the first and second side trails.

BLAIR RIDGE

From this trailhead, the trail starts along a ridge that is easy to walk, and then slowly descends down, winding through an older hardwood forest area, evident by the large size of the trees. At 1.5 miles you will reach the unique expanse of glades that characterize this wilderness area. Again, please take care to preserve it by staying on the main trail only. From the glade area, the trail winds down a steep incline through some cedars and eventually back out into the hardwood forest again. At 2 miles in you will see a campsite on your right and a trail just before it that heads left. Take the trail to your left and follow the creek. The trail crosses a small stream and then across an old road before reaching another campsite. Past this campsite you will see Long Creek Falls, a beautiful drop in the creek which makes for an excellent lunch or relaxing spot, and a definite BTV. To return, follow the trail back past the first campsite turn right and go up to glades and through the hardwoods back to the trailhead. The trail is 5 miles in total length.

Hiking Tip – Fuel

The general rule of thumb for fuel consumption on a packing trip is 5 ounces of white gas per person, per day. If using fuel to melt snow for water, or cook three times a day, you might want to allot for a bit more.

11. Klepzig Mill Trail

LOCATION: Klepzig Mill is actually located along the Current River section of the Ozark Trail, and begins at the Powder Mill Ferry trailhead off HWY 106, between Ellington and Eminence Missouri. Coming east from Eminence, turn right just before crossing the bridge that crosses the Current River. This is Powder Mill Ferry. Should you wish to start here, park at Owls Bend and walk across the bridge to start. If however, you want to save yourself a couple of miles, drive on down this road to a parking place and trailhead located just across the river from Blue Spring.

LENGTH: From the trailhead just below Powder Mill, the trail to Klepzig is approximately 5 miles in length. From the bridge, 7 miles.

COMMENTS: This is a cool trail! Klepzig Mill, in and of itself is worth the hike, and is also accessible via Rocky Falls, however, the hike to Klepzig from this direction is absolutely gorgeous, lending spectacular views of the Current River and covering some beautiful terrain. The hike is tough, offering some challenging climbs that earn you the right to stand atop the 200 foot bluffs aligning por-

The authors on the Rocky Creek

tions of the Current River, but take it slow and I think you'll find the work well worth it!

Below the heights of the bluffs, the trail meanders down into the stream valleys that can create some wet crossings in springtime. Be prepared. Whether hiking the 5 or 7 mile option, it would be recommended to either plan this hike as a backpacking overnight, or start early allowing for ample time to handle 10+ tough miles in one day. You can camp anywhere along the Ozark Trail, keeping in mind the leave "no trace" philosophy of overnighting in the wilderness (see the front section of this book).

Klepzig Mill, an abandon mill, built back in the early 1900's, is situated within a setting of rocky shut-ins, waterfalls, mini pools and fabulous rock formations. The sense of being hidden within the western mountains somewhere is very much present, and combined with the soothing sound of the rushing water choosing its path down through multicolored rocks, you are captivated and relaxed, disappointed only by the thought of leaving when you embark

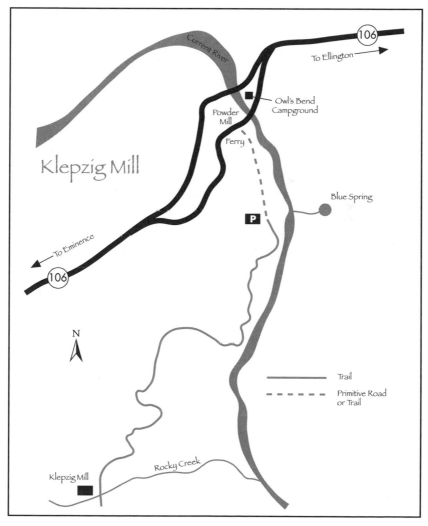

upon the return hike. The weathered wood building of the remaining mill still stands, as well as an old well house and a crumbling concrete dam. Bring your camera and plan to stay for a bit to enjoy this very pleasant, and somewhat historic spot.

TOPOGRAPHICAL MAPS: Powder Mill Ferry

From the trailhead below Powder Mill Ferry, the trail heads south and alongside the Current River. As the trail winds through the pines and other hardwoods, views of the Current River valley emerge. From here some of the climbing begins as the trail gradually leads up to the ridge and bluff area that rises up from the river banks below. Two miles in, and you will reach the first in a series of BTV's. As the main trail makes it way across this ridgetop section, some little spur trails leading to the edge of the bluffs allow for the best vantage point for the views below. Veer off to the left when you can, snap some photos, or take a breather as you soak in this area's awesome topography. As the trail and ridgeline continues, so does the view. Continue hiking and watching, taking in the view and enjoying the scenery. As you come down off the ridge, the trail brings you down across a couple of spring fed creeks and beside some large beaver dams, more BTV's and some very pleasant spots.

At about 3 miles in, you meet up with Indian Creek. Look up Indian Creek and take in the Smokey Mountain or even western feel that this area offers— between the beaver dams, the rushing water and the pine forest surrounding, it might take a moment to remember that you are in Missouri! Following Indian Creek for just a short distance, the trail finally crosses it, and takes to the left up an old road momentarily. Watch for the drastic left the trail takes off the road and back onto a foot path as it kind of jogs over quickly. At 4 miles you will begin the trek around the base of Barnett Mountain. The trail winds through some gorgeous pines stands around this area and remains gentle in terrain as it follows some of the Indian Creek valley and basically skirts around the entire mountain. Follow this as it winds its way down and around, eventually leading you Rocky Creek, the gorgeous shut-ins there, and Klepzig Mill. Enjoy your stay returning via the same route in reverse!

Hiking Tip — Condensation

When you sleep, you crank out quite a bit of heat and moisture. As this moisture passes through the tent walls it usually accumulates on the inside of the rainfly. If the rainfly isn't staked taunt, then it sags, causing that moisture to seep back in through your tent walls and create condensation. Venting a small air intake or two will help minimize this, as will staking out your rainfly to be tight.

12. Letter Look Trail

Eleven Point River Section

LOCATION: The trailhead to begin this hike is located off FR 3152. From the crossing of HWY 19 over the Eleven Point River at Greer Recreation Area, travel north just a few miles to FR 3152 located on the east side. You can also access FR 3152 from HWY 19 by traveling south about 15 miles from Winona. From either direction, drive 6 miles east down FR 3152 where you will find the trailhead. The trail's exit point is at Greer Recreation Area off HWY 19 and the Eleven Point River.

LENGTH: This section runs 10 miles in length, and is a one-way trail.

COMMENTS: Although not the official name of this trail, Letter Look is a beautiful hike through one of the most fabulous areas in the state via a portion of the Eleven Point River section of the Ozark Trail. When you arrive at the trailhead of FR 3152, signs will indicate that you are at the beginning of this Ozark Trail section, so don't be confused if there is nothing identifying the trail to be the "Letter Look Trail"; it is most commonly known to be just a section of the much larger Ozark Trail. Regardless though, of how one titles this 10 mile stretch, it resonates with bluff-top vistas that descend into deep enchanted hollows, and rugged uphill climbs rewarding you with beautiful scenery. It is not the easiest of trail sections, but the scenery packed between the roller coaster terrain is well worth some extra expended energy and time spent in the wilderness.

The actual Letter Look point is only one of the many gorgeous BTV's that overlook Hurricane Creek, the Eleven Point River, and other deep rooted hollows situated below. Running just below, and east of Letter Look, lies the beautiful Hurricane Creek which holds potential for being a wet crossing during springtime months, so hike prepared. Start your day early if you plan to make this trip a one day excursion, otherwise, if you wanted an evening out doors, this trail could be ideal in length for a relaxed overnighter. Water could be a problem, camping wise however, so plan accordingly.

TOPOGRAPHICAL MAPS: Greer

From the starting point at FR 3152, the trail starts you off easy as it heads south and down into the first hollow, passing through some large standing pines lining the trail, that pave the way under foot with fresh smelling needles. The 900 foot elevation that resided at the trailhead, gently eases downward through typical Ozark scenery, to arrive at the base of the first hollow. Soon after your arrival in this lower lying area, Hurricane Creek comes into earshot and the trail

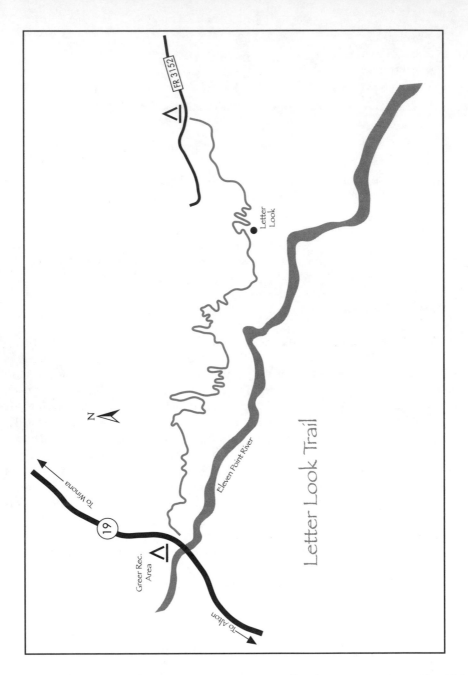

crosses it about 1.5 miles in. Large sycamore and oak trees are situated within this creek bottom creating a peaceful scene as well as a respect for the age of growth spread throughout this bottomland valley. Look to your right when crossing, and if the beaver are as tenacious and withstanding as the hardwoods, then evidence of their presence might still be there into the form of a larger dam extending across the river's width. The area is very pleasant and if it were not so close to the starting trailhead, it would be ideal for pitching a tent and staying a while.

Immediately after crossing the creek the first of many climbs takes you up to 950 feet to the bluff titling (or rather nick-naming) this trail as "Letter Look". Named as such because of its "postcard picture" view, this BTV overlooking the surrounding area provides as awesome look at Hurricane Creek below and gives him to the potential nature of this trail's other scenic highlights. Up a little further the view continues, and as you reach the top of this ridge, you cross a logging road at 3.5. Gratefully on top for just a while, the trail relaxes from it's climb and continues across a level area that merges into the ridgeside, following the Eleven Point for a bit while sneaking glimpses of the beautiful river through the trees as you go. At 5.0 the trail drops down a bit through a rocky field area strung with a large boulders—an exceptionally beautiful area, especially in springtime when their already bold presence is accented by running streams of water. Just past the boulders, at 5.1, another BTV to the left opens up, this time providing a more full fledged view of the underlying Eleven Point River. Switchbacking to the left, the trail continues along the ridge carrying with it this outstanding view.

It is from here, that the trek along the ridgetop comes to a momentary close as it drops down into Haokleton Hollow. The easy downhill is short lasted however, and soon the trail leads back up a short but steep climb that returns to the ridge and BTV's on your left. The amazing view carries as it continues with you across the next ridge. At this point, the heart of the trail as well as the bulk of the hefty climbing is complete, and the final ridge stretch eventually graduates into an easy descent down into, and across Graveyard Hollow. Climbing only slightly to exit the Graveyard Hollow area, the trail makes its way towards your ending destination at Greer Recreation Area.

Hiking Tip — Seamsealing

Waterproofing, DWR coatings and waterproof fabrics are only effective if seams are waterproofed as well.
What should you seamseal?

- Seams on the hiking boots of cloth or Cordura boots.
- Any untaped or internal seams of raingear.
  (Keep in mind that this makes the garment less breathable.)
- Seams inside your tent; floor seams and rainfly seams in particular.
- Any seams on your pack that are exposed and might compromise its waterproofness.
- External seams of sleeping bags or bivy sacks if camping without a tent.

13. Loggers Lake

LOCATION: Loggers Lake is located 6 miles south from Bunker on FR 2221 in Shannon County.

LENGTH: This trail is a short one mile hike around the lake.

COMMENTS: The entire Loggers Lake area is quite pleasant and offers spacious, shaded campsites right along the shore. The area characterizes a nestled hideaway for a campground, providing a setting that is somewhat more remote and private than most "drive-in" camp spots. For the backpacking purist who doesn't ordinarily agree with the concept of car camping, this place isn't too bad. Camping spots designated around the lake are nestled between trees and allow shoreline access that provide the necessary ingredients for an enjoyable stay. Plus, having extended packing room from your back to the car, you can even splurge on a fabulous meal of something other than freeze dried, dehydrated, carefully rationed entrees! If all sites are full however, or if your preference lies with the higher elevations, move uphill to the above Oak Knoll Campground which also provides sites—"lakeview" style, rather than "lakeside". Whatever your choice, Loggers Lake is a pleasant visit, and with picnicking, swimming and hiking all permitted, an excellent family overnight, backpacker's break, or weekend stay.

TOPOGRAPHICAL MAPS: Loggers Lake

The hiking trail begins at the south end of the lake and begins its trek along the lake's shoreline. Being relatively short in length and basically encircling the perimeter of Loggers Lake, the trail is easy to follow as it winds back and forth from the shoreline to timber, mapping a path around the water. An additional campground, Oak Knoll, sets up above Loggers Lake and from the lake's west shore there is a trail spur that leads up to this little ridgetop camping area. Pine trees and rock outcroppings make this a nice campsite location as well.

Another trail spur, located towards the trail's beginning, leads down to Logger's Lake dam. A nice view overlooking the lake is offered here, and the tailrise for regulating water overflow is in working order during wet weather. Also during wetter weather, this trail can be a bit sloppy in spots. Be prepared for a few minor swampy type places down close to the water. It does cross a few intermittent streams along the way as well, including Mill Creek, a small little stream that feeds from the lake. Overall, this is a beautiful trail and relaxing area.

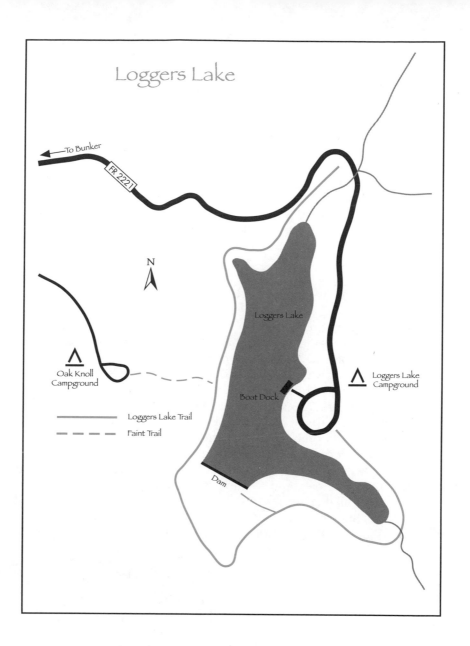

Loggers Lake

To Bunker

FR 2221

N

Oak Knoll
Campground

Loggers Lake

Boat Dock

Loggers Lake
Campground

Loggers Lake Trail

Faint Trail

Dam

14. Marble Creek

LOCATION: Marble Creek campground is located directly off HWY E west out Fredricktown and Route 67. This is the start and trailhead for Marble Creek. The exit point is at Crane Lake. Crane Lake turn-off is 3 miles down from the Marble Creek Campground on HWY E. Turn west down FR 124 (FH-69), a dirt road and travel 4.5 miles. Turn south onto Crane Pond gravel road to the picnic area of Crane Lake.

LENGTH: Marble Creek to Crane Lake is 8 miles in length.

COMMENTS: Standing on the bridge peering down at Marble Creek is much like standing on top of some boulder on an eastern whitewater river scouting out the best line to paddle a kayak or open boat through the rapids. Although not quite as intense or as powerful as Class III to V water, Marble Creek is strewn with pink and gray boulders that are simply electrifying as water rushes over and between them. The scene from this bridge, which isn't even really part of the trail at all, is a BTV and view worth catching in and of itself.

The trail, named after this awesome little creek, is an 8 mile section of the Ozark Trail that will become a 21 mile section at some point, upon completion. Easy to follow, this trail is marked with the typical OT white and green trail markers. The 8 miles here extend southwest to Crane Lake, a pleasant place to spend the day and hike as well. Terrain along this route carries a few heavy elevation changes but climbs are not overwhelming and you are rewarded with extensive views and wonderful gladetop treks across flattened ridges.

TOPOGRAPHICAL MAPS:
Des Arc NE

The trailhead starts across HWY E at the campground and wastes no time at all before climbing, moving slowly in elevation gain for the next 1.5 miles. The 200 foot gain settles along a flattened trek across the ridge making for a pleasant hike with some nice views on either side during periods of leaf off. Hardwoods dominate most of this area providing typical Ozark scenery. At 2.5 miles in the trail crosses a gravel road to proceed

Marble Creek

downhill slightly through much the same scenery with a creek bed at bottom. The next road crossing encountered requires a quick jaunt to the left before returning to the woods on the road's other side. Up on the ridge still, the trail opens up into a beautiful BTV traveling across a gladed clearing featuring lichen colored rocks, wildflowers and outstanding views of surroundings across and below. Trail markers convert from the familiar OT square tag on a tree to piles of rock scattered along the glade revealing direction and path. Moving down from this gladed ridge, the trail disappears again into the timber, descending down to a creek bottom that holds a streambed and old roadbed crossing in one. The trail then temporarily shares this roadbed for its path following the creek a bit as it moves back up through an area rich in Azaleas during spring. Down once more to cross another road and creek, the trail repeats this move once more to exit out from the woods and into a field at Crane Lake. Follow through the field to your left and the trail junction at Crane Pond Creek gives option to take either direction as a path around the lake and to Crane Lake Recreation Area.

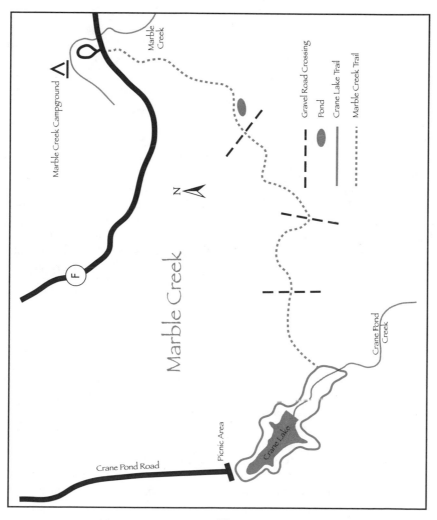

15. McCormack Lake

LOCATION: The trail to McCormack Lake runs from the Greer Recreation Area to McCormack Lake Recreation Area. Greer Recreation area is located on the Eleven Point River at HWY 19 bridge between Winona and Alton. McCormack Lake is located on FS 3155 off the west side of HWY 19 just north of the bridge.

LENGTH: This trail is a one-way trail that is 4.2 miles in length.

COMMENTS: If you want a small taste of the Ozark Trail with all of its surprising Missouri treasures, then this is the ideal trail for you. Short in length, yet packed with some superb views of the Eleven Point River, the hike from Greer to McCormack is not only reasonable, but also serves as a nice appetizer for the entire Eleven Point section of the Ozark Trail. Most of the trail parallels the river, either at its banks or at the ridgetops above. Also, across the river from this route is Greer Spring Branch—a tributary flowing into the Eleven Point River that is itself fed by Greer Spring, Missouri's second largest spring. Before or after your hike take a quick side trip to the river's other side, and take a look at this magnificent wild spring that plunges so much fresh ground water into the river that it inflates the Eleven Point river level and keeps it flowing even during dry seasons.

If you wish to hike this section of trail all in one setting, you can start at Greer Recreation Area and proceed to the lake and back, or with camping available on either end of this route, you could easily pitch a tent for an overnight stay. Although the hike is short, elevation climbs are pretty drastic, creating some rather challenging terrain ascents, but rewarding you with a ridgetop full of terrific BTV's and river valley overlooks.

TOPOGRAPHICAL MAPS: Low Wassie

From the Greer Recreation and Campground Area the trail starts with two options; right leading to the Highlands Trail, and the left, taking you alongside the Eleven Point River. Assuming that the Highlands option was created for trail passage during times of high water, and the other being an option anytime, it doesn't particularly matter which route you take as they both end up merging together later down the trail, leading on to McCormack Lake. Remember that this trail constitutes a portion of the Ozark Trail and thus it is well marked with the familiar green and white OT trail markers. Although the highlands route begins the steady incline a bit sooner, both stretches, especially once merged, graduate into a rather challenging trek up, as the trail pushes towards the top of the towering bluffs that start their rise from the riverbank. From the gravel bar under the bridge to the ridgetop exposing tremendous views, the trail climbs about 400 feet before residing on top for just a bit before gradually bringing you back down.

Returning to the valley, and 3.1 miles from where you began, the trail intersects with the option to either continue down the Ozark Trail, or proceed right up towards McCormack Lake. Select the trail right and you will again be on the incline as the trail leads towards your destination. The hike up to McCormack is much milder than your past uphill battle, and as you get closer it is evident that some of the small stream beds crossed are home for the beaver. Be careful not to disturb their habitat, but enjoy and watch as you might very well catch a glimpse of one tugging a tree limb through the water to patch up his log home. The lake is not much more than a mile from the trail intersection just passed, and it sets in an open area up on the hilltop. A beautiful and peaceful area, this lake is perfect for a picnic stop before heading back, or a campsite to enjoy a full sky of stars.

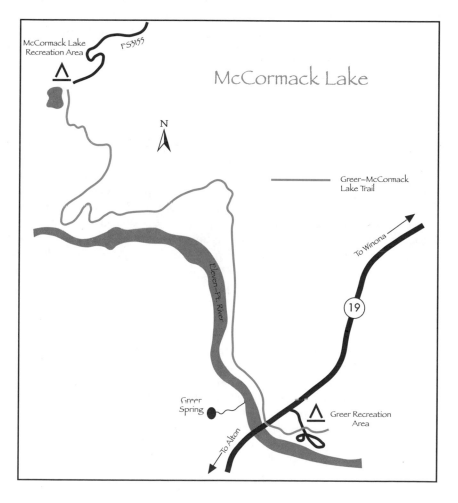

McCormack Lake Recreation Area

FS3155

McCormack Lake

N

Greer–McCormack Lake Trail

To Winona

Eleven-Pt. River

19

Greer Spring

To Alton

Greer Recreation Area

16. Noblett Loop

LOCATION: The Noblett Trailhead is located at the Sugar Hill Campground off FR 857, just before reaching the lake. From Highway 181, turn south on State Road AP. FR 857 is on your right leading to the campground.

LENGTH: This trail is an eight mile loop trail.

COMMENTS: Noblett Loop is the eight mile northern loop section of the Ridge Runner Trail. Portions of the trail circle beside the banks of Noblett Lake, leaving the remainder to continue on through woodlands and natural spring areas. Much like its southern counterpart, Noblett Loop becomes less distinctive and difficult to follow at times due to the lack of heavy hiking traffic, but holds some areas, unique and scenic, that make the hike worth the effort. Carrying a map and compass is suggested.

TOPOGRAPHICAL MAPS: Dyestone Mountain

The trail takes off as the beginning section of the Ridge Runner Trail and heads almost straight south, through a forested area situated somewhat on a ridge amidst a topography of gently rolling hills and shallow basins. During spring season, the blossoms of redbud, dogwood, and wild plum accent the surrounding oak and pine forest environment. As you come off the ridge, the trail joins the crossing of Spring Creek. Possibly high during wet season, crossing the creek to join the trail on the opposite side might be easier through the aid of a gravel bar below the beaver dam downstream. A large incline greets you across the creek, leading up to the next ridge and across, only to head back down the hollow towards Galloway Spring which stands at the 1 mile mark. After Galloway, the trail hops across an old logging road and descends down a bit in a southeasterly direction passing a survey mark on your left and edging back up. As you come to the top of the ridge at 3.0 miles, the Noblett trail forks to the right, diverging away from the Ridge Runner Trail, and begins traversing northwest, maintaining its position on top of the ridge. (If you cross a road reaching Horton Cemetery, you've gone too far.)

No longer sharing route with Ridge Runner, the trail quickly becomes less distinct and is pieced together connecting marker to marker, in order to follow its path. The trail, on top of the knoll, crosses an old logging road into a exquisite stand of beautiful, large pines which accompany you down the trail with their fresh "mountain air" fragrance. Traversing across the ridge through the pines and hardwood forest, the trail again joins up with the crossing of a logging road; this time causing the location of the trail's other half to require a bit more of a search. Look for the blazes however, and the trail will follow. From here the trail leaves the ridge, descending down to meet up with Noblett Creek at just under 4 miles. The crossing here will most assuredly require the assistance of water sandals, and maybe the aid of the gravel bar down to your left as well. Down in this river bottom area, the trail can again become confusing, seemingly lost in the crossing of the stream. Markers on the trees are present, however, should you miss them, the trail follows the bluffline on your left crossing a spring, and continuing up. On top of this bluff, a unique rock outcropping appears, covered with mosses and ferns to create a minor BTV. Continue on up, and as the trail regains its position on top of the ridge, it passes through some more beautiful pine areas that, mixed with blooming dogwoods in the spring, create a gorgeous scene, pleasant to hike in. The trail will wind down into Cord Hollow and emerge once more to the ridge top, where it treks north, leading towards Hellroaring Spring. As you come closer to approaching Hellroaring Spring, the trail comes to a point and switchbacks down to the spring, displaying several BTV spots along the way. The trail crosses the spring, following it along the eastern bank and heads up. At this point you have hiked 6.5 miles.

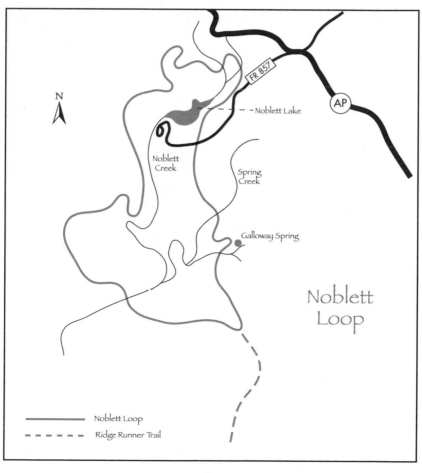

N

FR 857

AP

Noblett Lake

Noblett Creek

Spring Creek

Galloway Spring

Noblett Loop

——————— Noblett Loop

- - - - - - - Ridge Runner Trail

The remainder of the trail, from Hellroaring Spring back to Noblett, becomes very difficult to follow as markers dwindle and become sparse, leaving more empty ground in between. Look for markers carefully, and use your compass! Off the ridge, the trail leads down across a creek and after coming back up the adjoining side, meets up with a road on your right. Stay on the hiking trail, rather than the road which is used as an equestrian route. Your next rendezvous is with Noblett Creek again (only this time its on the other side of the lake), and an orange marker will be visible in the middle of the river. Past this orange marker, across the creek and across a road, a yellow marker designates the direction of trail travel, and will continue to do so the remainder of your hike. From this creek crossing, the trail leads up a hefty elevation climb, that when flattening out on the ridge, rewards you with a fabulous BTV view highlighting Noblett Lake in the background. The trail continues, following the ridge and eventually coming to the banks of Noblett Lake where you will enter Sugar Hill Campground. Proceed on past the campground where the trail officially ends at the parking lot.

Indian Paintbrush

Hiking Tip — Camp Recreation

You've got to have some campside entertainment, upon reaching your hiking destination for the day. Two lightweight toys serving as favorite extras are the hackey sack and the frisbee. Both are easy to carry, add little to no weight, and can be used for further "group bonding" (as if trekking those strenuous, backcountry miles together wasn't enough)! Besides, the frisbee can double for a dog dish or a plate!

17. North Fork Loop

LOCATION: The North Fork Loop begins at Hammonds Camp, located on the north side of Highway CC, 5 miles east of Highway 181 at Dora.

LENGTH: The loop trail is 12 miles in length.

COMMENTS: The North Fork Loop is the southern portion of the Ridge Runner Trail that connects the loop with its northern counterpart, Noblett Lake Loop. The trail passes through typical Missouri hardwood forest accented by sections of large standing pine. The trail can be difficult to follow at times due to minimal use, but can be pleasurable because the low impact has provided a sense of isolation and solitude.

TOPOGRAPHICAL MAPS: Dora

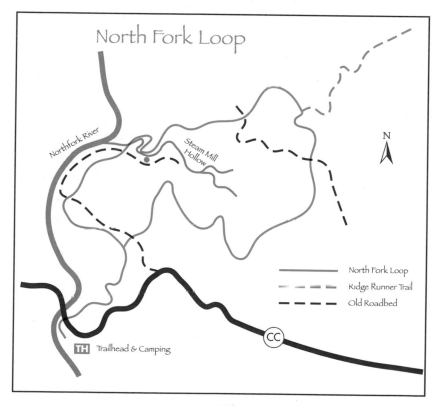

From the trailhead at Hammonds Camp, the trail heads north, crosses Highway CC and enters into hardwood forest, scaling along the side of a broad hollow. After a solid first mile, the trail comes to a fork designating the official beginning of the loop. Proceed right and hike the loop in a counter clockwise direction. Most of the trail on this first half of the loop remains in the hardwood forest setting, and traverses up and down Steam Mill Hollow. At 5.5 you cross an old logging road and at 6.0, a fork which is the trail intersection with Ridge Runner, North Fork Loop and Ozark Trails. Take the trail to your left and you will be entering into the second leg of this 12 mile loop. The trail drops a bit in elevation before rising to a plateau which you remain hiking on for about one mile. You will cross the other end of the same logging road crossed on the first half of the loop while on this plateau. As the trail descends at 8.5, you are dropping down into Steam Mill Hollow, a deep hollow area possessing a beautiful natural spring, running year round and emptying into the North Fork River. While hiking down the hill into Steam Mill, watch for a road on your left. This will take you to the spring, and must also be taken back the same way to continue on in the trail.

Now at the base of the hollow, the trail proceeds to lead uphill back to the ridgetop. As you move up in elevation, an overlook of Steam Mill Hollow and surrounding area comes into view creating a beautiful BTV during leaf-off periods. The trail comes back down to a stream holding water most of the year and then follows along the North Fork for ¼ a mile before veering back off into the woods and up a steep incline. Watch for markers on this last stretch of trail, as direction of travel can become confusing when the trail comes to an old roadbed joining it for about 15 yards going east, and then heading off to the right and back into the woods. The junction and fork signaling the completion of the loop arrives soon after the road, at the 11 mile mark, and a right turn here leads back to Hammonds Camp.

Hiking Tip — Emergency Firestarters

When the three-day backpacking trip that you've planned for months lands on a rainy weekend, here are some ideas for starting a fire with wet wood.
- Compressed balls of dryer lint mixed with or covered with paraffin creates a real fireball underneath a strategically built "tee-pee" of wet wood. The same is true for Vaseline-impregnated cotton balls stored in your spent film canisters.
- Bring along small strips of waxed cardboard to intermix with the damp wood.
- Purchase a tube of fire-starter gel and squeeze dabs of it along the strips of wet wood. It will burn long enough to get the rest of you damp wood started.

18. Paddy Creek Wilderness

Big Piney Trail

LOCATION: Big Piney Trail begins at Paddy Creek Picnic and Campground. To get to the campground, turn onto Paddy Creek Road (also known as Forest Road 220), located 13 miles west of Licking and 3 miles east of Success on Highway 32. Once on Paddy Creek Rd, continue straight down for about five miles until you reach the low water bridge. Before crossing, turn right, and you are at the campground.

If you wish to enter the area via Big Piney Trailhead at Roby Lake, travel 1 mile north of Roby on Highway 17 and travel southeast down FR 274 for half a mile.

LENGTH: The trail is a 15 mile loop, 17 miles if the spur to Roby Lake is taken.

COMMENTS: Big Piney is an impressive Missouri trail and an excellent choice for backpacking due to its length, refreshing spring water, inspiring vistas, and gorgeous pines. The trail does contain some good sized elevation climbs taking you to the vistas and also two stream crossings, one on either end, that are almost sure to require water sandals. With the markers, the trail is easy to follow and water accessibility should not be a problem.

TOPOGRAPHICAL MAPS: Slabtown Springs and Roby

The trail begins at the trailhead located behind the restrooms on the south side of the campground. At the official trailhead there is a place to sign in, some brief information, and a sign that is a bit deceiving because it indicates a north loop, and a south loop. The entire Piney Creek Trail, however, is one single loop with simply a north and south side. Begin to the right, or along the south side. Heading south, the trail begins uphill, crossing Forest Road 220 almost immediately, and then continues uphill for a while until reaching a small knoll, and heading back down to a fork of the Big Paddy at about half a mile. This crossing will most likely be a wet one. Upon crossing the creek, the trail has a small fork to the right with the main trail continuing left and back uphill a bit. At one point the trail forks with a sign that indicates you can proceed either direction. Staying to the right is the better route. At about 3.5 to 4.0 miles the trail reaches a fork at what seems to have been an old military road. There is also what appears to have been an old homestead here. If the road is taken right it leads to the north side of Piney Creek Trail. Stay straight and to the left, following the sign that points towards Roby Lake. From here the trail moves slightly uphill again and weaves through some delightful new growth pine stands. At the 5 mile mark, the trail extends up alongside a ridge that holds some fine overlooks of Paddy Creek and the wilderness area below. From this little ridge, the trail heads down, crossing one of the small tributaries of Paddy Creek only to extend back up to a beautiful BTV overlook on the left that consists of a small bluff line accented with distinguished rock outcroppings. Continuing on from here, the trail brings you across the plateau. During leaf off periods one can see some more of the rock outcrops and a few small waterfalls below. At 6.2 you reach another fork. This fork marks the turn around point of the trail as it completes the south side of the loop. If you go left, the trail takes you to Roby Lake, and right, back towards Paddy Creek Campground via 9 miles of the north side of Big Piney Trail.

The spur to Roby Lake takes you about a mile down the trail to the left. You will reach the Big Piney trailhead first and then a fence with a gate accessible for hikers and horseback riders. From here, the lake is almost straight south. Walk straight down the gravel road about 50 feet until you cross another road and see a small trail directly on the other side. By now you should be able to see the lake straight ahead and to your right. The trail takes you across a field and to Roby Lake and campground.

Back to the main trail and the fork at 6.2. Take the fork right and you will be beginning the north side of the loop. At 6.4 you will reach a fork, stay right and the trail will wind down and past a small spring on your right. As you continue past the spring, the trail takes you around past a lovely little campsite on the left. Go past the spring and campsite, and the trail will take you slightly uphill. As you hike, look down at the creek to your right—the water flows down some huge rock slabs and makes a few nice drops between ledges, creating a some beautiful little waterfalls and an ideal summertime swimming hole as well.

The trail takes you up to a small plateau and then back down to the creek a couple of times. At 9.1 you will intersect the old military road connecting from the south side of the trail where there is a small pond having a deer stand and the appearance of a food plot. Continue ahead and the trail will widen following alongside the military road for about mile before forking left back down into the woods. Your next big landmark to watch for is the crossing of Forest Road 220 which is at 12.1. Prior to this you will be hiking on the plateau and will reach a place where the trail appears to widen and fork either straight or right. Continue straight and soon after you will cross the graded gravel road of FR 220. The trail connects directly across and there is another trailhead sign at this point. As you continue hiking the trail will eventually follow in alongside Slabtown Road and at about 12.6 it almost intersects. There is a spot here that appears to have been an old homestead area with foundation remains and large yucca plants. The road is directly to your left, and the trail continues straight ahead. At this point you are hiking in and out of some very nice pine stands, and will continue to do so for the remainder of the hike. The pines are beautiful and their mountain air scent can give you the illusion of hiking out West somewhere.

At about 13 miles in, you will come out of one of these pine stands, around and to the right of a small pond and then back into the pines. To your left will be the Big Piney Trail Camp, complete with hitching areas to be used by many of the equestrian groups. At this point you are about 2.5 miles from

Paddy Creek Campground and the finish of the trail. This last 2.5 miles contains more pine trees, rock outcrops and beautiful overlooks, making it one of the prettiest sections of the entire trail. The vistas off to your right start at about 13.5 and continue in and out for the next mile. Your elevation at this point is about 1200 feet, giving you a view of the surrounding wilderness and Paddy Creek campground below at 950 feet. The trail continues along this bluff line and then merges back into the pines along a ridge before heading back down to the creek. You will hike alongside some of the creek bed tributaries below before finally crossing Paddy Creek at 15.2 miles. It may be a wet crossing, but you are just about at the end of your hike because the campground finishes the trail at about 15.5.

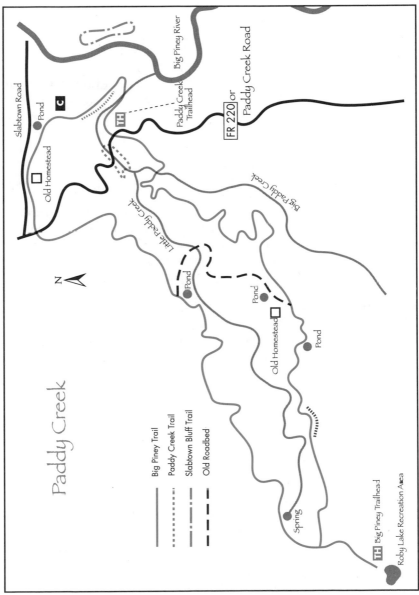

19. Piney Creek Wilderness

LOCATION: There are several access points to the Piney Creek Wilderness Area, with the main one being the Pineview Lookout Tower Trailhead. To get to the tower head east from Cassville down Lake Road 76-6 about 20 miles. In addition to the Pineview Tower Trailhead, the area can be accessed from the south side via Lake Road 39-1 which is located off Highway 39, southeast of the Highway 39 and Highway 76 junctions.

LENGTH: Piney Creek Wilderness Area has a network of trails that total 13.1 miles altogether. You can choose how long you wish to hike by creating loops within the network.

COMMENTS: Piney Creek, from which the wilderness area earns its name, runs through the center of this 8,142 acre section of Mark Twain National Forest. The creek contains several small springs and extends five miles in length to empty into the James River Arm of Tablerock Lake. The area is rugged, particularly on the south side, with hollows extending down 400 feet or more from the ridgetops. Trails can be hard to distinguish and a map and compass should be used. The area is beautiful, however, and can give one a sense of remoteness that is peaceful and relaxing. Since this area encompasses Piney Creek it can involve wet crossings during the spring season.

TOPOGRAPHICAL MAPS: Shell Knob and Cape Fair

Begin the trail from the tower and traverse down the ridge to the creek area for a 5 mile loop. If you wish to explore the area further, there are many side trails that allow you to lengthen your day of hiking. As you begin hiking south from the tower, you will first pass an old abandoned foundation on your right, and then head down the ridge for the next mile with plenty of nice views and scenery along the way. At the bottom of the ridge about 1.5 miles in, you will cross the creek and head back up a steep incline that levels off and merges to the left along an old logging road. The logging road takes you about ½ mile before crossing over Piney Creek. Stay to the left upon crossing and you will be in the bottomlands along Piney Creek. This is a popular area for backpackers to make camp as the creek provides water and creates a pleasant atmosphere for an overnight. A few yards after crossing Piney Creek, you will reach Siloam Springs Creek. When you cross Siloam Springs there is a trail situated to the right, leading down to the more rugged south side of the wilderness area. Stay straight, however and head east, crossing Piney Creek for a second and third time. Bring your water sandals! About ¾ of a mile after your third creek crossing, the trail forks. Stay left. This takes you around to crossing the creek yet another time and heads uphill. The climb is steep and rocky but offers some nice views similar to what you had when going down. Once you are on top of the ridge the trail turns into an old logging road. You will want to stay to your left. When you reach a pond on the left, the trail will fork. Either way will take you to a gravel road where you turn left and head about ¼ of a mile to the tower.

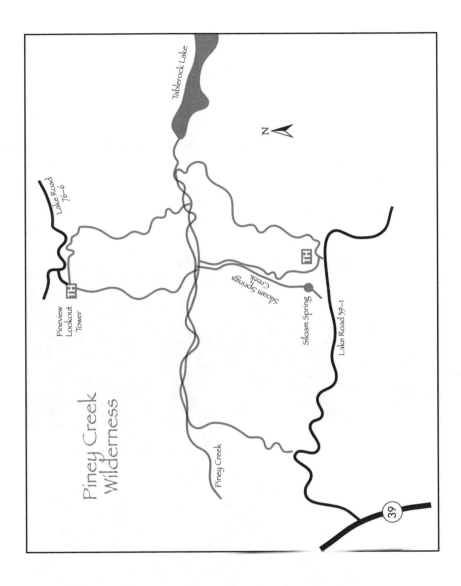

20. Raccoon Hollow

LOCATION: Raccoon Hollow is located just west of the Devil's Backbone Wilderness and can be reached off Highway CC west of Hammonds Camp, about 3.5 miles east from Highway 181 at Dora.

LENGTH: The trail is a one way trail, two and a half miles in length, for a total of 5 miles.

COMMENTS: This trail is perfect for day hikes or a casual afternoon picnic, as the terrain is mild allowing for an easy and pleasant hike. The area resembles that of Devil's Backbone with some nice hollows and waterfalls during the wet season. The trail culminates at a bluff line BTV overlooking the North Fork River below.

Phlox

TOPOGRAPHICAL MAPS: Cureall N.W. and Dora

From the trailhead go south slowly descending from the ridge at which you start. At the one mile mark the trail turns sharply to your right entering into a pleasant valley through which a stream runs, creating waterfalls during the wetter months, and providing adequate moisture for the many gorgeous ferns decorating the area during springtime—a very peaceful spot and BTV. Leaving the valley, the trail takes you up an old logging road until reaching a fork where you want to stay to the left. Stay on the logging road for another mile and a quarter until you reach a second fork. Either direction leads to the trail's end and also a impressive view overlooking the North Fork River. Stop and enjoy the scenery for a bit before heading back the same way you came in. The total trail is 5 miles in length.

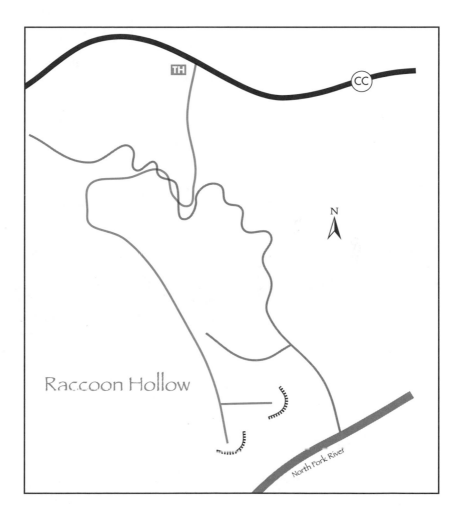

21. Ridge Runner Trail

LOCATION: The Ridge Runner Trail extends from Noblett Lake to Hammonds Camp at the North Fork River Area.

Noblett Trailhead: To get to the Noblett Trailhead take Highway 181 and turn south onto AP. On your right will be FR 857 leading to Sugar Hill Campground. The trailhead is on your left before reaching the lake.

Northfork Trailhead: Hammond's Camp is 5 miles east, down Highway CC from 181 at Dora, and located on the north side of the road.

LENGTH: Ridge Runner Trail is approximately 22 miles in length and has an additional loop on each end (Noblett Lake and North Fork Loop).

COMMENTS: Ridge Runner Trail is a one-way trail that can be hiked either direction and connects the two loops of Noblett and North Fork. True to its name, the trail heads up, and leads across ridge top areas that provide one with glimpses of the fantastic scenery characteristic of the Ozarks. Climbs are steep and rocky but reward you with some excellent vistas and areas of rock out-croppings. Although the trail is well marked, it can be tough to follow at times due to overgrown brush and fallen trees in spots. During dry seasons, carry in water because it will only be found on either end, being scarce in between.

TOPOGRAPHICAL MAPS: Siloam Springs, Dyestone Mountain and Dora.

From the Noblett Trailhead, the trail begins to the left of the sign-in box taking you through a pleasant hardwood and pine forest stretch along a ridge, wind-ing around the hollows that reach to the bottoms below. As the ridge drops down into the valley, Spring Creek emerges across the trail creating a wet crossing. Upon crossing the creek, the trail immediately rises up a steep incline to regain position on the ridge for a short while before dropping back down to Galloway Spring at the one mile mark. From the spring, follow the trail as it winds up and back down a couple of times before reaching a fork with an accompanying sign. Taking a right will continue you through the Noblett loop and back up to the trailhead in 5 miles. You want to proceed straight, maintain-ing course along the Ridge Runner Trail as it continues through a pine forest area and past a small pond to the Horton Trailhead. Proceeding straight, the trail crosses a road, and encounters Horton Cemetery, a small older cemetery settled beneath the shade of a few large oak trees, and off the trail a bit to your right. At this point you have hiked 3.3 miles.

The trail stays on the ridge for a bit with the emergence of a scenic over-look on your right at 5.5 miles, providing views of the Dry Creek basin area and Sue's Hollow—a definite BTV. From here, the trail heads down into Horton Hollow and crosses Dry Creek at about 6.0. The name is more than appropriate for this creek bed as it doubtful that much water is ever contained in it. After crossing it, stay left and you'll find the marker identifying where the trail continues. (There is a logging type road on the right that is not the trail.) From here the trail becomes rough and rugged, crossing ground not well marked and seemingly very much undermaintained. Terrain is rocky with numerous fallen trees and excessive brush overgrowth, causing average hiking pace to be reduced to a minimum. Keep your eyes peeled for markers though and you'll find your way as you somewhat bushwhack down the trail! At about 8 miles in the scrambling over brush and trees ceases, and you will cross a gravel road to find a small but welcoming spring fed creek running through the base of Blue Hole Hollow. This small spring, which might run intermittently over the course of a year, is the only water source for quite a ways so it serves as a good rest stop or overnight area.

From the gravel road crossing and the spring, you will hike about ¼ of a mile or less before reaching a point where Ridge Runner Trail merges with the Ozark Trail. This section of the Ozark Trail originated from the Blue Hole Trailhead and would be found about a quarter of a mile down the trail if you kept hiking straight. The Ridge Runner Trail takes a right uphill tying in with the Ozark Trail for the remainder of the hike. Head right as the trail switchbacks uphill to the ridge where you will stay for a while, weaving through some very scenic, pine forested, rocky areas that add a rugged feel to the trail and atmosphere alike. You will cross an old logging road at 10 miles, continuing into the pines for a bit longer before heading back into hardwood forest prior to the crossing of Highway 14. At this crossing is a mini trailhead with a sign. Across the highway the trail heads back into the woods and stays on top of the ridge for the next couple miles, bringing significance to the name "Ridge Runner Trail". The trail crosses several logging roads up here and is less distinct making it tricky to follow, so remember to keep your eyes open for the markers. You'll know you're at the end of the ridge because it tapers off almost to a rocky point with a fantastic view of Hay Hollow on your right and Mine Hollow on your left, the combination of which creates a fabulous panoramic BTV. At the end of this point, the trail winds downhill through a rocky cedar grove continuing the BTV with a view of the hollow below. The downhill run continues, ending at a gravel road at about mile 13.5.

The trail continues directly across the road into a clearing, but if you follow the road to the right for a short distance you will discover Braddock Lake—a pleasant little spring fed lake with a huge beaver dam in the middle. Cross the road and the trail heads across a small field and back uphill along the ridge. During leaf-off you should have some more vista spots off to your left as you hike—very scenic. At mile 15 you will reach a fork in the trail. Right leads to Tabor Creek Trailcamp and left continues the Ridge Runner Trail. Almost immediately afterwards, the trail forks again signifying that you have reached part of the North Fork Loop. You can go right or left, as either direction takes you to Hammonds Camp, but for this guide, proceed left. This part of the trail is again, a bit hard to follow in spots, requiring your full attention in locating markers. It takes you up and down a few hollows for almost 6 miles before reaching the next fork and sign that designates where the loop would begin. From this fork go left and the trail continues for another mile and a half (the sign says only 1 mile), down and up a hollow and along a ridge, before heading down and across the road to the trailhead at Hammonds Camp.

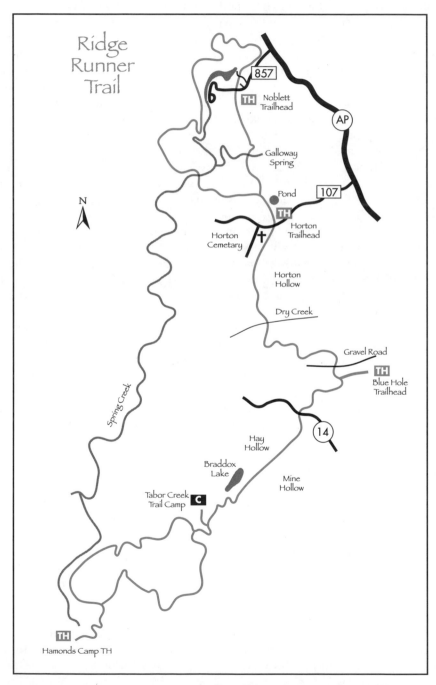

22. Ritter Springs

LOCATION: Ritter Springs is located just north of Springfield and can be reached by traveling north down Highway 13 from the Kansas Expressway, Highway 44 junction. Follow the signs for Fantastic Caverns as they share the same route. From Highway 44, take Highway 13 north for 1½ miles. Turn left onto Fantastic Caverns Road and follow it 1½ miles to FR 129 where you turn right. FR 129 comes to a "T" shortly and you turn right on FR 92 which leads you straight into the park.

LENGTH: Ritter Springs contains a network of small trails with the outermost loop covering approximately 2 miles.

COMMENTS: This place is a wonderful little park with a beautiful pond situated in the lower half that is home for a flock of Canada geese each spring. The surrounding area is all undeveloped and your almost sure to see deer, turkey or maybe even beaver, as is evidenced by the gnawed off tree stumps in the creek bed region. The trails are fairly short with some following the creek and around the lake, while others lead up to the ridge. It would be a wonderful place for family outings or just a relaxing afternoon.

TOPOGRAPHICAL MAPS: Ebenezer

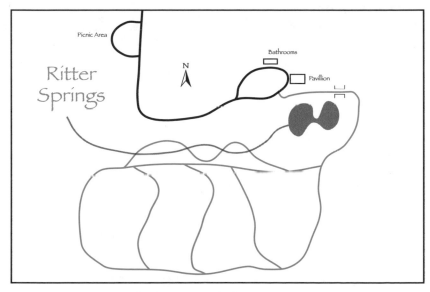

23. Roaring River

LOCATION: Roaring River State Park can be located by traveling 13 miles south on Highway 112 from Cassville.

LENGTH: The state park has 6 trails to offer:
    Firetower Trail—3.5 miles
    Eagles Nest Trail—2.3 miles
    Devil's Kitchen Trail—1.5 miles
    Pibern Trail—1.5 miles
    River Trail—.7 miles
    Deer Trail—.2 miles

COMMENTS: Roaring River, carving a narrow path through the wooded hills of the Ozarks, and possessing a spring which gushes over 20 million gallons of water per day, has long since been an area of activity and recreation. Situated in the heart of Missouri Ozarks, Roaring River provides a beautiful setting perfectly suited for the combined activities of camping, hiking, fishing and swimming. The park also houses a fish hatchery, nature center, cabins for rent and 2,075 acres of land protected as a Missouri Wild Area. Trails for the area are well marked, easy to hike and easy follow.

TOPOGRAPHICAL MAPS: Eagle Rock

FIRETOWER TRAILHEAD
The trailhead for the Firetower trail begins off Highway F in the state park at the Wild Area parking lot. The trail is well marked with yellow and brown arrows. From the Wild Area parking, the trail starts up, splits to the right at the first fork (left leads to the stables), and begins a steady climb, passing a small pond and a grove of cedar trees. Continuing up, the trail becomes steep in places but flattens out at 1400 feet displaying an array of rock outcroppings and rewarding views. At 1.5 the trail meets a small path on your left leading to the firetower lookout which offers spectacular views of Ketchum Hollow if you walk up to the top. Past the tower and a little over two miles, the trail reaches a fork and sign designating a side trail to the right marked with brown arrows and leading to the bluffs above the Roaring River spring. The main firetower trail continues straight and begins to descend down slowly to where the trail ends at Camp Smokey and Highway F. The Wild Area parking, where the trail began, is approximately half a mile to the east, down Highway F as it follows the river.

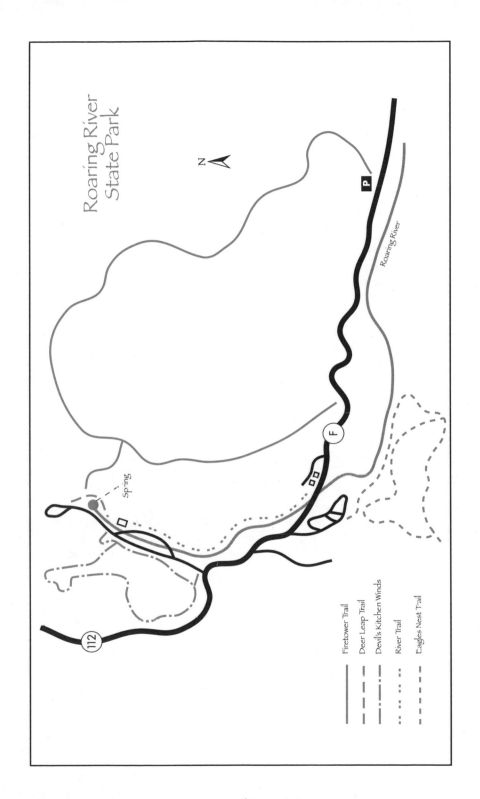

Roaring River
State Park

N

Roaring River

P

Spring

112

Firetower Trail
Deer Leap Trail
Devil's Kitchen Winds
River Trail
Eagles Nest Trail

EAGLES NEST TRAILHEAD

Eagles Nest trail starts behind Campground 2 and carves a pleasant path alongside Roaring River for half a mile before turning away and ascending up to one of the highest points in the park. At ¾ of a mile the trail forks with option right bearing green markers. Stay to the left, following yellow markers and enjoying the view of Roaring River far below. At the trail's top, you will again merge with the green marked trail and just beyond that some huge limestone bluffs bearing splendid views of the landscape below. Take a right on the green marked trail which leads back to the yellow in creation of a loop. Turn left, back onto yellow, where the two come together, and it leads back along the river to the beginning trailhead.

DEVIL'S KITCHEN TRAILHEAD

This trail begins to the north of the junction of Highway 112 and the hatchery road. Granting this trail its name, the featured highlight is a large rock outcropping forming an enclosure ideal for use as a hideout for outlaws. The trail is well marked in blue and yellow arrows and has an interpretive guide available for pick-up at the park's nature center.

PIBERN TRAIL

The Pibern trail begins at one end of the Campground 1 and ends at the other, requiring a short walk back by way of the road. The 1.5 miles of trail curves up to 1200 feet and traverses the length of the ridge before descending back down. Varied terrain and habitat is encountered within the area drawing unique beauty and a pleasant atmosphere to this small trail.

RIVER TRAIL

The name is self-explanatory as this trail simply follows alongside the river from the park store to the cabins for a pleasant walk of less than a mile.

DEER LEAP TRAIL

Deer Leap is the shortest of the trails within this park, but leads to the namesake, Roaring River Spring, as well as an overlook just above the fish hatchery. The trail can be accessed at the fish hatchery pools and the waterfall.

Hiking Tip — Emergency Blanket

Reflective mylar, and or an emergency blanket should be carried in every first aid kit. This lightweight emergency tool can aid in prevention of hypothermia on cold and/or wet trips where conditions can easily cause hikers to get chilled from the combination of exertion and cool temperatures.

24. Rocky Falls

LOCATION: Rocky Falls is located in Shannon County, south of Ellington, along the Current River. From HWY 60 at Winona, take HWY 19 north, to a quick right onto HWY H. Follow H about ten miles to HWY NN where you take another right. Two miles down, lies County Road 526. This takes you straight to the parking lot and picnic area for Rocky Falls.

LENGTH: From the parking lot, there are various short hikes available up and downstream along Rocky Creek that can easily create a days worth of exploration and mini side trips. The Ozark Trail intersects here, allowing for a two mile option to the south up Stegall Mountain, or a two mile option to the north, leading to Klepzig Mill. For an even longer option, the hike from Rocky Falls all the way through to Powder Mill Ferry is 9 miles, one-way.

COMMENTS: More like a huge cascade, Rocky Falls isn't so much a straight drop of water off a cliff, as it is an impressive rush of whitewater carving its way down through the igneous rock into a giant pool below. This spectacular display is the highlight of a incredibly scenic surrounding area that should definitely be explored and hiked if you have the time. Day hikes around the falls and along Rocky Creek offer some nice scenic stops, and hold a multitude of hidden treasures as well. Portions of Rocky Creek resemble the famed Johnson Shut-ins, as it holds the mix of igneous and sedimentary rock that create rock chutes and pools for water to flow through in a myriad of patterns and paths. Further south from Rocky Falls, down the Ozark Trail, lies Stegall Mountain which offers a splendid BTV of the surrounding area, should you be adventurous enough to hike, or rather climb a couple miles to get there. Beavers and beaver dams are common to the area and evidence of their habitation can readily viewed if you venture just a few yards down the old dirt road towards the west bank of the giant pool below Rocky Falls. Hold still and be patient long enough, you might even catch a glimpse of one at work!

TOPOGRAPHICAL MAPS: Winona

Once you have arrived at the parking lot, you have reached Rocky Falls. The hiking for this enchanting and pleasant place revolves around the Ozark Trail which passes through here and allows some "out and back" side trips in either direction. If you're up for a bit of an elevation increase, the climb up to Stegall Mountain rewards you with some awesome BTV's and a beautiful panorama of the surrounding area. From Rocky Falls, follow the creek down below the pool to the intersection of the Ozark Trail.

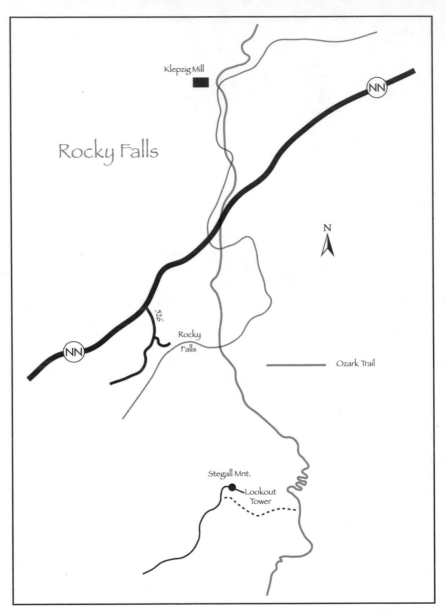

There is a sign here, and markers with the traditional green and white OT symbols label the trail to lead you in either direction. Take the trail south or to your right and you will make the first portion of your side trip easy as it passes through Kelley Hollow before crawling up the hillside in the formation of switchbacks. The top of Stegall Mountain is a uniquely scenic gladed area strewn with rocks jumbled in color and type. The vegetation is limited and fragile, resulting in OT trail markers being replaced by mini rock piles scattered along the trail's edge. Bring a picnic lunch and spend some time up here soaking up sunshine and enjoying the scope of this mountain's panoramic view; the trek back will be "cake" compared to the upward climb of your approach!

The other side trip option from Rocky Falls is to head north, or left from that trail intersection, and hike towards Buzzard Mountain and Klepzig Mill. Unlike Stegall Mountain, this portion of the Ozark Trail remains a bit more level as it follows Rocky Creek, veering away and then back at points, but not climbing too much. Not long into this trek, and you will exit onto HWY NN. Follow NN east, or to your right for a small detour, and watch for the green and white OT markers, indicating continuation of the trail on the road's opposite side, shortly after crossing the bridge. From here the trail winds to and from the creek, bringing you through some very pleasant little shut-in areas at points, particularly as you funnel through the hollow formed by the flank of Buzzard Mountain on your left and Mill Mountain on your right. Catch this section during the spring or after a rain and you will thoroughly enjoy the series of rapids and mini falls that are created from the rocks varied in color and type. The continuation of the trail away from the creek forces you to leave this pleasant spot, as it edges across the lower portion of Mill Mountain through the hardwoods for about the next mile. Hike in anticipation, however, because the best is yet to come! As the trail exits the forested area once again to join Rocky Creek, it brings you to Klepzig Mill, a definite photo shoot and BTV. Built in the early 1900's, this mill was once powered by water diverted from Rocky Creek via a flume, to be held by the then existing concrete dam. Crumbling remains of the dam are still visible as well as an old well house, some other foundation ruins and of course the mill itself. This entire area is fantastic and well worth the trip, especially during times of rain, when the shut-ins are running full throttle. Klepzig Mill can also be accessed via the other side of the Ozark Trail that leads along the Current River bluffs. If you were to continue down the Ozark Trail from this point, you would arrive at the Powder Mill Ferry trailhead in 7 miles. Directions and highlights from Powder Mill to here are given elsewhere in this book under Klepzig Mill Trail.

Rocky Falls

25. Sam A. Baker State Park

Mudlick Mountain Trail

LOCATION: Mudlick Mountain Trail is located inside Sam A. Baker State Park, off HWY 143, 4 miles north of Patterson. HWY 143 can also be accessed from HWY 49 at the town of Des Arc.

LENGTH: Mudlick is a 12 mile loop trail.

COMMENTS: Located in the St. Francois Mountains, Mudlick Mountain Wild Area is a 4,180 acre wilderness preserve contained within the boundaries of Sam A. Baker State Park. Established in 1926, by Governor Sam Baker, this rugged, yet majestic wilderness area which was originally preserved as a wildlife refuge for the rebuilding of the then endangered deer and turkey population, is now one of Missouri's classic state parks. Offering everything from a night under the stars atop Mudlick Mountain to a cozy stay in one of the park's historic cabins, this entire park is worth the visit, and is a haven for any outdoor enthusiast.

The 12 mile Mudlick Mountain loop can be reduced to a shorter hike as the park offers many different trailheads, spurs and smaller loops. The BTV's atop the 1,313 foot Mudlick Mountain however, are worth the winding trek upward and should be witnessed by any hiking visitor. Should you be hiking between October 1st and May 15th, check on the availability for one of the parks 3 backpacking shelters, located along the mountain's ridgetop. These shelters may be used by hikers on a first come, first served basis, and should you be fortunate enough to claim one for a night, you will enjoy a beautiful view and ideal setting.

For the more family oriented park visitor, Sam A. Baker's northeastern border, Big Creek, provides fishing and floating. Cabins are rentable April 1st through October 31st, and dining is available in the old rustic lodge. For more park and activity information, call 314-856-4223.

TOPOGRAPHICAL MAPS: Patterson

The trailhead for Mudlick Mountain originates across from the old dining lodge. It is here too that one can opt for a shorter one-way hike down the mile and a half Shut-Ins Trail instead. With allowances for both hikers and equestrians, the Mudlick trail loop heads northwest away from the dining lodge along the flats of Big Creek. With Mudlick Mountain base to your left, a canopy of forest vegetation hides the bluish-gray granite boulder outcrops that are the mountain's make-up. Springtime visitors will enjoy glimpses of hidden waterfalls that cascade down these outcrops as well as the beautiful yellow leaves and white blossoms of the park's unique yellowood trees, a species more Appalachian native.

As the flat land slowly evolves into more challenging switchbacks across the mountain, the thick vegetation opens up into glades, grasses and rocky soil. Watch for openings on your right that carry a definite BTV of the Big Creek Valley and surrounding St. Francois Mountains. Continue upward and you will soon arrive at the first of three shelters. Ruggedly built out of stone and timber, and strategically designed to be molded into the mountainside, these overnight shelters mimic what one might see along the Appalachian Trail. The views are spectacular, tagging these mountainside lean-two luxuries as a primo camping stop.

Catch the BTV's all along the trail as it passes each of the three shelters and plateau's somewhat on top. Eventually, 2 miles in at the third shelter, the trail intersects. Allowing for a shorter loop left, this intersection leads to a completed hike of 7 miles, and also goes by the firetower spur. The continuation of Mudlick Trail's 12 mile loop proceeds right, down to Mudlick Creek. Stay right for the longer trek. Mudlick Creek is a very pleasant Big Creek tributary that holds a couple unofficial, yet secluded gravel bar like campsites right next to the water, which is a plus should you wish to camp along this trail. Once you're past this creek, the next creek crossing doesn't appear until the park's opposite southern end. Mudlick Creek also offers a hiker's springtime BTV as the trail follows up alongside this steep creek run displaying all kinds of cascades and waterfalls twisting down and around the rock jumble of sporadically arranged granite boulders. The water show is spectacular, and worth a few photos.

Sam A. Baker State Park

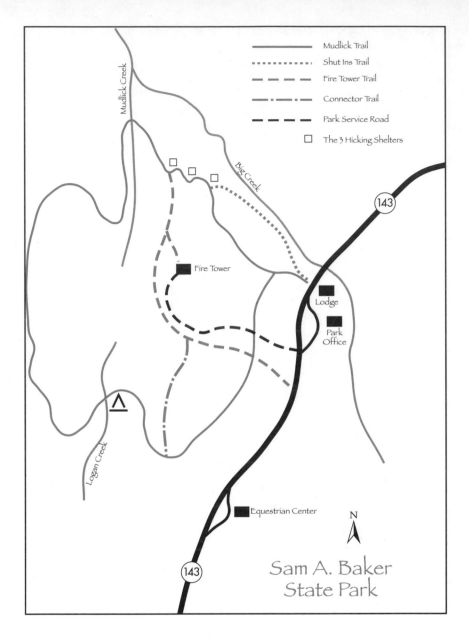

From the creek, the trail does climb a bit, passing by a corner of private land and then plateauing out close to 1,000 feet. It is at this elevation that the trail remains level, as it heads directly south, graduates into the remains of an old roadbed for a while and then switchbacks down towards the crossing at Logan Creek. The trail doesn't stay down long, immediately heading upward once more upon the crossing of Logan Creek. Up at the 1,000 foot elevation mark again, hikers have an option to proceed left, back north towards the fire-tower road via an old roadbed, or follow the trail around till it gradually heads north, looping back to the cabins.

26. Springfield Nature Center

LOCATION: Located in Springfield, close to HWY 65 and HWY 60, travel west down HWY 60, one mile from the HWY 60 and 65 junction, to the Glenstone exit. Go south, over the highway, and turn left onto the outer road that heads back east. This outer roads leads straight to the nature center.

LENGTH: There are plenty of options here for hiking length. Trails range from .5 to 2 miles in length, but can be intermixed for longer hikes. The Springfield Greenways Trail also connects, allowing for additional miles.

COMMENTS: For being an "in town" conservation area, located basically at the corner intersection of two major highways, this area is surprisingly quiet, peaceful and in spots, even a bit on the remote side. Portions of Lake Springfield border the area, offering nice viewing spots for wood ducks, eagles and other waterfowl. Terrain is varied with some wonderful high-point vistas, glades, bottomland field areas and rustic wooded acreage as well. The lower portion of this area connects with the Springfield Greenways, a trail connecting project still in progress for the entire Springfield area. Connection from the nature center though, is complete all the way through to Sequiota Park, with another side portion leading to an old abandon bridge crossing over Lake Springfield. The entire mini-network of trails here offers tremendous variety and plenty of mileage, and is all within a pleasant setting that is excellent for day hiking, or an afternoon outdoors with the family.

TOPOGRAPHICAL MAPS: Galloway

With a good-size trail network available, many route options can be chosen, but described here will be the Long Trail and Fox Bluff Trail combination to total 2 miles. From the base of this trail combination, all other sidetrips, alternate trails, and connections can be made. Long Trail starts at the pavilion, along a paved surface that winds into the woods very quickly to an intersection that is basically a mini loop of the Savannah Ridge Trail (all paved and .2 miles long). Either direction here will lead you to the continuation of Long Trail that graduates shortly onto a woodchip path and heads downhill. More into the woods now, the pleasantness of this trail begins to set in, and as you wind around towards the bottom, the trail flattens out to come alongside Galloway Creek, a stream that flows into Lake Springfield. It is down in this area that you are likely to see deer feeding by the water or standing motionless in the thick of the woods.

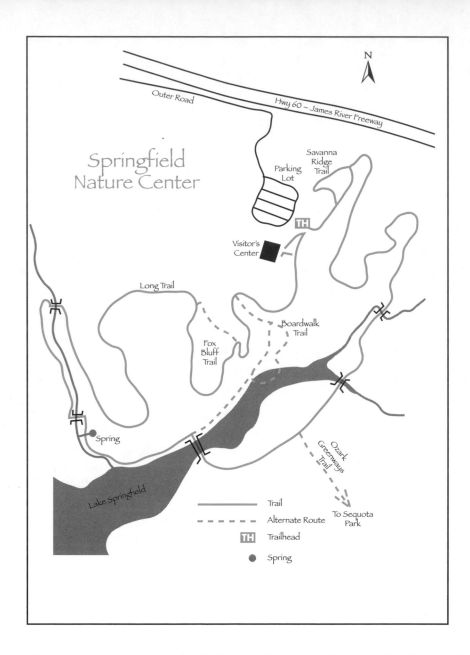

Crossing over a wooden footbridge and then another wooden boardwalk, the trail empties out into the open grasslands. It is mid-way across this field that the Greenways Trail intersects, giving you the option to veer away from the nature center, to the left and hike along the level path leading approximately 2 miles to Sequiota Park. This popular stretch of the greenway is flat with a chat-like surface ideal for walking and biking both. (You will probably see a few bikers out on this trail portion.) The setting is not quite as rustic as inside the nature center, but the walk is very pleasant, and if you want to add some mileage to your hike, it is a great trail add-on.

To remain on the Long Trail through the nature center, rather than opting for the Greenway's route, stay straight at the intersection and it will lead out of the grasslands, passing by the birdwatching, Photo Blind Trail on the left, and over a wooden bridge that expands across a portion of Lake Springfield. This is an excellent spot to stop and watch the ducks, catch a blue heron in action or spy out a muskrat or two! The bridge's opposite side gives another trail intersection, allowing a shortcut route to the right, or the continuation of Long Trail left. The right shortcut leads back to the visitor's center faster, but it also provides access to the Boardwalk Trail which is a tiny little loop on pavement and boardwalk that leads around a marshy area of the lake allowing for some additional wildlife viewing. It's really a cool little side loop.

The main trail proceeds left and becomes a bit rockier as well. Watch out during wet weather because this little stretch really gets slick! Following along-side the tail end of the lake's arm that graduates into a stream, the trail leads past a spring and over a small bridge to continue following the stream's other side. This section holds a more "remote" atmosphere, and is especially beautiful when water from the creek is passing over the large limestone rocks that line the stream bed. Curving right, the trail crosses another wooden footbridge and takes you across the nature center's glade area via a wooden boardwalk lead-ing slightly uphill. The boardwalk ends where the trail enters back into the hardwoods, but the incline intensifies a bit, leading up to a bench and vista point on your right, and then up and on around to the top of the hill. This is another popular spot to sight a deer or two. In fact, as the trail moves down slightly, it passes by a fenced in portion of land on your right which has been put up by SMSU in efforts to study the effect of deer on the environment.

Just past this area is the official end of Long Trail, as it empties out onto the Fox Bluff Trail—a ⅓ of a mile loop. The right option is prettier and leads around to another vista point overlooking Lake Springfield below. Just past this tiny lookout, the trail intersects. Take a right, and follow the switchback down-hill to where the trail crosses a small wooden bridge and merges with the pave-ment. Right will lead to the Boardwalk Trail loop and the intersection after the larger bridge that you crossed earlier. Straight and uphill will lead back to the visitor's center for a total of about two miles (without side trips).

Hiking Tip — Boots and Whistles

Whistles are always a good idea to carry while hiking in the woods. Hikers can use their whistle to alert of an emergency, or to call out for help if injured or lost. Placing the whistle around your neck with an extra boot lace not only makes it easily accessible, but also provides you with a back up shoestring, should you break one on the trail.

27. Victory Horse Trail

LOCATION: The Victory Horse Trail is located approximately 8 miles northwest of Popular Bluff. The trailhead begins near the old Victory School site which can be found on County Road 410, 2 to 3 miles west on US 60 from US 67, between Cane Creek and the US 60-67 junction. Turn down County Road 410, a gravel road and go less than a mile before turning right on FR 3117. The trailhead is ahead about 100 yards.

LENGTH: This trail if hiked from the Victory School to Highway A, is 18 miles long. There is, however, a six mile loop on the southeastern end that can be accessed from Victory School as well.

COMMENTS: Most of the Victory Trail is part of the Ozark Trail and known as the Victory section of the OT. Hardwood forests scattered with some good sized pine stands, typify this pleasant hiking trail. The six mile loop section of the trail at the southern end is commonly hiked by itself but is also used by equestrians. From Victory School to Highway A, hiking is gentle due to mild inclines and fairly easy terrain. The trail winds among and across several logging roads that make it easy to veer off in the wrong direction. Hikers should pay close attention to markers and bring map and compass with them. Water is also scarce. There are a few creek crossings, but they are most likely dry during most of the hiking months. If you have a good water filter you could access water from a couple scattered ponds along the trail.

TOPOGRAPHICAL MAPS: Ellisnore, Williamsville, and Stringtown.

The trail starts through hardwood forest in a northwest direction and continues that general direction for the entire 18 miles. The beginning part of the trail, which is also the beginning for those just hiking the loop, is wide and with a combination of wet weather and equestrians, can be muddy and difficult to manage. At about ½ mile you will come to a small stream crossing and shortly thereafter the beginning of the loop. Take a left here, although you can head either direction and still connect with the Victory Trail. The trail continues with some more spots vulnerable to equestrian traffic and as you approach the 2 mile mark you will head uphill along one of these areas where the trail will veer off the cart path to the right and into the woods. Pay attention to the markers, less you end up at a "T" at the top, with a cart path leading either direction. If you reach this T, you missed the turn by a couple hundred feet. The correct trail winds through the trees, off the beaten horse path, and will lead across the first of many logging roads. The trail is fairly level for a bit until you head down hill and cross another creek, this one being a tributary to Crane Creek. Immediately after crossing at about mile 3, the trail T's and you can go right or left. Right takes you east towards the Wrangler Trailhead of the OT, and is also the direction to take if you are doing the loop. Stay left if you are wanting to continue the trail. It will take you across another gravel logging road and then down into a pleasant little area known as Wiley King Hollow. The trail weaves back and forth across a couple of streams. During wet season it might make following the trail a little difficult. The entire hollow area is really a charming place and if water is present, would be an ideal overnight spot. From the Wiley King Hollow, you proceed back up and across another gravel road. Shortly thereafter is one of the small ponds, to the left, that is a

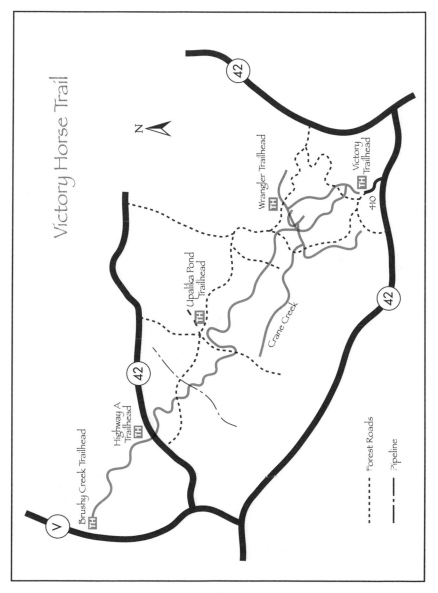

possible water source if one has a filter. If you pass the pond and hike down a bit, you will enter the Dry Creek Branch area—true to its name most of the year. At this point you have hiked about 7.5 miles.

Once across Dry Creek, the trail curves slightly up and passes some private property on your left and a pond overgrown with shrubs on your right. You will hike along the ridge for a bit before heading down and up through a couple of nice little hollows. The trail takes you through a mix of hardwood and pine stands for the next couple miles passing by ponds and across a few open field areas. Eventually the trail follows alongside a gravel road for a while before finally winding slightly away and downhill to where you cross it and meet an Ozark Trail trailhead. You are at the 13 mile mark. Victory Trail continues from the back of the field that lies at this trailhead and continues uphill. The next 5 miles from here to Highway A crosses alot of old logging type roads, and at places where they have cut trees, the trail is easy to lose. At 14.5 you'll cross an area where the pipeline has been run through and about mile after that you'll cross a slightly raised gravel road that was once a railroad bed. Most of the confusion as to where the trail proceeds lies after this old railroad bed, however, it weaves through some very pleasant pine stands and is marked, so just keep your eyes peeled. The trail takes you down into, and north along Wet Hollow, then back up and almost straight west down along Seed Tick Hollow, which is your last stretch before heading uphill to Highway A.

An additional 5.5 miles can be hiked if you continue from Highway A to the Brushy Creek Trailhead.

Hiking Tip — Kitchen Clean-Up

When cleaning up camp after a meal, there are a few outdoor etiquette rules to keep in mind. First, do all your cleaning, and personal washing at least 200 feet from any water source. Fill one of your clean cooking pots with water necessary to wash the remaining dishes. Second, all kitchen scraps, trash and meal remains should be placed in a plastic bag – not thrown in the woods. Pack it in, pack it out! Third, "camper clean" is usually achievable without soap, however, if necessary, use a biodegradable brand such as Campsuds, or Bronners. Just a few additional cleaning tips:

- Use soap sparingly, and do not empty soap rinse back into creek or water source.
- If fuel amounts allow, heat some water on your stove to make washing easier.
- Pine Cones are an excellent scraper for wiping excess food from the sides of cooking pots.
- It's not a bad idea to cook away from your tent site; and never leave food out overnight—it attracts critters, and in some Northern Arkansas areas, even black bears.
- Recruit the help of your furry four-legged friend—dogs are always the best dishwashers in the place!

28. Wappapello Lake Trail

LOCATION: Lake Wappapello is just north of Poplar Bluff Missouri. From the junction of HWY 60 and HWY 67, take HWY 67 north for 13 miles to HWY 172. Turn east onto HWY 172 and it will lead to the trailhead in 7.5 miles. Look for the trailhead sign on your right, turning left onto the gravel road that leads to the trail's start.

LENGTH: The Wappapello Trail is a solid 15 miles in length.

COMMENTS: Lake Wappapello stands along with Table Rock, as one of the Army Corps of Engineer's oldest reservoir parks. The controversial damming of the St. Francois River in 1941 formed this 8,400 acre body of water, which today is the playground for all who enjoy the resultant contrast of quiet lake-side serenity, with the surrounding rough wooded acreage. Rugged in terrain and seemingly longer than the recorded 15 miles, the Wappapello Trail can provide one with a challenging hike, but its lake-side border and aged timber setting offers some beautiful scenery, large trees and a remote atmosphere. Sharing paths with bikers and equestrians, backpackers may discover others on this loop trail as well, but with overall trail usage being minimal, your on your own.

The trail's lake-side portion is by far its highlight, rising up and down with changing topography as it hugs the shoreline edge to allow frequent glimpses of water through the trees. Possessing a few challenging uphill climbs, this 15 mile loop can be a tough day-hiking adventure, but if tackled in the form of an overnight, the length is much more reasonable. Campsites are available along the trail specifically for this purpose, so take advantage of their availability and plan a weekend in the woods.

Aside from this more hard-core 15 mile loop, Wappapello offers a series of shorter trails as well, ranging from the .5 mile Lake View Trail, to the 2 and 3.5 mile trails of Asher Creek and Allison Cemetery. With the center attraction for Wappapello being the lake itself, there is of course plenty of water recreation activities available during the summer, as well as cabin rentals and a camp-ground. Overall this park provides plenty of family oriented amenities available for the provision of an excellent daytime visit or weekend stay.

TOPOGRAPHICAL MAPS: Wappapello

Tagged with yellow markers, the trail starts off heading in an easterly direction, meeting up with a creek almost immediately that has a nice little footbridge to lead you across. Down in the bottoms of Allison Hollow for a short bit before working your way up, the trail leads into a pine forest stretch to settle upon the ridge. Moving through the hardwoods now, this stretch brings some of the beginning glimpses of Lake Wappapello into view—a scenery bonus that will follow the trail for much of this eastern half. It is within the first mile that this lakeside view graduates into an "up close" picture, as the trail leads around a mini point and down to the shoreline. Departing from the shoreline, the trail then leads into the wooded depths, across a little creek bottom and uphill to intersect with an old road. The sign here directs you left. Continue down this retired logging road as it should lead you past the first campsite. As you hike up this road, watch for tree markers to the right indicating the trail's exit off the road, back into the single track and through the timber to proceed uphill. The steep climb continues a bit but lake views emerge, rewarding your effort as you reach the top. Flattening out on the ridge, the trail's elevated vantage point brings about some nice BTV's of Wappapello below. This lake panorama continues for a good stretch, edging closer to the water to contour with the lake's shoreline in places, as it winds around a few shallow peninsula points.

The momentary level trek drops down at about the 3 mile mark to cross a creek that could very well be a wet crossing during rainy months. Taking advantage of the water availability, it is here that the second backpacking campsite resides. This little spot already set-up with a firepit and a few large rocks for resting, is an excellent area for an overnight stay. Just past this campsite the trail moves across a little wet area, and as you traverse this section, take note of a huge American elm tree just off the path—one of the first of several very large trees that can be sighted along this trail.

Climbing again, the trail moves "up over and around" to skirt another waterline portion of the lake as it maintains its position along the ridge. Intersecting with a road at 6 miles, a sign pointing right indicates another camping area. Follow it down to an awesome little scenic peninsula where it appears that an old homestead once resided. A couple of old stone fireplace remains, now utilized as fire pits, are available for use if camping. The peninsula here opens up a wide view of Wappapello, creating a BTV as well as a very pleasant site for pitching a tent. Whether camping or just lunch-breaking at this pleasant spot, when your ready to be trail-bound once again, re-trace your steps back to the main trail to continue.

A slight incline up leads to the next ridge where the trail borrows a level trek for only a short bit before climbing once again. With the lake northeast of you now, small glimpses of water shine through the trees as you hike across the flattened ridgetop, head back down, and wind around the low drainage areas of Lilly Hollow. A steep climb originating from the depths of one of these basins leads you to a road crossing at the 8 mile mark, which you will want to take to the left. The road leads about 50 yards up to an old cemetery entitled Chaonia, to which the trail skirts around to the north. You are now into the western section of the Wappapello Trail. Continue down the trail as it will move around the hollows with only a few short but steep little inclines. Winding through the hardwoods, the trail drops down slightly at just under 9 miles to cross a portion of Snow Creek and around to a trail intersection at 9.5. The option right is a side-trail leading to the Chaonia Landing, while the trail left is actually the main route and the one you will want to take.

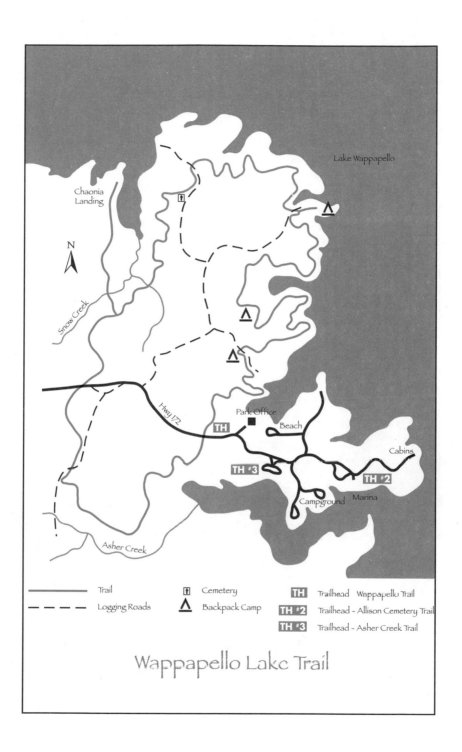

Wappapello Lake Trail

Legend:
- ———— Trail
- - - - - Logging Roads
- 🏠 Cemetery
- ⛺ Backpack Camp
- **TH** Trailhead Wappapello Trail
- **TH #2** Trailhead – Allison Cemetery Trail
- **TH #3** Trailhead – Asher Creek Trail

Map labels: Chaonia Landing, Lake Wappapello, Snow Creek, Hwy 172, Park Office, Beach, Cabins, Campground, Marina, Asher Creek

Be prepared as the next mile produces another large incline leading up to a BTV and rewarding overlook during leaf-off times. Notice here that upon reaching the top of this ridge, you also enter into a "no camping" zone, which due to the lack of water up here, should not be a problem. You can welcome the somewhat flattened section as the trail remains on top for a while, dropping down gently to intersect with HWY 172 at about 13.25. It is at this intersection that the option to shorten this trail by just a bit lies. Although the short-cut back to the original trailhead requires a walk down the highway, you can proceed left here to return in under 14 miles. The main trail actually crosses HWY 172 though, which will be slightly longer but quite a bit more scenic as it continues through much of the same hardwoods and rolling terrain. With a more mild trek to the ridge and back down on 172's other side, the trail leads out of the "no camping zone", and intersects with another old road that the trail merges with to the right. Sharing paths for a short while, the trail leaves the road rather suddenly with a sharp turn-off to your left as it traverses across the Asher Creek area. Not in the lower elevation for long, the trail moves up once again and across a couple of ridges to enter back into the official state park land for Wappapello. From here the trailhead is just ahead, along a mainly level bench for the remaining mile. Follow the trail around the end of the lake's marina arm to HWY 172 and the trailhead parking. Congratulations, you've completed one heck of a hike!

Wappapello Lake

29. White River Bluffs Trail

Shepherd of the Hills Fish Hatchery

LOCATION: White River Bluffs Trail is located at the Shepherd of the Hills Fish Hatchery off HWY 165 south of Branson.

LENGTH: This is a short trail, covering 1.6 miles in length, with an even shorter loop option of .6 miles.

COMMENTS: Run by the Missouri Department of Conservation, Shepherd of the Hills Fish Hatchery is the department's largest running trout facility. Created and opened originally to supply trout for Lake Taneycomo once Table Rock Dam was completed, this hatchery has been in operation since 1958. In addition to the site's main purpose of trout production, Shepherd of the Hills Fish Hatchery sits adjacent to wilderness acreage managed to protect wildlife, and is therefore an area for hiking, fishing and bird watching as well.

The White River Bluffs Trail is a gorgeous little trail that rises up over 200 feet above the White River Valley, extending some spectacular views and offering a beautiful setting for this short hike. The fabulous overlook views originating from the top of this trail's bluffs do require somewhat of a climb, but the ascent is gradual, and not too strenuous. After completing the hike, you might consider touring the hatchery as it is open for exploration, along with the opportunity to trout fish. Other trails located here are also available for hiking, and covered paths winding in and around the hatchery grounds.

TOPOGRAPHICAL MAPS: Table Rock Dam

From the parking lot east of the fish hatchery, the trail takes off on its mission to rise to the bluffline overlooking the White River Valley. Running through a small pine stand and cedar mix, the trek to the top begins via a gentle incline along a well maintained trail. As you slowly ascend, a trail coming in on your left marks the return route, so stay right, or straight and enjoy the openings for the nice views that begin to emerge. From various trail stops, glimpses of the dam as well as the White River come into view. Another trail connector allowing a shorter route option if taken left emerges, creating a total of only .6 miles if desired. Stay more right for the longer loop and by the time the trail tops out, flattening out upon the bluff's highest point, you will have covered such a neat little section of the trail that its surprising to remember how close you are to Branson.

Up on top now, the trail splits off, leading to a private residence on the right. Stay left for the continuing loop and the trail moves through another small cedar area. You will pass the trail from the shorter loop emptying out

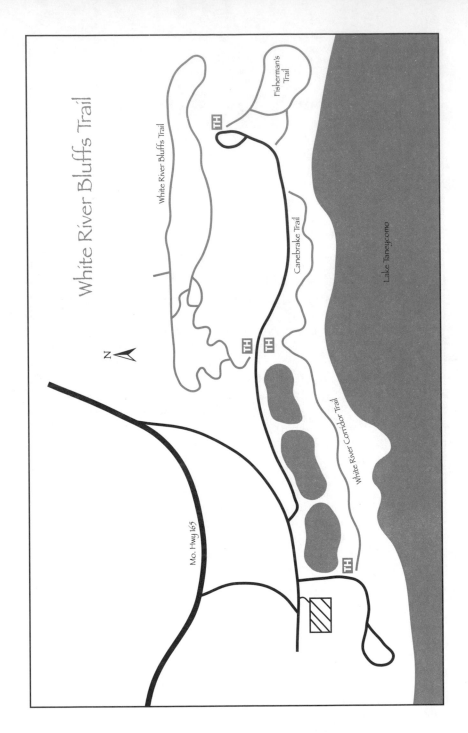

onto the main trail, so stay right again and you will maintain course. A few more scattered views and pleasant vantage points reside along the return stretch, and soon the trail winds back down to the parking area where you began.

30. Whites Creek Trail

LOCATION: The trailhead is located off Highway J, which is off Highway 60 at Fremont, 10 miles west of Van Buren and 22 miles east of Willow Springs. From 60, go south on J about 15 miles to the Camp Five Pond turnoff, which is a gravel road on your right.

LENGTH: The trail is a loop of approximately 21 miles in length.

COMMENTS: Commonly known as the Irish Wilderness Area, Whites Creek is a wonderfully pleasant backpacking trail that traverses some of Missouri's common hardwood forest areas scattered with a few pine stands, and rocky cedar glades. The wilderness area is characterized by the karst topography so common in the Ozarks featuring sinkholes, caves, disappearing streams and natural springs. The trail holds many highlights, one of which is the breathtaking view from the trail's west side overlooking the beautiful Eleven Point River. Steep limestone bluffs house a handful of caves for the area, the largest of which is Whites Creek Cave, a popular cavern for exploring, but closed September to April in efforts to preserve endangered bats.

TOPOGRAPHICAL MAPS: Riverton and Wilderness

The trailhead at Camp Five begins behind the pond itself where there is also a nice campsite nestled in the trees, overlooking the pond. There is a sign at the trailhead that marks the beginning of the trail, and from here the trail heads west. The entire trail is well marked with white blazes and should be fairly easy to follow. About fifty yards past the trailhead comes the first fork. Take a right and you are beginning the loop. This first section of trail is mainly hardwood forest, and winds around along some small ridges, crossing hollows and a few dry creek beds. Dry Prong Creek is one of the first of the dry creek beds you reach and is ½ mile into the trail. As you continue past Dry Prong, Camp 9 pond is to the north of the trail although there is no official side trail leading to it. At 3.0 miles, you will cross Whites Creek and enter into Larimore Hollow.

Shortly thereafter, the trail turns into a old logging road and at about 4.5 miles, heads slightly uphill to a fork with a sign designating Brawley Pond to the right and Bliss Spring straight ahead. Continue straight toward Bliss Springs on the logging road. Approximately 1 mile past the fork, you pass through a shaded pine forest stand resembling the beautiful, large lodgepole pines out west. The trail hooks left around this pine stand and remains fairly level until you come off the top of Tumbling Shoal Hollow where the terrain becomes rocky and a bit more rugged. The trail proceeds down to Bliss Spring Hollow where there is another fork and sign. This is at 8.5 miles. To the right, about 25 or 30 feet is the origin of Bliss Spring; a beautiful natural spring that flows out from the large rock formations situated behind it. To the left, the trail continues to complete the loop back to Camp Five. If, however you proceed right, straight past the spring, the trail will take you to Bliss Spring Campsite—a most excellent BTV and a wonderful place to spend the night. The campsite itself appears to have been an old homestead at one point with the foundation and stone fireplace being the only remains. You can easily see the reasoning behind the choice of homestead location because directly below the campsite is the Eleven Point river, a superb place to play in the water after a long day of hiking.

To continue the trail from this campsite you must hike back to the fork at Bliss Spring and take a right. The trail climbs up from Bliss Spring and follows along the bluff line for a short while overlooking the Eleven Point River and creating another BTV. As you pass the bluff vistas, the trail goes up for about a mile and a half and becomes steep and rocky at points. When it finally flattens out, you're on top of the ridge and the trail blends into an old logging road that will provide for some much appreciated level hiking. Continuing across this even terrain, the trail leisurely heads down through a isolated cedar glade and then across Whites Creek where there is a fork without a sign. Turn right, off the logging road and follow the blazes on the trees. The trail is in the valley and follows an extended bluff line across Whites Creek (on your right), that displays a series of overhangs, pockets, and small caves ideal for the Irish immigrants or soldiers to have hidden in during the Civil War. (A bit of history regarding the Irish Wilderness name.) The area here is unique, possessing a remoteness and splendor that declares it as a BTV. Continue alongside the creek and bluff line until you reach a sign and another fork. The trail to the right goes across the creek and takes you all the way to Whites Creek Float Camp. This is a canoe campground on the Eleven Point River with fire pits and picnic tables. At this fork, however, continue straight and to the left, it will take you up past White's Creek Cave. This cave is located up the hill a bit to your right, and is closed from September 15th to April 30th due to the Indiana bats which are endangered.

Continuing on past the cave the trail goes uphill until it eventually flattens out into another old logging road which stays on top for only a short time before descending down to another fork and sign. To the left is the side trail leading to Fiddler Springs, a refreshing site featuring the spring which comes out from the rocks creating a mini BTV. This is scenic spot and a nice place to take a rest break. To the

Whites Creek

right the main trail continues down, following an old creek bed for a while and then crosses the creek at a couple different spots, possibly with wet crossings depending on the season. At some points upon crossing, the trail can appear to veer off in two different directions, so watch for blazes as they will indicate the proper trail, and keep you headed in a northeasterly direction.

Out of the creek bottom, the trail starts uphill again and runs into an old logging road. At this point you are about three miles from Camp Five Pond. Stay on the logging road as it makes its way across the flattened ridge top thick with hardwood forest. During leaf off periods, there are some nice views through the trees to the left. Eventually the logging road tapers back into a basic trail. At this point you are close to the end. Your next division in the trail is the very first one that began the entire loop. If you wish to do the 21 mile loop again, take a left. If not, proceed to the right and it will take you back to Camp Five.

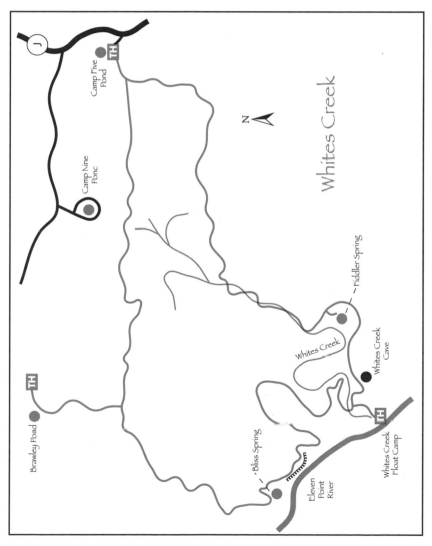

31. Bell Mountain

LOCATION: Bell Mountain Wilderness is located south of Potosi and can be reached by taking Highway 21 south, to Highway 32 west to Highway A. There are three trailheads granting access to the area:

Trailhead 1: Shortly after turning onto Highway A, look for FR 2228 on your left. It is a gravel road and there is a sign for Bell Mountain here. Take FR 2228 about 2 miles to the trailhead.

Trailhead 2: If you continue down Highway A, past the turnoff to Trailhead 1 by about 5 miles, you will find a small parking lot and trailhead on the right, directly off the highway.

Trailhead 3: A newly developed trailhead also resides further down on Highway A. Check with the Potosi/Fredricktown Ranger District for details on this new access.

LENGTH: The trail is 9 miles long between trailheads, with a partially maintained connector trail creating a loop and adding extra trail mileage.

COMMENTS: Bell Mountain Trail is characteristic of the entire St. Francois area as it is full of creative rock formations and fantastic scenery. The trail is a bit rough, being rocky and having a couple good climbs, but it is well worth the

The view from Bell Mountain Trail

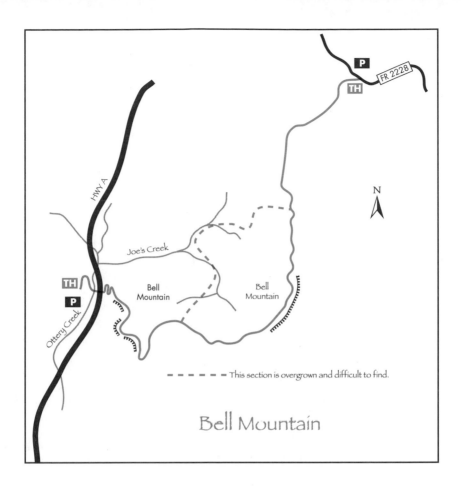

Bell Mountain

- - - - - This section is overgrown and difficult to find.

effort. Except for the small section that is part of the Ozark Trail, Bell Mountain is unmarked and should be hiked with a map and compass. Although it is without markers, the trail is distinct and fairly easy to follow with the exception of the loop, supposedly at midsection, which is very faint due to overgrowth, and easily confused with the logging paths. It is recommended that you stay on the main trail traveling between the trailheads and either hike out the way you hike in, or have a shuttle. There is no water accessibility on the trail so all water should be carried in.

TOPOGRAPHICAL MAPS: Edgehill, Johnson's Shut-Ins, Banner, Johnson Mnt.

From the parking lot of Trailhead 2, find the wooden sign that marks the Ozark Trail. As you face this sign, you will want to begin Bell Mountain to your right, or east. The trail crosses Highway A almost immediately and heads up the hillside. This is the steepest part of the trail, so once you get to the top you're through with the hard part. The trail switchbacks up for about ½ mile and as you proceed there are various rock outcroppings to peer up at that lie in wait at the top. Once on top, these outcroppings create a beautiful rocky plateau with huge moss covered boulders and a fantastic view—a definite BTV!

The trail heads south and slightly east along this entire bluff line, allowing one to enjoy the view while hiking for the next mile. At about 1.5 miles in, the trail turns away from the bluff line and heads up into the woods towards the first fork which is the turnoff for the Ozark Trail. Stay to the left to continue with Bell Mountain as the trail leads slightly uphill with some nice views on your right. You will pass a small gladed area on your left at just over 2 miles and at 2.5 a faint remainder of a trail to the left. Stay to the right, or straight on the main trail.

Just as the trail flattens off, you will come to a logging road marked 8B on your left (you have hiked 3 miles). This is the first of many short posts labeled with a number/letter periodically seen on this trail, as well as trails throughout the area. These were formally used to designate "fire-roads" accessing the area should a fire occur. Now, however, they serve no real purpose since these areas are reserved as a wilderness area, with motorized vehicles and/or equipment being prohibited.

This woods road, labeled 8B, leads to the left, and grants access to Joe's Creek as well as an old logging road following through the creek basin area. This is the old trail forming the loop, however, it has not been maintained or seen much use and is thus overgrown making it difficult to follow. The recommendation is to stay on the main trail, which is followed by continuing straight, unless you have a topo map and compass.

From the junction, the trail passes a pond and another fireroad on the right, continues through hardwood forest broken up by a few cedar glade patches, and begins a gradual climb up to the top of Bell Mountain. You will reach the top at 5 miles and also a campsite which is to the right. Sidetrip off the trail beyond the campsite area and you will be 1700 feet up at the top of Bell Mountain experiencing a widespread, breathtaking view—a definite BTV all the way!

On past Bell Mountain, the trail continues through hardwood forest and at 6.0 reaches another rocky clearing, skirts around the edge, heads downhill and eventually flattens out into a widened path. There is another fireroad fork labeled 9A on your right and just after that, one on the left, but stay on the main trail as it continues through the forested area and remains fairly level for the next two miles (8.0). The remainder of the trail maintains the wooded atmosphere and thus creates pleasant surroundings through which to hike. As you near FR 2228, the trail moves up in elevation slightly until reaching the parking lot situated somewhat on a plateau, at a little over 9 miles.

Hiking Tip — How Much Can I Carry?

The appropriate weight of your pack will definitely be somewhat a function of your backpacking experience and physical condition, however, a good rule of thumb is that a fully loaded pack should equal one-fifth to one-fourth your body weight. If your strength permits, it's possible to carry as much as one- third of your body weight. This author's advice: always volunteer to carry the food – it's the only item guaranteed to lighten as you go!

32. Berryman Trail

LOCATION: Berryman can be accessed from two different trailheads:

Brazil Creek Trailhead: This trailhead is located south from Sullivan on Mo. 185. Go 17 miles down Mo 185 to County Road N. Head west down N for approximately 8 miles to CR W. Turn south down W and follow it for 9 miles before reaching Brazil Creek Campground.

Berryman Trailhead: This trailhead is 17 miles west of Potosi or 19 miles east of Steelville on MO 8, to Forest Road 2266. Take FR 2266 north for 1 mile to Berryman Camp.

LENGTH: Berryman Trail is a 24 mile loop.

COMMENTS: Berryman Trail loops through some of the Ozarks most impressive large standing pines, and advances in elevation to display a scenery of bottomland timber types situated in the hollows below. Because this trail is 24 miles in length and runs in a loop, backpacking is ideal. Keep in mind though, that hikers share the trail with bikers so paths can be rough and rutted. Water is difficult to come by on this trail, as most of the creeks remain dry throughout the summer requiring that all water be carried in during much of the year.

TOPOGRAPHICAL MAPS: Berryman and Anthonies Mill

We will be starting our hike from the Berryman Trailhead. From the trailhead, we will proceed east, hiking the loop in a counter-clockwise manner. The trail crosses 2266 right off and then continues east. This section leading up to Brazil Creek Campground crosses several "fire roads" formally used as a means of access to the wilderness area for fire fighters. As the trail passes through the beautiful large pine stands characteristic of Berryman, it switchbacks for a while and leads to a pond on your left at almost the one mile mark. Up on the ridge, past the pond and directly ahead, is a diamond marker with red painted over it. Go right and it takes you a little south and along a dry creek bottom for a while. As you come out of the creek bottom you will proceed up the first of two inclines before crossing one of the fire roads (14B) at the top of a ridge. Continue in a northeasterly direction and the trail switchbacks down into Smith Mill Hollow, passing by a pond and across Clear Creek. The trail seems to diverge in a couple different directions here. Stay to the right after crossing and follow the trail as it crosses the creek again to head back into the pine forest.

From here to Brazil Creek campground the trail is rugged with spots washed out because of excessive use. Heading north, the trail crosses FR 2265 at 6 miles and begins a slight descent to the underlying hollow where it

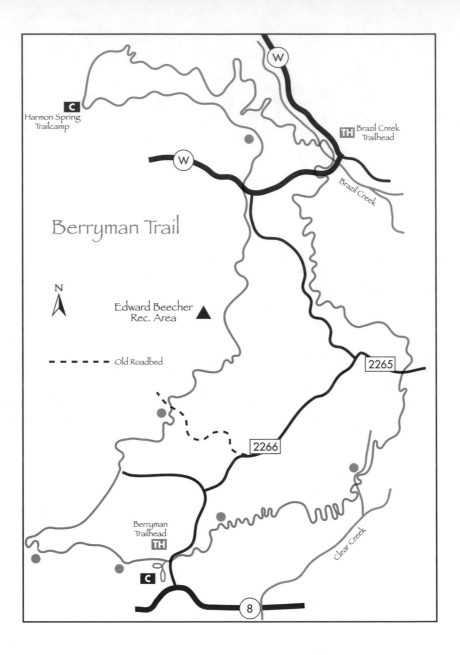

remains only temporarily, moving in and out of the hollows and following the topography of the land. At 8.0 miles, the trail begins to traverse and maintain position along the ridge for a bit, until approaching Brazil Campground where it switchbacks up and back down again to cross a blacktop road (Highway W), and eventually Brazil Creek by way of a small bridge. For much of the year this is the trail's only creek running with water, making this location a definite place to fill water bottles.

Immediately after crossing the creek, and at mile 10, you will approach the campground. As you pass through the picnic area of Brazil Creek Campground, the trail gets a little confusing. It crosses Brazil Creek again and you can pick up the trail by watching where it goes up the bluffline on the other side—and it does go up for a pretty good climb. You will top off at a plateau that takes you right back down to a creek that takes you up again via switchbacks through another gorgeous pine forest. The trail crosses a gravel road at 12 miles and passes a deer hunter's camp on your left hand side. It then descends down to a neat creekbed area with a scenic bluff line and nice waterfall displays when the season permits.

Your next stop is Harmon Springs, where Berryman and the Ozark Trail intersect. The Ozark Trail heads north; Berryman south. Harmon Springs, at 14 miles from the trail's start offers a nice place to camp with a spring and pond as well as scenic surroundings. Leaving Harmon Springs, the trail leads almost directly east, following the creek bottom for about a mile before proceeding up to over 1100 feet again. Once on the ridge, the trail merges closely with a logging road and passes by a survey marker identifying Township 38 N. Stay to the right, on the trail, and at 16 miles, it will lead down past a small wildlife pond, and ½ mile further cross FR 2265. Just as an interesting note, if you were to go west here, down FR 2265 for ½ mile, you would discover the heliport location for the area.

From the crossing of FR 2265, the trail proceeds straight south winding through fresh smelling pines while traversing up and down the hollows. At 18.5, the trail arrives at Edward Beecher Recreation Area where an artesian well resides. The trail continues on south here, following the creekbed briefly before turning slightly east and resuming the task of maneuvering through the pine stands and hardwood clusters scattered between ridges and hollows. During wetter months, the mile marker 20 will bring you to three stream crossings in a row, after which the trail leads across a fire road, past another wildlife pond and down along the next hollow. Another creek crossing comes up a half a mile further, after which, the trail continues southwest before creating a horseshoe shaped curve to the left, looping back around to follow the creek bottom east, headed towards Berryman Camp. Moving away from the creek, the trail cuts across another old road and makes its way to the completion of the loop at 24 miles.

Hiking Tip — Duct Tape

Duct tape is always an excellent item to carry while on the trail as it can be used for many trailside emergencies such as repairing a ripped tent or fly, taping together a broken tent pole, or constructing a brace or stretcher. On external frames, Duct tape can be carried by simply wrapping excess amounts around ends of the frame that are out of the way. If packing with an internal frame, wrap an adequate amount of tape around an empty toilet paper roll.

33. Cedar Creek

LOCATION: Cedar Creek is nestled between Jefferson City, Columbia and Fulton. From Jefferson City take HWY 54 north 12 miles to the New Bloomfield exit, turning left onto HWY J. Continue to follow J as it curves off to the right at 1.8 miles. Eight miles from this intersection is County Road 353. Turn left and follow it less than a mile to the trailhead on your right. This is the Boydsville Trailhead. Cedar Creek has other access points from this direction as well. The Pine Ridge Trailhead and campground is off HWY Y, 2.3 miles down J. Dry Fork is 6.8 miles down J off County Road 356.

LENGTH: Cedar Creek is a giant network of trails offering many routes of varying lengths. This trail is 9 miles in length, with a shorter and longer route both available.

COMMENTS: With just over 15,000 acres of wilderness land, Cedar Creek is Central Missouri's largest tract of National Forest land. The original trail here runs through much of the southern section of Mark Twain, covering 22 miles of trail in the form of one giant loop. The northern section now has a couple shorter loop options making it more accessible for less lengthy hikes and thus more adequate for a single afternoon on the trail. The Cedar Creek loop described here is a sort of mid-section loop that covers some fabulous territory offering vistas of the surprisingly bold Cedar Creek from atop the incredibly massive bluffs and rock outcroppings that hover above. A few caves, some awesome rock formations and splendid little tributary creeks scattered throughout much of this trail, make it a wonderful day in the woods. Cedar Creek's one drawback, if there is one however, is that longer routes here connect via gravel road, requiring some stretches between remote timber areas to connect through the path of a road rather than trail. The road connectors are not bad though, most being scenic and somewhat remote themselves.

Camping is not available at the Boydsville Trailhead, but the nearby Pine Ridge and Dry Fork Trailheads both offer camping facilities, should you wish to overnight before or after your hike. It may also be worth noting that during a period of heavy rains, the crossing of Cedar Creek may be next to impossible, so the route avoiding this crossing is advised during rainy months of the year. Cedar Creek is marked fairly well with gray diamonds, but with so many connectors and road intersections attention needs to be given to where you are, and where you are going, less you get lost in the network of the entire trail system. A compass and topographic map might be handy, especially if you wish to explore the area beyond this trek.

From the Boydsville Trailhead, the trail heads into the woods in a northwesterly direction. Without much introduction you will quickly become aware of the reasoning behind titling this area Cedar Creek. With a small tributary of Smith Creek to your right and a heavily cedared field to your left, the name for this district of the Mark Twain National Forest becomes more than appropriate. The beginning of this trail wanders through field and forest, exchanging one scene for the other, and holding the common bond of cedar trees throughout. A couple beautiful "cedar corridors" accent the hike, as does the fresh cedar scent that accompanies them. At .7 miles you will arrive at the first trail intersection, behind which you can detect through the trees a backdrop of bluffs belonging to Smith Creek. Stay to the right and the trail soon crosses this beautiful little rock bottom stream that qualifies as a mini BTV. Connecting diagonally across to the right, the trail moves up into the woods and through more of the cedar thickets common to this forested tract. For about the next mile, the trail remains mostly level covering ground through the timber of hardwoods and crossing streambeds via a sort of earthen walkway. At about 1.6 miles in, the trail seems to end at the junction of an old roadbed. There is a metal guard here to prevent vehicles from going trail-bound, and a National Forest post. Take a left down this road that appears to be a 4-wheeler's playground, and follow it for about half a mile. Watch on your left for the turn off. It is on the downward slope of the road and marked not only with a sign but also a trailhead register and a map signaling "you are here".

From this post, follow the trail that takes off behind it as the surprising portion of this trail begins. The first side trail to the right leads to a campsite overlooking the farmland and beautiful surrounding landscape below. This is a definite BTV, but it gets better. Continue down the main trail as it will lead through a pleasant little hollow area with a creek to the right and a cedar field to your left. Dipping down slightly to cross this steep rocky creek, the trail moves up to one of its highlights. The ridgetop it resides along consists of a series of pronounced rock outcroppings powerfully protruding from the bluffline to overlook Cedar Creek in action below. Various side paths along this route venture out to the bluff's edge giving view to details of the rock strewn display of art below. Hidden within the bluffs here somewhere lies Rutherford Cave, a site for some future adventure given a topographic map and a headlamp.

Moving away from the intense and continual BTV bluffline, the trail graduates into the more subtle, although equally as pleasant wooded hollow. A small boulder outcrop greets you at a small creek crossing, followed quickly by the ford of Cedar Creek. At Cedar Creek's opposite side, a cool rock slab, etched almost with a natural set of stairs, introduces you back into the forest. Rock formations scattered within the hollows of this next stretch of hardwood forest, create a BTV for hiking. Reaching down to cross another small creek, the trail passes by a huge boulder like cave residing above and to the left. A matching "rockhouse" resides just on the other side of the creek crossing as well. Through the trees and on the right as the trail meanders back up to the ridge, are views once again of Cedar Creek. It is also at this point that the trail comes to a 'T'. The sign indicating straight for Cedar Creek is the one you want to follow, which is good because the trail here continues along the bluff providing an awesome ongoing BTV of Cedar Creek, especially during "leaf-off" periods.

Moving down through the forest after the ridge is complete, the trail arrives at a four way intersection. Mileage hiked thus far is about 4.5. Straight leads onto private land and isn't an option. Right continues the longer loop and requires a rather large crossing of Cedar Creek below. Left is the shorter route back that empties into the second Boydsville Trailhead just a few 100 yards down from the first one (where you parked).

Continuing right, the trail moves downhill to cross Cedar Creek. It is here that the size of Cedar Creek becomes amazing (and maybe a bit overwhelming if water levels are high!). The trail connects directly across this wide expanse of a creek, but if water is swift, go back to the last intersection and head back via the shorter but drier route! Glance both directions down the creek bed and notice the beautiful blufflines outlining it's banks—this is a gorgeous creek. Moving away from Cedar Creek the trail winds through the cedars as it covers half a mile of flat ground. Rock outcroppings signal the presence of another stream tributary which you will cross twice before heading uphill and intersecting with a gravel road at 6 miles. Turn right, follow about half a mile to it's 'T', and turn right again. (This one actually has a name: Englewood.) Heading straight east now, the road takes you another half mile to its end.

The end of the road meets up with the crossing of a cool little metal footbridge carrying a bit of history with it. Known as Rutherford Bridge, this old steel structure was utilized by residents way back, to cross Cedar Creek. Abandon for years, the bridge was reconstructed by Eagle Scouts in 1983 to be used as a foot bridge. Putting it to its intended use therefore, cross this unique bridge that carries you over a very scenic portion of Cedar Creek, and follow the abandon road that begins, and heads uphill to the left. Views of the creek follow the beginning length of this road, and soon you will recognize your whereabouts. Emerging on the right as the road heads up slightly is the trail register and turnoff taken earlier in the hike. Pass this following the road one-half mile to the equally as familiar metal guard on the right signifying a right turn that brings you back to the trailhead.

If you desire to lengthen your hike, or increase your workout for the day, you can proceed straight here and loop back to the trailhead via a longer route. Much of this route however is gravel roads, so returning the way you came in, although repeating miles already hiked, is much more scenic. If you were to stay straight here however, the roadbed ends at trail parking area making a 90 degree turn right, heading straight east. Walk this road for one mile, until it too makes a 90 degree turn, this one to the left. At this point the trail exits the road to the right requiring that you crawl through a fence, to enter into what appears to be a private field, while at the same time creating real doubts in your mind about whether or not you're lost. Head straight back, however, skirting the right flank of this field and you will actually see an occasional gray diamond assuring you that this is the correct route. Stay with the markers, that basically lead a path through somewhat of a gully area, slightly downhill and to another fence crossing that exits this field. If you get a bit lost, follow the telephone poles—they lead directly to the second fence crawl through. Out of the field now, the trail crosses Smith Creek, returning to a gravel road. Rather pleasant for a road, this last stretch isn't too bad as a thick plot of cedars line and hover over the rock bottomed Smith Creek that follows the length of the road. Follow this about one mile till it intersects with County Road 353. Take a right here and it leads straight to the trailhead where you parked.

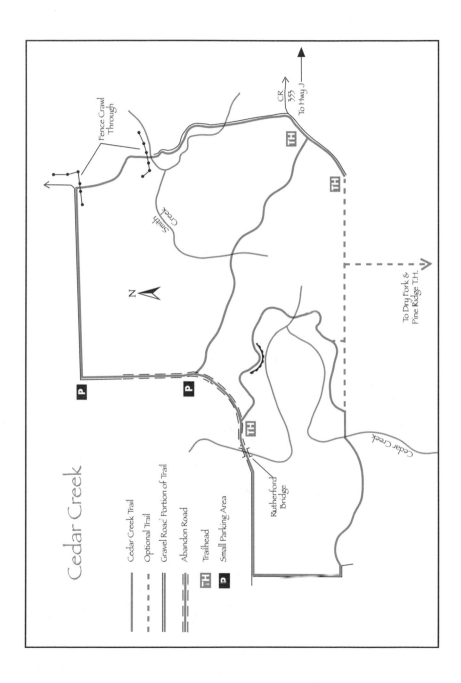

34. Coakley Hollow

LOCATION: The Coakley Hollow Trail is located just outside of Camdenton, at Lake of the Ozarks. From Camdenton, travel north on HWY 54 to Lake Road 54-65. Take LR 54-65 east till it ends at A-33. Turn south on A-33, following signs to the left-handed side turn-off for Ozark Caverns. The caverns, visitor's center and trailhead are all at the end of this road.

LENGTH: Coakley Hollow is a one mile loop that has an added half-mile side trail leading to the lake.

COMMENTS: A favorite short hike for this author, Coakley Hollow is unique in that its modest one mile loop covers some solid variety in terrain and landscape, with a setting that not only offers picturesque hiking, but a cave and lake access as well. In fact, along with the nearby Ha Ha Tonka State Park, Coakley Hollow is the only other trail accessible by boat, as well as car! If you're on the lake, hop in the boat or on the waverunner and head to the Grand Glaize end of the state park. A small wooden dock across the cove from the state park's camping point can be used to tie your watercraft to while hiking the trail. An old roadbed there leads straight to the trail and visitor's center.

Aside from the beauty of this trail, Ozark Caverns is a neat little non-commercialized cave to tour as well. Although closed through the winter, tours run during fall, spring and summer, so it is worth checking out times if you wish to run through the cave in addition to your hike. You can contact the Ozark caverns at 573-346-2500.

TOPOGRAPHICAL MAPS: Camdenton

From the visitor's center, this trail begins across Mill Creek via a neat wooden swinging bridge that accents the already beautiful hidden setting of this place. The spring which feeds into Mill Creek is just upstream from this point, and although you need to walk up to it by road, it is worth seeing. Coming out of the rocks clear, cool and surrounded by watercress, this spring is a mini BTV and a bonus side trip.

Back to the trail! Cross the bridge and immediately the trail skirts up through moss covered boulders to gain some elevation and move along the side of the hill. The shallow hollow to the left is eventually hiked around as the trail curves to the left and moves down to an intersection with a double track path at .5 miles. Diagonally across is the continuation of this loop, but if you have some extra time, it is worth side-tripping to the right, down the sodden road, to a beautiful point and shoreline of Lake of the Ozarks. This BTV and

Grand Glaize arm of the lake is by far the prettiest of sections, boasting of tall bluffs to the left of the point as you look out, and pristine land to the right looking up the Grand Glaize Creek entrance. The side trip here is only a half mile long, which actually doubles the trail length, but being a short hike to begin with, this detour is well worth it.

Returning from the lake, the trail continues, marked in yellow and proceeding west diagonally across from where you came out of the loop originally. It crosses first a small bridge, and then the larger and super cool swinging bridge that carries you over the stream and its low-lying area. The opposite side begins some of the varied and unique terrain of this trail. First a savannah, then a glade, each mixed within the middle of the Ozark hardwoods. The contrast is amazing, and creates a beautiful setting. Continuing around, the trail passes by the remains of an old earthen dam built originally in the 1800's by the settler now responsible for this trail's name—Coakley.

Just after the dam spur, and before your return to the visitor's center, the trail adds one final highlight that verifies it's unique diversity. This finale begins via a small section of boardwalk that carries hikers through an area similar to a bog, yet slightly more elevated and fed by moving groundwater. This geologic phenomenon is known as a fen and deserves special mention due to its rare occurrence for this part of Missouri. Passing the fen, Coakley Hollow returns to the visitor's center where you can buff up on some nature information or opt for a cave tour!

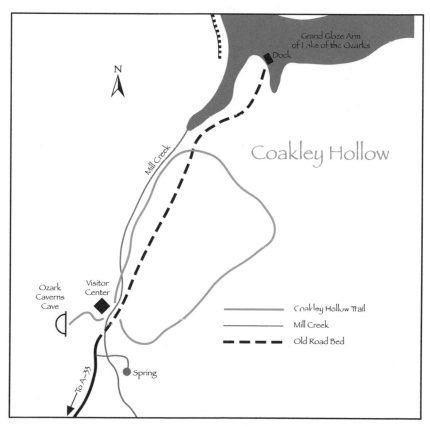

35. Grand Glaize Trail

Lake of the Ozarks State Park

LOCATION: The Grand Glaize Trail is located just outside of Camdenton, at Lake of the Ozarks. From Camdenton travel north on HWY 54 to lake road 54-65. Take LR 54-65 east till it ends at A-33. Turn back north on A-33, and the trailhead is a half a mile down on your left.

LENGTH: Grand Glaize is 2.5 miles in length.

COMMENTS: This is a short but very pleasant little trail winding mainly up and down through the hollows of hardwood forest that typify the nature of this area. Actually part of Lake of the Ozarks State Park, the timber throughout this trail is virgin forestland, natural with some towering trees and giant oaks. Catch this loop during the fall full color bloom and you're in for a festival of reds, oranges and yellows that create a splendid afternoon hike. The terrain is gently rolling with only mild elevation changes. Follow the road on which the trail-head is located all the way down and you will arrive at McCubbins Point, a beach, picnic and access area for the lake. Bring hiking boots, swimwear and the makings for BBQ and you're in for the perfect combination of activities for your day!

TOPOGRAPHICAL MAPS: Camdenton

The trail moves straight into the woods from behind the sign at the parking area and soon crosses a corridor clearing where telephone lines have passed through. Passing back into the woods, the trail intersection defining the beginning and ending point for this loop is encountered. Take a left here and the trail curves around a bit to catch sight of, and cross the first little creek. It then winds up a bit and settles out for a while on the ridge, where it stays, with only some minor dips into shallow hollows before really descending down to the lake and creek area. Although not right up against the lake, glimpses of water through barren trees can be seen on the trail's northern corner. This portion of the lake is actually the extreme back end of a cove that houses a recreation area and army base. The hollow down in this area is deep with terrain extending upward creating walls that give the feeling of being buried within the forest. The trail crosses a creek down in this valley of the hollow and then continues with a pattern of "up the hollow, down the hollow" skirting ridges and contouring the topography of the wooded acreage. Enjoy the pleasant serenity of this forest along with the mini-views of opposing ridgetops through the trees during leaf-off. At the top of the ridge is the connection that began the loop. Take a left to return from here to the trailhead.

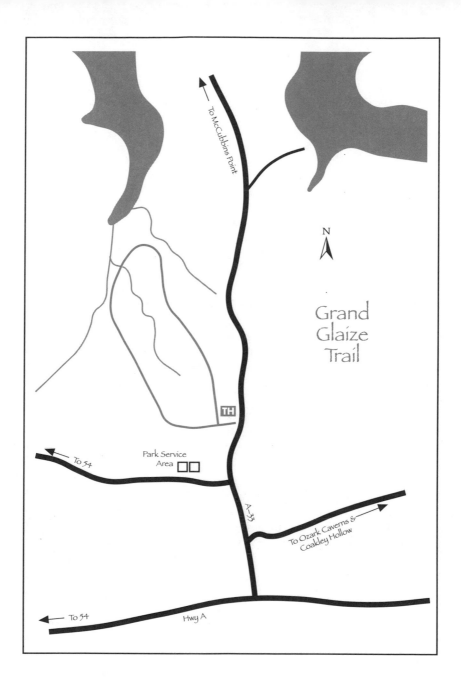

To McCubbins Point

N

Grand
Glaize
Trail

TH

To 54

Park Service
Area

A-33

To Ozark Caverns &
Coakley Hollow

To 54

Hwy A

36. Ha Ha Tonka State Park

LOCATION: Ha Ha Tonka is located 2.5 miles down Highway D, which is about 5 miles southwest of Camdenton via Highway 54, just west of the bridge crossing the Niangua Arm of Lake of the Ozarks.

LENGTH: The park has 9 different trails providing access to the major features of the park. All of the trails are fairly short, varying from ½ mile to 1½ miles in length and merging together at some points.

COMMENTS: Ha Ha Tonka consists of 70 beautiful acres situated on the Niangua arm of the Lake of the Ozarks. The castle remains, for which the park is named, was a magnificent 60 room mansion that burned down in 1942. The castle, however, is just a small part of what this geologic haven has to offer. Featuring the karst topography so characteristic of the Ozarks, Ha Ha Tonka consists of a landscape filled with caves, sinkholes, natural bridges and springs. Among some of the noteworthy features is the spectacular Ha Ha Tonka gorge that is a result of a collapsed cave, creating a chasm and island lined by 250 foot bluffs. It is in this gorge that the 12th largest spring in the state resides flushing out almost 50 million gallons of water each day. Ha Ha Tonka also contains six different caves and two large sinkholes, one of which forms a quite impressive natural bridge reaching over 50 feet high and spreading almost 60 feet across.

Ha Ha Tonka provides an excellent spot of recreation, geologic features and history. Hikers, outdoor enthusiasts and families will all enjoy this remarkably unique area of the Ozarks.

TOPOGRAPHICAL MAPS: Ha Ha Tonka

DELL RIM TRAIL — ½ mile (one way)
This is a scenic boardwalk trail leading around one of the two major sinkholes, Whispering Dell. It also allows access to the 80 foot water tower, part of the original estate that was burned by vandals in 1976. Since this trail connects the castle with Dell Rim, Spring and Colosseum trails it is most commonly used by visitors and offers a compact tour of the park.

CASTLE BLUFF TRAIL — ½ mile (one way)
This trail can either be used by boaters wishing to hike up to the castle, or by hikers wishing to walk down to the lake. The trail passes by one of the quarries from which stones for the castle were taken.

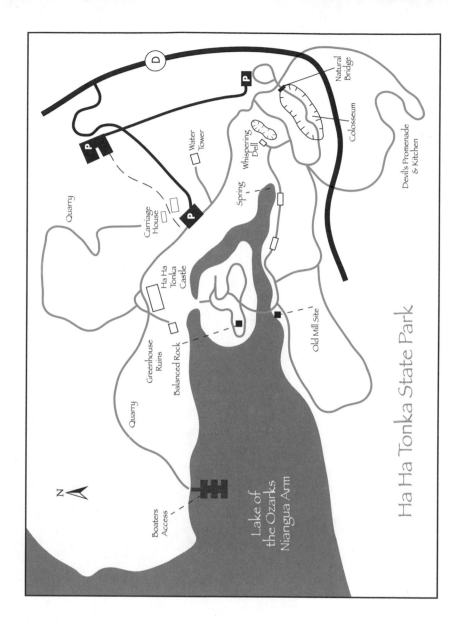

COLOSSEUM TRAIL — ½ mile

Named after the impressive Colosseum Sinkhole, this trail first takes you under the large natural bridge, which is a feature in itself, and then ascends up to the ridge merging with Dell Rim and Spring Trails to offer a viewpoint of Whispering Dell.

ISLAND TRAIL — ¾ mile

This trail loops around the island created by the collapsed cavern and holds excellent views of the huge bluffs, the spring, and Balanced Rock. It can be reached by taking either Spring or Dell Rim Trail down to where you join the lake, which is also the site of the old mill.

TURKEY PEN HOLLOW TRAIL — ¾ mile

This is a pleasant little trail, designed as an interpretive trail, and takes you through a maintained savannah area, featuring bluestem and Indian grasses among a forest of various oak species. It begins at the parking lot on the east side of Highway D and is accessed via Devil's Kitchen Trail.

DEVIL'S KITCHEN TRAIL — 1 mile

If you like a little more remoteness, this trail provides it, leading through some of the characteristic geologic features of the area. Devil's Promenade, a series of ledges alongside a cliff, and Devil's Kitchen, a window opening in a cavern, are both located along this trail.

QUARRY TRAIL — 1 ½ miles

Starting at the castle, this trail takes you up on the glade allowing you some lake views. It also takes you by the second quarry used to excavate stone for the castle.

SPRING TRAIL — 1 ½ miles

Spring Trail originates from the lower parking lot down by the lake and old mill sight, and extends along the spring all the way up to Dell Rim, looping back around through the woods to the parking lot. The lower portion leading alongside the spring is paved, making it easily accessible to the handicapped, and while pleasantly following the curvature of the spring, also offers some impressive views of the castle above. The upper section, leading up to Dell Rim, is boardwalked but steep, and although it can be a slight workout getting to the top, rewarding views of the spring below make the trip up well worth the effort.

Castle ruins at Ha Ha Tonka State Park

37. Hawn State Park

LOCATION: Located east of Farmington, and west of St. Genevieve, Hawn State Park is located on Highway 144 which is off Highway 32.

LENGTH: Hawn offers two different trails:
Whispering Pine Trail: This trail consists of 2 loops, a north loop of 6 miles and south loop of 4 miles, creating a 10 mile hike.
Pickle Creek Trail: 1 mile

COMMENTS: Hawn State Park is part of what is known as the LaMotte sandstone basin. The area is characterized by rock formations, sandstone cliffs and canyons, lofty pines, and picturesque scenery. Such a unique blend of geology and nature creates a wilderness environment unmatched in splendor anywhere in Missouri. The trails are very well marked and colored coded to head you in the right direction. Hiking is fairly easy with water being plentiful. There are spots reserved for backpackers on the trail for overnights, as well as designated areas within the park for camping.

TOPOGRAPHICAL MAPS: Coffman

WHISPERING PINES TRAIL

From the picnic grounds the trail begins in a southeasterly direction over a wooden footbridge and then heads west as you cross a second bridge over Pickle Creek. You can start the north loop in a counterclockwise direction, following the red markers. From the crossing of Pickle Creek you head up unto a knoll and almost immediately begin to have some nice vistas overlooking Pickle Creek. The trail extends along this ridge, an extended BTV, for about ¼ a mile before heading back down and crossing Pickle Creek at the 1 mile mark.

At this point the Whispering Pine trail connects with the one mile Pickle Creek trail which is marked in green so stay left on the red trail after crossing the creek. Just past this junction lies a beautiful display of cascading waterfalls created by the rock formations within Pickle Creek. The trail continues alongside the creek for a while to produce a very scenic hike and then passes through a huge stand of gorgeous Savannah Pines for about ½ mile.

At 2.5 the trail crosses Pickle Creek for the second time then heads right to the top of a small knoll. Look to your right and you will see a nice size beaver dam creating a little pool of water. The trail widens as it continues on top and re-enters the savannah pine area. These tremendous pines are amazing in stature as they tower along both sides of the trail—this is a truly unique spot

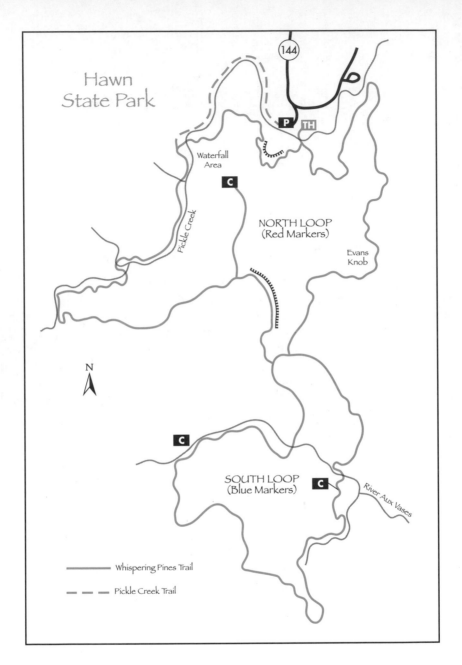

Hawn
State Park

Waterfall
Area

Pickle Creek

NORTH LOOP
(Red Markers)

Evans
Knob

N

SOUTH LOOP
(Blue Markers)

River Aux Vases

——— Whispering Pines Trail

– – – Pickle Creek Trail

hidden within the Ozarks. Mingled within these stands are dogwoods, redbuds and other flowering plants that create an absolutely gorgeous scene in the spring. As the trail exits this area it opens up into a clearing and to your left will be a sidetrail to a trailcamp area. Stay to the right to continue down the trail and it takes you up a fairly steep grade to a fabulous BTV to your left of the surrounding valley. Continue up and the scenery continues as well, this time on your right. As the trail comes down off the bluff it drops rather sharply and blends into an old logging road. At 4.5 you will reach the intersection of the north and south loops. Take a right to continue the trail on around the southern loop and stay to the left if you wish to finish only the northern half and head back to the picnic area.

Proceed to the right along the southern loop, following the blue markers. The trail takes you back into the pine forest and eventually across a small stream. After crossing, there is an area to your right that appears to be a low impact camping area. On the opposite side of this campsite is a pleasant little waterfall area creating a wonderful spot to spend the night. There is no fire ring allowed here so be careful when camping to preserve this pretty spot and practice "no trace" backpacking. Right after this spot there is a place where the two streams meet creating a small pool and then about 50 yards beyond lies the designated camp area marked with the white blaze and a sign reminding you of no fires allowed. As the trail moves off from the camping areas it heads uphill and passes a nice spring on the left. It continues up above it on past to another spring that cascades down. It is at this point that the beauty created by the water formations is complimented by wild azaleas, which when in bloom, are one feature the trail is known for.

From the springs, the trail takes you to the top of a boulder glade that offers some more nice scenery and rock outcroppings—another BTV! Down to the right is the creek, and the trail follows alongside and above it before curving at the base of the ridge, and dropping down to the left, keeping in step with the bend in the creek. There are some beautiful rock outcroppings along side the creek viewable from the trail creating some nice waterfalls; a definite BTV all along the way.

As the trail weaves away from the creek it heads up towards the next campsite which is at about 7 miles. The creek is just below the campsite for water accessibility. At the creek bottom you enter into yet another stand of huge pines, and if you look to the right there appears to be an old hand-dug well from a past homestead. The trail continues, engulfed by pines and eventually leads back into the clearing which is the junction again of the 2 loops. You have hiked about 8.5 miles. Stay to the right and begin following the red markers again to take you back to the picnic area. The trail widens and you will see evidence of controlled burning on the right. The wild flowers and azaleas flourish here since the burning keeps underbrush at a minimum. As you proceed up and over Evans Knob the scenery continues. There is a creek on the right with another beautiful display of cascading falls. The trail continues on up to the campground area and around it to the picnic area where you began.

PICKLE CREEK TRAIL

This little one mile trail also begins at the picnic area and is a nice wide path that follows alongside Pickle Creek offering delightful views of the shut-ins stream area. The hike is not a loop although you can create a loop by returning to picnic are via the Whispering Pine Trail, lengthening the hike to about 2 miles long.

38. Johnson's Shut-Ins State Park

Shut-Ins Trail

LOCATION: Johnson's Shut-Ins State Park is located on Highway N, 8 miles north of Lesterville and Highway 49, or 10 miles south down Highway N, from Highway 21.

LENGTH: The Shut-Ins Trail is within Johnson's Shut-Ins State Park and is a beautiful 2.5 mile trail encompassed in a loop.

COMMENTS: The "shut-ins" were created when volcanic eruptions sent volcanic debris down the mountainous area, layer upon layer, forming igneous rocks exposed today in the swift current of the Black River's East Fork. The water cuts through the maze of boulders in varying channels, funneling through chutes and creating rapids. The Shut-Ins Trail provides an easy hike along the East Fork of the Black River, providing an excellent view of this unique geologic feature and spectacular area.

Johnson's Shut-Ins State Park also provides an excellent spot for camping, fishing, swimming and picnicking. In addition, it holds trailheads for the Ozark and Taum Sauk Trails which offer backpacking opportunities.

Johnson's Shut-Ins State Park

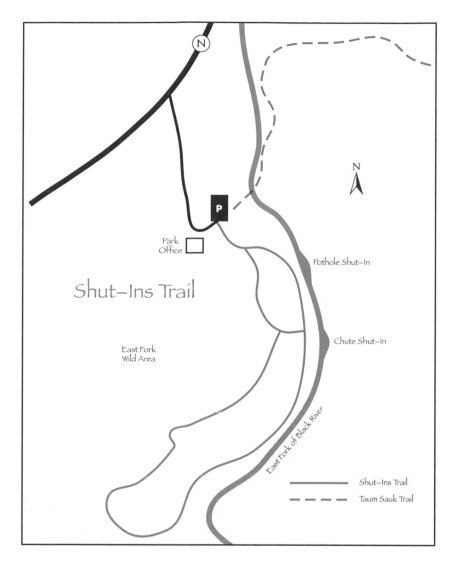

TOPOS: Johnson's Shut-Ins

The trail begins at the south end of the large parking lot, just east of the Park Office. The first quarter of a mile is covered via a wooden walkway that follows alongside the Black River's East Fork allowing excellent access to shut-ins, and providing observation decks for viewing and photos. You may choose to take a leisurely stroll along this boardwalk and return the same way, but if you wish to see more of the East Fork Wild Area, continue on past the walkway to complete the full 2.5 mile loop. The trail is easy to follow and at the half way point forks right, away from the Ozark Trail, thus looping back to your origination point.

39. Kaintuck Trail

LOCATION: Kaintuck is located near Rolla Missouri, just south of the little town of Newburg. From Rolla, take I-44 west to the HWY T exit and take T to the left, or south, through Newburg. After crossing the railroad tracks and the Little Piney Creek in Newburg, turn right onto HWY P. Travel 2.7 miles down HWY P to County Road 7550 (gravel), which is on your right. Drive another 2.7 miles down 7550 which will take you straight to Mill Creek Picnic Area. The trailhead is actually across the low water bridge there, and up the gravel road a bit to your right.

LENGTH: This trail has many loops and therefore length options allowing for hikes as short as 3 miles and as long as 15.

COMMENTS: This is an excellent little trail. The network of loops make it absolutely ideal for all types of hikers—long enough to backpack in and make a camping overnight of it, or very reasonable in length for a wonderful day hike and picnic lunch. Kaintuck is shared by mountain bikers and equestrians, so some non-hiking traffic may be encountered, but the network spreads out visitors to this area well, leaving you a remote and isolated feeling. Be sure to bring this guide and/or a map and compass, as the trails are well defined but unmarked. The map in this book is sufficient to lead you through all the intersecting points and trail highlights; however, if you wish to explore the area more, the topographic map for this area is Kaintuck Hollow.

In addition to the pleasant stands of tall pine trees that line the trail in many sections, and beautiful ridgetop stretches that offer leaf-off period views, Kaintuck possesses two rather unique and spectacular sites to which it can boast: Wilkin's Spring and the 175 foot natural bridge. Located at the trail's southwest corner, Wilkin's Pond lies situated beneath the serenity of several large oak trees and is fed by the amazing Wilkin's Spring that pumps out over 3 million gallons of water every day into the pond, eventually overflowing into Mill Creek as well. The spring is gorgeous, and so is the pond, with water so clean and clear that one can look straight down into either one and see a bit of a sandy bottom as well as the large amounts of growing watercress. This area, once homesteaded by a family, was donated to the park service when the last of the family passed away. Although the house that once stood here has been torn down, one can still see remains of the old spring house, and if you look closely at the sides of the ledge where the spring pours over into Wilkin's Pond, grooves in the rock tell of the old water wheel that used to be in place here. The entire pond and spring area is wonderfully pleasant and an excellent place for a mid-day trail break or overnight stay.

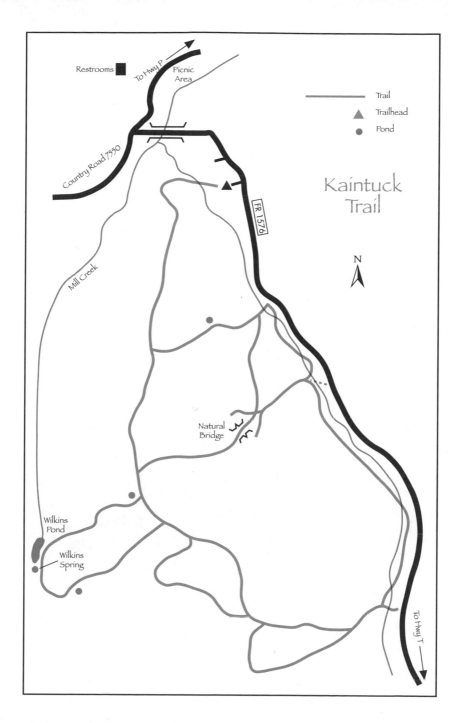

The second spectacular feature of the Kaintuck Trail is the amazing and grand natural bridge situated almost dead center within this hiking area. The natural bridge, measuring 175 feet in length extends as an expansive rock ledge with openings on either end that give the appearance of this structure to be a cave, not a natural bridge. Wander in just a bit, though, and soon light from the other side is apparent, and the path made clear. Formations like this are always amazing, and the immense size of this natural phenomenon is striking, making it a real jewel and showpiece for the Kaintuck Trail—don't miss it!

Pulling into Mill Creek Picnic Area, you will notice bathrooms and a small parking area with a trailhead on your right. This trail is NOT the Kaintuck Trail beginning, although if you wish to add a bit of an extra side trip to the day, this little short hike extends about a mile or so to a cave area and then continues on past a bit further, requiring you to return the same way you came in— worth some exploring if you have the time.

TOPOGRAPHICAL MAPS: Kaintuck Hollow

Kaintuck Trail begins at a trailhead location further down. Take a left at the end of the picnic area and cross Mill Creek over the low water bridge following the gravel road (FS 1576) past the first pull-in with metal guard on your right, and on up to the second little pull-in on your right. A huge pile of large rocks have

Hiking along the Kaintuck Trail

been dumped here to prevent ATV use and a small cleared area is available for parking. The trail begins to the right at the small trailhead sign and moves across the cedar field area down towards the woods and Mill Creek. Mill Creek is fed by this trail's famed Wilkin's Spring, and thus is flowing steadily even during dry times. During periods of wet weather or springtime rains, its quite possible that this creek could represent a wet crossing, so be prepared.

After crossing Mill Creek, the trail doesn't hold out too long before making its ascent up towards the ridge. The climb is steep with rocky terrain, and if you begin to tire a bit as you climb, feel grateful that you're hiking and not on a mountain bike. In mountain biking terms, this climb would be designated as steep and technical! Sharp in incline, but rather short, this upward scale to the ridge doesn't last more than a quarter of a mile before leveling off into a nice pleasant ridgetop walk down a widened path with gorgeous views on either side during periods in fall and winter when leaves are off the trees. This scene pretty much continues as it extends for a little over a mile to the first trail intersection. The turn-off here to the left leads straight across the area to FS 1576, further down from where the trailhead was, and has a turn-off option from there that leads down to the natural bridge. (See map and this will be clearer!) Straight at this intersection is the direction to opt for as it continues southwest towards the turn-off and loop for Wilkin's Spring. The next trail intersection, again leading left, is the one to take if you wish to proceed straight to the natural bridge. The path from here, when taken to the left, leads to the natural bridge within about one-fourth of a mile. If you just want to see the bridge and are at Kaintuck for a short day hike, this is a good trail route option to take.

Staying straight once again, the main trail will lead to a third junction, which is actually a "T" junction, with options of right or left. Go right, this will pass by a small pond immediately to the right and head down about one half mile. As you reach the bottom, the trail crosses a little stream and passes through half of a fence opening to a clearing. This is Wilkin's Pond. The clearing and area surrounding the pond is the picture perfect setting for a fall afternoon or spring picnic. Two giant oaks reside just in front of the lake, extending branches that shade a couple of picnic tables beneath them. A path just to the right of these tables circles around the pond with an outflow of water into Mill Creek being encountered first on the pond's north end, and the beautiful Wilkin's Spring pouring into the pond on the south end. The amount of water that consistently originates from Wilkin's Spring is amazing—even during the driest of seasons, water gushes out and into the pond, feeding Mill Creek on the opposite side. Looking down into the spring, the water gives a view to the vegetation growth below, but it's hard to determine an exact point where the water comes up from the ground—amazing!

When you are ready to leave this most pleasant setting, proceed left from where the trail entered the clearing, skirting the back side of it (past the outhouse, if its still there!) up alongside the trees and into a wooded area where the trail eventually leads. There is an intersection after the pond where you want to stay left, following the trail as it makes it's way uphill. A beautiful pine forest stand emerges as the widened path for the trail leads up and around, making a slight incline as it climbs back towards the ridge just above the Wilkin's Pond area. Passing through another clearing, an old homestead and pond, the trail moves through a section of the most gorgeous stand of pine trees. Tall, straight and dense, they appear almost perfectly spaced apart. In addition to resembling a scene from the Smokey Mountains, they also send out a wonderful scent of fresh pine, while lining the trail with a soft bed of needles. Once on top, the trail comes to another intersection that requires a choice of hiking length. The longer route, covering a stretch of three miles, is to the right. Once this route establishes itself in the valley, the trail loops around a flat and easy segment, that moves in and out of timber to the next trail intersection near FS 1576 (see map). A left taken here proceeds back past the turnoff to Wilkin's Pond and can be hiked all the way back to the trailhead in just over 2 miles. The ideal route would be to go left here, pass a dead-end roadbed intersection on your left, pass the junction to Wilkin's Pond that is also on the left, and go to the next intersection, which is on the right and take it about ¼ of a mile to the natural bridge.

You will know you are at the natural bridge when the trail steps down over a couple of tiny rock ledges and out to an intersection. Just to the left at this point is the one opening to the incredible natural bridge. Taking on the appearance of a giant cave mouth opening, the bridge can be entered, and as it curves, light from the opposite end shines through, leading to the exit on the other side. Natural bridges are always amazing, particularly one of this scope and size—be sure and spend a few moments here exploring and enjoy this natural wonder. Walking under the bridge, which is much more like passing through a tunnel, takes you under and across the trail so that if you take a left out the other side and follow the trail all the way around you will be back at the other side. There is also the option, however, of taking a left out this exit and moving straight down the trail until it meets another crossing of Mill Creek, a trailhead and a gravel side road leading to FS 1576. This is where the longer southern route section of the trail empties out.

After a short stay at this Kaintuck show piece, the trail (from the first opening) proceeds straight or left, and heads slowly upward as it moves away from the bridge. Hiking about a half mile up and over the ridge, the trail intersects again at the bottom across from a cedar clearing. Right goes back to FS 1576 which can be used to return to the trailhead, but, it's more scenic to return via trail rather than road, so take a left. Left goes uphill for about ½ mile to intersect with the original ridgetop trail that led in. Take a right at this intersection and follow it back the way you came—you will be back at your vehicle in just over a mile!

Hiking Tip — Teamwork

Packing in pairs or groups is a great way to activate some quality teamwork. Helping one another over logs, across streams and through tight spots is a very necessary part of a day on the trail. Aside from this however, packers can also team up ahead of time on gear organization. Since the name of the game is "go lite", collaborate on who is in charge of carrying certain "shared" items such as cameras, cooking gear, water filters and fuel.

40. Lake of the Ozarks State Park

LOCATION: This section of the park, located on the extreme eastern end of the Grand Glaize arm of Lake of the Ozarks, is found by traveling 3 miles southeast down Highway 42 from the junction of Highway 42 and Highway 54, to Highway 134. Highway 134 travels south and is the entrance to the park.

LENGTH: Five trails are offered in this area:
Woodland Trail — 6 miles
Trail of 4 Winds — 6 miles
Fawn's Ridge Trail — 2.5 miles
Squaw's Revenge Trail — 2 miles
Lake View Bend Trail — 1 mile

COMMENTS: Hidden along the shorelines of Lake of the Ozarks, and tucked deep within the quietness of the lake's Grand Glaize arm, resides a portion of Missouri's largest state park. Encompassing more than 80 miles of lake frontage within its 17,000 acres, Lake of the Ozarks State Park provides a secure haven for a wide range of wildlife species, while also offering recreation opportunities for those wishing to enjoy the outdoors.

Due to this parks immense size, trail options remain largely divided by acres of protected forestland and miles of fabulous lake front. Rocky Top Trail, also covered in this guide, lies within the park on the Osage Beach end of the lake while the remaining trails and campground areas (as discussed here) are situated on the lake's extreme eastern end, where the Grand Glaize arm tapers down into Grand Glaize Creek.

The facilities in the park at this end of the lake are many; ranging from campgrounds (both primitive and electric), picnic areas and stables, to a boat ramp, cabin rentals and a general store. Trails within the area all offer something unique, and are well marked.

TOPOGRAPHICAL MAPS: Toronto

WOODLAND TRAIL
Woodland Trail winding through Patterson Hollow Wild Area, is the park's official backpacking trail with the provision of a primitive camp spot located on the trail's southern end. The trailhead for Woodland is 1.5 miles in from the park's entrance at Highway 42 and 134, and is located just behind the trail information cabin situated on the road's right-hand side. The trail is 6 miles in

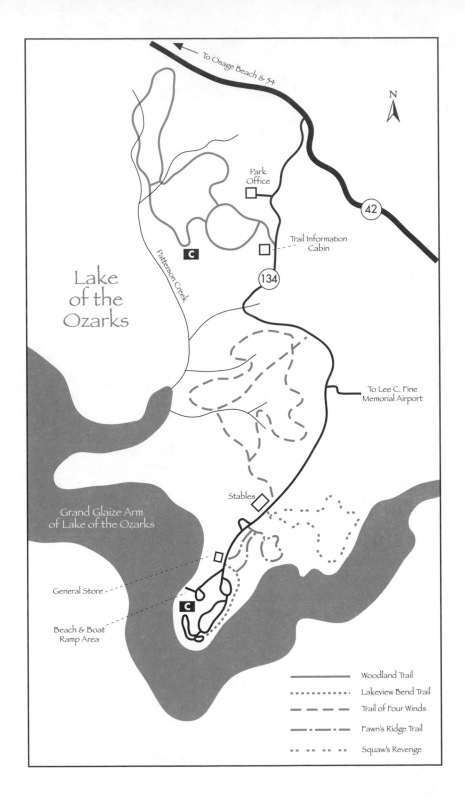

To Osage Beach & 54

N

Park
Office

42

Trail Information
Cabin

C

134

Lake
of the
Ozarks

Patterson Creek

To Lee C. Fine
Memorial Airport

Stables

Grand Glaize Arm
of Lake of the Ozarks

General Store

C

Beach & Boat
Ramp Area

——————— Woodland Trail

·············· Lakeview Bend Trail

— — — — Trail of Four Winds

—·—·—·— Fawn's Ridge Trail

– – – – Squaw's Revenge

length, yet broken up into three 2 mile loops in provision of shorter options for those not wishing to hike the entire 6 miles. Marked with blue arrows in a counter-clockwise direction, the trail remains easy to follow as it passes up and down the rock terrain typical of this area.

From the trailhead, the trail begins in a northwesterly direction passing down into the hollow and back up to the ridge where the first fork resides. To your left, and marked in orange, is a connector trail that brings you to the other side of the blue trail and back to the trailhead. Stay to the right in continuation of the larger 6 mile loop, and the trail resides along the ridge for a short while before heading down into Patterson Hollow. At the base of this hollow to the left, just after crossing Patterson Creek lies the second connector trail marked in yellow that loops back around to total 4 miles. This connector might be harder to distinguish due to the brush overgrowth and the creek's path. Patterson Creek runs most of the year and could create some wet crossings, particularly in the spring season.

From the creek bottoms, the trail proceeds up, eventually settling briefly along the contours of the ridge, where it loops around to head south at the trail's half-way point. This outer most section of the trail, characterized mostly by forested oak and hickory, also holds stands of Eastern Red Cedar that is scattered throughout the area. The trail heads down from the ridgetop and crosses Patterson Creek a couple of times before rejoining the yellow connector trail at the base of Patterson Hollow again. Up from the hollow, the trail makes its way towards the backpack camp. Before reaching the trailcamp however, the trail first brings you alongside one of this area's natural springs, which is off the trail on the left. The water originates above the trail and forms a tributary that passes under a large rock across the trail and makes its way into Patterson Creek. At approximately 5 miles in, the trail comes to a low impact backpack camp on your right, with the nearest water source coming from the natural spring just crossed.

Leaving camp and continuing on to the trailhead, the trail varies in elevation as it passes across the hollows and moves through a small cedar growth area to the fork that originated the loop. Take a right and it will lead back to the trailhead at the trail information cabin.

TRAIL OF FOUR WINDS

Although identical in length to Woodland, this trail is not designated as a backpacking trail and should be done as a long day hike. There are two entry/exit points to the trail, with the main one located on the west side of Highway 134, past the Woodland trailhead, and the second option located at the stables.

From the trailhead and parking area of 134, the trail starts southwest and quickly comes to the first junction. The trail option taking you straight ahead, cuts through the middle of the 6 mile loop, bisecting the trail into two smaller loops: a 3.2 mile loop marked in blue covering the northern section, and a 4.1 mile yellow loop circling the more southern portion. Take a right at this fork to proceed with the original 6 mile trail, or to begin the 3.2 mile loop of the trail's northern half. Easy hiking at first, the trail holds steady on the ridge, traveling through oak and hickory forest dominating the few scattered cedars. The trail dips down into a hollow crossing a tributary to Patterson Creek, and at just under 2 miles, reaches a fork designating the yellow trail again that bisects the area. The pleasant and scenic area within this hollow holds natural springs as well as intermittent tributaries to Patterson Creek, causing the ground to be wet, and at times marshy, during periods of rain. The trail junction at this point allows you the option of returning to the beginning via the yellow trail, or continuing on the main route towards the trail's prettiest section. Shortly after the passing of the yellow trail, another short-cut option marked in red lies to the left. Stay to the right however, for the main trail and it will lead up to a fabulous BTV overlook. Situated to the right of the trail, the overlook consists of a large sandstone bluff, with an abrupt drop that extends views of the lake to the west, best seen in spring and fall. The display of colors from the trees in fall is especially pretty, qualifying as an BTV. From the overlook, continue down the trail until it forks again. Take a left here following the loop, because staying right leads you out of the area via the trailhead located at the stables. Left takes you back down into the hollow and stream area, at which point the trail curves a bit dramatically to head southeast. It moves up to the ridge almost overlooking the road (134), and then skirts off to the north, making its way back to the trailhead through wooded area for about 1.5 miles.

The Grand Glaize arm of Lake of the Ozarks

SQUAW'S REVENGE TRAIL

The trailhead location for Squaw's Revenge automatically provides you with information concerning this trail's type. It begins across the road from the stables, heading downhill from behind the small paddock located there at the trail's starting point. Yes, this trail is heavily used by the horses as is evidenced by its generous width and less rocky terrain. The beginning section adopts the appearance of "horse trail" much more than does the completing half, providing you with an incentive to continue down this trail which offers fantastic scenery from on top of the bluff along the southeast section.

If, from the trailhead, you follow the trail as it winds its way down into the valley, it will lead you to a small, partially cleared area on your right that has the appearance of having been a family cemetery plot at one time as it contains at least one old headstone dated from 1882. It is past this area, that the trail heads up to the bluff where it continues, providing splendid BTV lake views to your right as you hike for the next fourth of a mile. Upon completing its course along the ridge, the trail eventually turns to the west and slightly downhill passing some small BTV views to your left along the way. From this point on, the trail's final ¾ of a mile lies flat or heads downhill, continuing to be easy to follow and finishing at the trailhead you began from.

FAWN'S RIDGE TRAIL AND LAKE VIEW BEND TRAIL

The Fawn's Ridge Trail, along with Lake View Bend, both start directly east of the campground registration booth located just beyond the general store. Sharing a trailhead and beginning portion of the trail, both head downhill for a short distance before coming to a "T" at which point they split off.

Lake View Bend Trail goes to the right and follows alongside the lake for one mile with a clear and very scenic view of the water to your left for the entire hike. At the completion of the mile, the trail exits at the lower portion of the campground requiring that you return by backtracking down the trail, or hiking up through the campground.

Fawn's Ridge Trail goes left at the "T", and immediately takes distant residence alongside a springtime tributary on your right that runs down the small hollow below, eventually emptying into the lake. The trail crosses a few creek beds that remain dry during hotter months, but could guide runoff water from heavier rain down to the tributary creek. The trail is rocky, typifying terrain common to the area, but is fairly flat, allowing for easy hiking. At ½ a mile in, the trail approaches the first fork, at which you take a right, followed closely by a second fork. At this second fork, right proceeds on with the trail and the second loop, while left takes you to another of the trail's entrance/exit points located across the road from the picnic areas.

Take a right in continuation of the trail and you will soon find the fork designating the second loop's beginning. This loop is about a mile long in its entirety and at its midpoint edges close enough to the lake to offer a fairly nice view of the water during leaf-off periods. This loop completes itself and leads you back again past the picnic area to a point where the trail has been widened. As it follows the wide path back towards the general store area, views of the woodland acreage begin to open up to your left, providing scenic walk back to the trailhead.

41. Mina Sauk Falls Trail

LOCATION: Mina Sauk Falls Trailhead is located in the Taum Sauk Mountain State Park south of Ironton. The State Park can be found at the end of CC, 9 miles southwest of Ironton, off Missouri Highway 21-49.

LENGTH: The trail is a 3 mile loop.

COMMENTS: Mina Sauk Falls Trail is an easy and pleasant hike through outstanding areas of scenery and leads to Missouri's highest waterfall state-wide, Mina Sauk Falls. The trail also serves as a segment of the Taum Sauk section of the Ozark Trail which leads 12 miles southwest to Johnson's Shut-Ins State Park.

Photo Credit: Missouri Department of Natural Resources

Mina Sauk falls on the Taum Sauk Trail

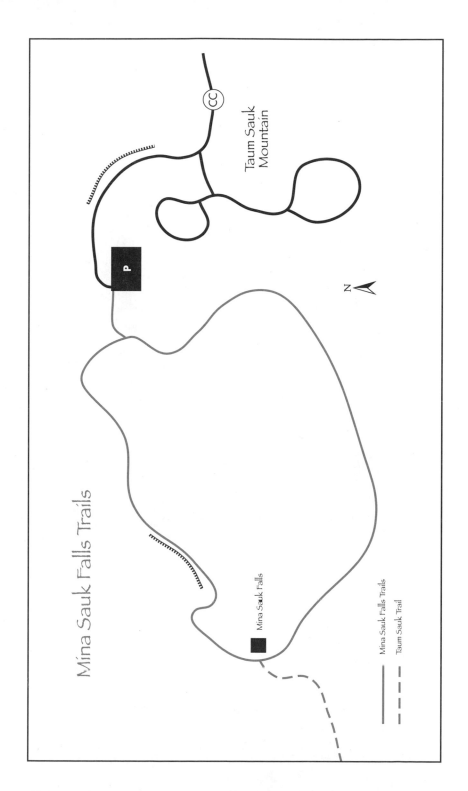

Mina Sauk Falls Trails

Taum Sauk Mountain

Mina Sauk Falls

P

CC

N

——— Mina Sauk Falls Trails

– – – Taum Sauk Trail

The trailhead can be found behind the restrooms located at the northern most parking lot of the park. The start of this trail is paved, and leads to the west. You will reach a sign and fork almost immediately that designates the beginning of the loop as well as the direction for the Ozark Trail. Take a right, heading towards the falls. The area here, characteristic of this St. Francois Mountain region, is covered with woodlands interrupted by rocky clearings known as glades. The combination is striking, and the landscape outstanding. As you approach the one mile mark, a tremendous view opens up to your right overlooking the hills and valleys for miles—definitely a BTV! The trail leads over and across the large flat rocks that create a nice ledge and vantage point for the vista, and proceeds slightly downhill for about two-tenths of a mile curving right up to the Mina Sauk Falls. Cascading 132 feet down a series of volcanic ledges, emptying its flow into the large pool below, this waterfall is impressive and earns the title of BTV! The fork in the trail at the top indicates the Taum Sauk and Ozark Trails, to the right away from the loop, and the continuation of Mina Sauk loop to the left. If you take a right at the fork, it will take you briefly downhill and to the base of the falls—a worthwhile sidetrip without question. If you're up for a longer sidetrip, continue down that same route past the base of the falls for approximately 1 mile, and catch a glimpse of the Devil's Tollgate, another fascinating geologic wonder featuring the splitting of a 30 foot high igneous boulder through which the trail runs.

Returning to the top of the falls and the fork there; take a left to continue the loop of Mina Sauk Falls Trail and it will bring you back around to the parking lot within a mile and a half.

Camp Recipe — Bean and Pasta Dish

An excellent combination of protein and carbs, this easy meal is a tasty trail favorite.

    Pasta (tortellini, corkscrew or muscacholi)
    Pinto Beans
    Cous Cous
    Red Peppers (dehydrated if on the trail for a while)
    Green Onions (dehydrated)
    Tomatoes (dehydrated)
    Garlic powder
    Parmesan Cheese

Soak the pinto beans while setting up camp and this will shorten stove time. Cook pasta and beans, add ingredients and spices. Leave out the parmesan and leave in the water, and you have an excellent trail-side soup. Be creative and add more if you'd like. Enjoy!

42. The Ozark Trail

LOCATION: The Ozark Trail begins south of St. Louis and extends across the southwestern portion of Missouri to connect with its Arkansas equivalent, the Ozark Highlands Trail. The trail currently contains 8 finished sections, with the missing pieces to be completed as land easements and funding allow. For detailed information on the Ozark Trail, its completed sections and trailhead directions contact:

    Missouri Dept. of Natural Resources, Ozark Trail Coordinator
    P.O. Box 180, Jefferson City, Mo. 65102
    (314) 751-2479

    Missouri Dept. of Conservation, State Forester
    P.O. Box 180, Jefferson City, Mo. 65102
    (314) 751-4115

LENGTH: When completed, the Ozark Trail will cover 500 miles of southwest Missouri. The finished sections vary in length from 20 to 30 miles each, with shorter options available in some areas.

COMMENTS: The idea for the Ozark Trail began in 1977 with a group of hikers, land managers and private land owners who each shared an interest in preserving and promoting the natural beauty of Missouri's Ozarks. The goal was to create a long distance trail that would traverse southwest Missouri, and someday link with the already existing Ozark Highlands Trail in Northwest Arkansas. The Ozark Trail Council was established in efforts to promote, organize and put into motion the plans to construct this vision. Large portions of the trail have been completed with the remaining sections requiring land easements and cooperation from private land owners. Eventually however, this trail will join St. Louis with the Arkansas border as it winds itself down through this state's fabulous Ozark wilderness.

    Much of this trail will surprise you, perhaps causing you to question your Midwest whereabouts for just a moment. The views along the Current and Eleven Point Rivers are breathtaking, and some of the backcountry-like wilderness unmatched. There are waterfall displays, rushing winding creeks, and creative rock formations that will all catch you off guard, pleasantly surprise you, and increase your appreciation for what this area has to offer. If you like to really escape, separate from the more casual outdoor crowd, and spend a weekend alone in the woods, then this is your trail!

    Plan your trip carefully. Obtain the recommended topographic maps for

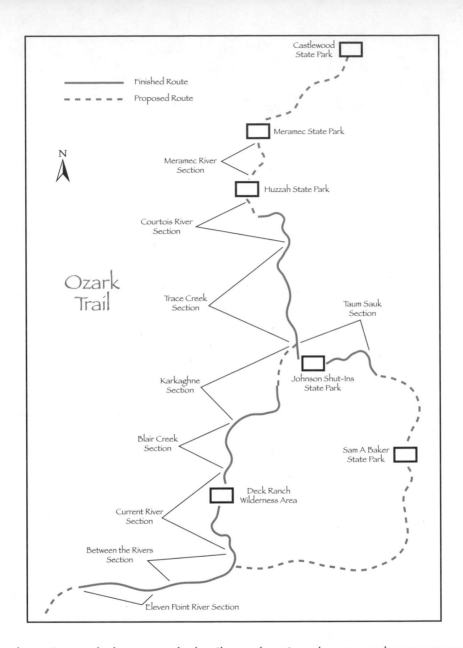

each section and observe such details as elevation changes and water stops. There are sections where water is limited, and planning strategically for your overnight stops is essential. For the most part this trail is well marked, identified by the signature green and white OT trail markers posted on trees along the route. Watch for turn-offs however, as much of this trail will utilize short segments of an old logging road only to veer off into the woods sharply at some point. Camping along the trail requires no permit and is undesignated, although evidences of particular camping spots along the trail are easily seen. Please try to preserve the area as much a possible, practicing "no trace" camping and being cautious not to over use the area.

43. Pickle Springs

LOCATION: Pickle Springs can be reached by heading east of Farmington down Highway 32 for 5 miles to AA. Pickle Springs is 1.7 miles down AA on the left.

LENGTH: The trail is a two mile scenic loop.

COMMENTS: Pickle Springs is probably the most unique and interesting 2 mile trail in Missouri. Although too short in length for a backpack trip it is perfect for a leisurely day hike, picnic spot, or family outing. The area offers unique geologic features, spectacular views and a few rare plants. The trail is wide and easy to hike. Because of the unique geology and vegetation, please remain on the trail at all times to preserve this wonderful little area.

TOPOGRAPHICAL MAPS: Coffman

From the trailhead you head north and start the loop in a clockwise direction. The trail is well marked with wooden signs explaining each of the features along the trail. The first of these is The Slot. The Slot is a series of strange holes and pockets along the sandstone walls formed by water moving through fractures caused by shifts in the earth's crust. The water has eroded away parts of the wall over time, causing the pockets to enlarge. As you walk on, there are some large "moundlike" sandstone formations known as "hoodoos" or rock pillars, but due to their appearance they are termed "Cauliflower Rocks".

The next unique feature of Pickle Spring is the Double Arch. The arches hold out a shelf of sandstone above and are a beautiful formation. Not much farther down from the double arches is The Keyhole, where two huge rock masses merge together at the top forming a keyhole to walk through.

As the trail moves past The Keyhole you will pass Terrapin Rock, cross Pickle Creek and come to the half way point at Mossy Falls, which only flows during

The double arch at Pickle Springs

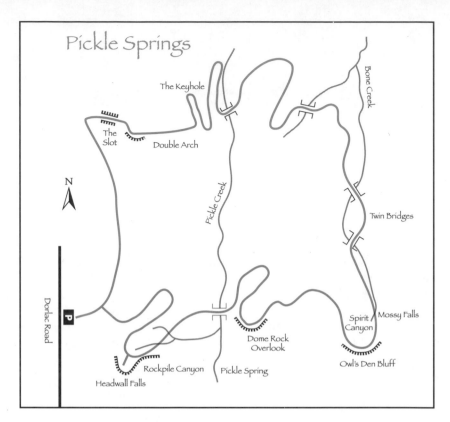

Pickle Springs

The Keyhole

Bone Creek

The Slot

Double Arch

Pickle Creek

N

Twin Bridges

Dorlac Road

P

Spirit Canyon

Mossy Falls

Dome Rock Overlook

Owl's Den Bluff

Rockpile Canyon

Pickle Spring

Headwall Falls

wet weather. From Mossy Falls you move on to Owls Den Bluff and Spirit Canyon. Owls Den Bluff is a large bluff packed full of history hidden within the horizontal layers of sandstone. Each layer, created by channels of water years ago, if separated, would tell which direction water flowed at that time.

Next is Spirit Canyon, and aptly named as it appears the perfect spot in which Indians might have dwelled years ago. Being constantly sheltered from sun this pseudo-cave remains moist and cool all year round and houses some of Missouri's most unique mosses and liverworts. Spirit Canyon leads to Dome Rock Overlook, which sets on top of the largest hoodoo formation and boasts of a beautiful overlook to the south—a definite BTV! Coming down from Dome Rock you cross Pickle Creek again only this time at the spring that gives this place its name. There is a nice little waterfall coming off the ledge in Pickle Creek and the spring is just to the left of it. Rare for this area because of the sandstone bedrock, Pickle Springs was well known among settlers in the 1800's who needed a water source. Down the trail from the springs is Rockpile Canyon, a group of large boulders to the left that is a result of a bluff collapse in 1959. The crash created the large bluff along the canyons south side as well as a few small natural arches. From Rockpile Canyon the trail passes a short spur to Headwall Falls home to more than 20 select species of mosses, ferns, partridge berries, and orchids. As you near the end of the trail it will take you through Piney Glade, where desert grasses meets woodlands. This is the last unique feature of the area and the trail leads you back to the beginning.

44. Rock Bridge Memorial State Park

LOCATION: Rock Bridge is located just 7 miles south of Columbia, in Boone County, off HWY 163.

LENGTH: Rock Bridge holds 5 well marked trails centering around the many geologic attractions that vary in length from .5 to 2.5 miles each. In addition, the neighboring Gans Creek Wild Area contains 15 more miles of backpacking, biking and/or equestrian trails.

COMMENTS: For central Missouri especially, this park is an absolute jewel. Thick with amazing geologic features and natural beauty, Rock Bridge is a treasured hideaway that not only flaunts some of nature's best, but also tells a story of past economic endeavors. Dating back as early as 1834, Rock Bridge held claim to being the first paper mill west of the Mississippi, producing pulp for newspapers distributed in Columbia and St. Louis. The mill was eventually converted into a whiskey distillery, and then when Boone County went "dry", Rock Bridge was purchased by a family who created a sort of mini amusement attraction out of the place. The birth of Rock Bridge into a state park came about as the result of the tragic death of a 9-year old little girl from Columbia who was struck by a speeding car. Established as a memorial to her, and preserved to be safe place for children to play, area residents raised money enough to purchase the original 1,100 acres of land, and Rock Bridge Memorial State Park came into official being in 1967.

The trails leading around this park contain so much to see. The karst topography that characterizes this area is displayed throughout the park in the form of sinkholes, springs, hidden underground streams and small caverns. In addition to the showcase of natural creation, Rock Bridge's history can also be pieced back together through the stone remnants of past building foundations, and crumbled dam layers of the once used mill. The actual "rock-bridge" that gives this park it's name, and accompanying Devil's Ice Box, are definite attractions to capture your attention, but are by no means the area's only highlight. Forested and gladed terrain, mixed among ridgetops and overlooks, provide a perfect complimentary backdrop to the entire haven of geologic wonder and formation.

Originally founded upon the idea of creating a safe "children's playground", Rock Bridge is of course, an ideal escape for the family. With trail length options being either short or combined into something more lengthy, this area is perfect for family hiking and/or picnicking. Rock Bridge does not

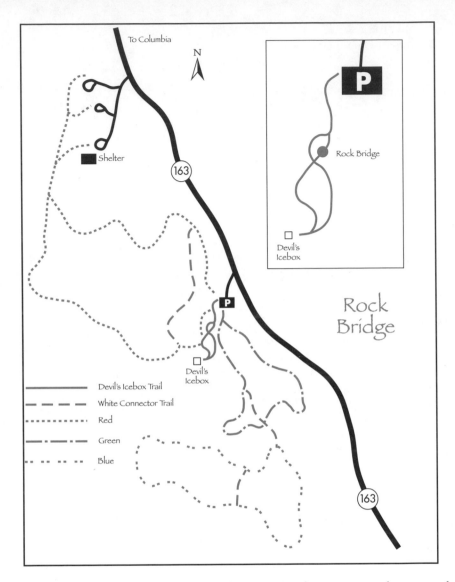

To Columbia

N

163

Shelter

P

Rock
Bridge

P

Devil's
Icebox

Devil's
Icebox

——————— Devil's Icebox Trail

– – – – – White Connector Trail

·············· Red

—·—·—· Green

·—··—··— Blue

163

P

Rock Bridge

Devil's
Icebox

contain area campgrounds, or primitive camp sites however, so plan to explore the area via a long day hiking trip. Rock Bridge also provides the unique offering of an orienteering course for those interested in challenge of endurance and topographic map reading combined. Maps outlining the course and its checkpoints are available at the park office. Check also for scheduled meets or training events. Even if you have no desire to orienteer through the course, the map itself, being colored and more detailed contour wise, is nice to have in exploration of the area.

Since the natural rock bridge is the area's main attraction, and since each of the other trails can feed off of, and/or interconnect here, we'll start with Rock Bridge Trail. Although short, at only .5 miles in length, this trail is packed with many of the park's highlights. The trail is boardwalked in efforts to protect the fragile area from erosion and deterioration due to heavy use. Rock Bridge

Trail situates itself in the park's mid section and can serve as a kind of "hub" for the other remaining trails. Each trail is marked well and color coordinated. Trails marked in white are designated as connector trails, allowing passage to and from each trailhead and linking the network together.

TOPOGRAPHICAL MAPS: Columbia

From the parking lot, head off down the Rock Bridge Trail following the yellow markers. Wasting no time, the trail leads you straight to the mouth of an immense cave opening which is actually the entrance into the giant "rock-bridge". The boardwalk leads right under the bridge along the stream to remaining portions of the original dam built to power the old mill back in the 1800's. Continuing on through the cavern, this boardwalk trail will skirt around to the equally outstanding steep rocky chasm of Devil's Ice Box. The blast of cool air originating from the iced spring water within gives hint to the name, and provides an excellent escape from summertime heat. Housing more than just nature's air-conditioning, Devil's Icebox is also home to the federally endangered gray bat, and is thus closed April 1 through August 31 to prevent disturbance to these creatures while nurturing their young.

Rock Bridge Memorial State Park

Going back to the cave-like entrance of the bridge, just before entering, should you cross the creek and head to the left, you will enter onto the Sinkhole Trail. Marked in green, this trail is approximately 1.5 miles and leads you up along the ridge. Along this ridge, the trail takes on the form of an old logging road and on your left is one of the first remains that this trail holds of old foundations left from the area's distillery days. Continue on the trail and the sinkholes that offer this trail its name soon come into view. Watch for Polly's Pot Cave on your left, which is actually a hidden opening on the surface, that extends down into a deep 40 foot vertical shaft, and eventually opens up into a quarter mile long cavern. As you head downhill slightly and arrive at the trail intersection, continue straight into Hog's Graveyard, another spectacular collection of huge sinkholes. Continue hiking, and as you pass the old water tower structure, you arrive at another trail intersection. Stay left to continue green, and pass the old large silo. Boardwalk steps lead down to the Devil's Ice Box on your left, or continue down green back to it's origination.

Spring Brook Trail commences at the Rock Bridge trailhead area as well, but can also begin near the picnic area of the park office side of the park. Spring Brook is about 2.5 miles long and covers the northern side of the park through a beautifully forested area of ridgetop and bottomlands mix. The markers are red with one white middle connector that allows for a shorter loop or access back to the Devil's Ice Box section. From the Rock Bridge Trailhead, the trail extends to your right and follows alongside the Little Bonne Femme Creek, which is sometimes tagged as "Rock Bridge Creek". Soon the trail crosses this pleasant little brook, and climbs slightly in elevation before heading back down to recross the same stream. Plan to get your feet wet during real rainy weather, otherwise crossing isn't a problem. The full loop continues this sort of "up, over and across the creek" pattern and will lead back to the Rock Bridge Trail. Up and over the scenic top of the rock bridge itself, and you are back to the start!

Hiking Tip — Garbage Bags

Garbage bags are a lightweight item that can be very useful "on trail."

- Lining the inside of your pack with a garbage bag can add extra water-proofing and protect the contents from a weekend of rainy weather.
- A garbage bag can also be used on the outside of your pack to act as a raincover.
- An extra bag can serve as a nice liner to an otherwise muddy or dusty vestibule floor.
- If you place your boots in the bottom of your bag during winter months in efforts to keep them warm overnight, put them in a garbage bag first and keep all that dirt out of your bed!
- Garbage bags can actually help you stay warm during extreme cold—they are non-breathable and trap body heat in.
- Garbage bags are also excellent for wet and or dirty clothes when on a longer trek.

45. Rockpile Mountain

LOCATION: Rockpile Mountain is located just south of Fredricktown. From Fredricktown, take US 67 south to County Road C on your right. Follow C for 5 miles to County Road 406, which is a gravel road on your right. Stay on 406 for about two miles until, on your left, you reach FR 2124. Take this until it ends at Rockpile Mountain trailhead.

LENGTH: The hike to Rockpile Mountain itself is about 4 miles, but if you continue on past Rockpile, the trail creates a nice 11 mile loop with some side trails along the way.

COMMENTS: Rockpile Mountain earned its name from a circular pile of stones stacked up on top of the mountain that some believe to be an Indian burial marker. The "pile" of rocks, stacked circularly, at one time stood approximately four feet in height, but has since dwindled down in size due to human interference and lack of preservation. The trail itself is a beautiful hike through hardwood forest leading up to some nice vistas amongst boulders and interesting rock formations. The gradients are fairly gradual making the trail easy to hike. If hiking the loop, water can be found at the halfway point, where a very pleasant tributary to the St. Francois River flows. If you're just hiking to Rockpile mountain and back, take water with you as there are only a few small ponds for water sources. The trail is fairly distinct but is without any markers.

Rockpile Mountain

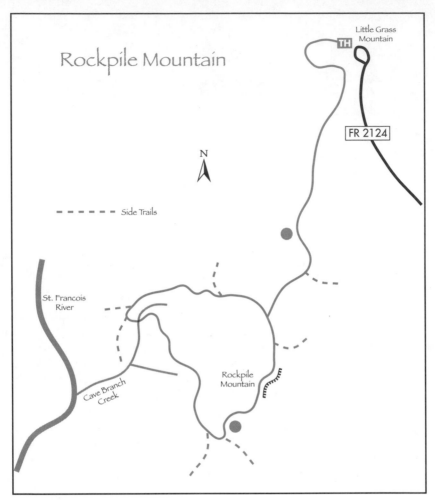

It is recommended that you take a topo map and compass with you to make it easier to follow.

TOPOGRAPHICAL MAPS: Rockpile

The trail starts on the west side of the boulder with "ROCKPILE MOUNTAIN" etched in it and curves almost directly south and downhill. For a short while the trail travels parallel with the road (although you don't really see the road) and then turns away to the south continuing to head that direction all the way to Rockpile.

Once the trail turns away from the road, at ½ mile, it goes up a small knoll and then remains mostly flat through a hardwood forest area scattered with an occasional boulder or two. Stay on this plateau for about a mile before heading up to the first little vista. The area is sort of a rocky clearing on the top of a mountain with boulders and a few cedar trees—a very pleasant BTV spot. The trail travels through the middle of this area and then heads back on into the woods. At about 2 miles you'll pass a small wildlife pond on your right, and at

2 ½ miles you will reach a fork in the trail. If you followed this trail left it would lead to Trace Creek, but only by way of crossing private property, so stay to the right and the trail will take you another half a mile to a second fork. This is the 3 mile mark and also the beginning of the loop which in itself is about 5 miles in length. The trail taken left leads up to Rockpile Mountain. You only have about a mile more to get there but before reaching it you have another fork. Stay to the right and the trail begins to climb a bit. You will see rock slabs, boulders, and rock formations on both sides of the trail before finally reaching the top. Once on top, look for the circular stack of rocks that sets to the right of the trail—this is the "rockpile" that gives the trail its name. Although very interesting, the "rockpile" is not the biggest attraction of this little mountain top. The rocky, high point plateau holds some terrific views on either side and is an excellent stopping point to enjoy this BTV.

If you wish to continue on the loop, the trail picks up again on the west side of Rockpile and heads back into the woods and downhill a bit. At 4.3 miles, you will pass another small pond on your left. At this point, the trail widens and starts to curve around to head a bit more north. With hollows on both sides and a nice view on your left, you feel as if you're hiking along a ridge. Eventually the trail descends down to a beautiful little creek area at 6.0 miles. This is a definite BTV and would make an excellent camp spot if one wishes to do an overnight. During periods of rain, this creek flows quickly creating some rushing little cascades and small waterfalls. Across the creek, the trail continues into an area resembling a wooded clearing. It is here that a saw mill once existed, but there are no longer remains of the sight. A trail veering left once led to a view of the St. Francois as well as caves from which materials were extracted to make gun powder during the Civil War. Proceed right and the trail goes uphill and winds around at the top of the hill to head east (right). Hiking then levels off into a very pleasant stroll through the woods, with some nice views of the hollows below to your right. You will come to a side trail on your left, at about 7.5 miles, but stay straight, and shortly thereafter the trail leads to another fork which is the completion of the loop. Take the trail left and you will be headed north again and back to the trailhead. Straight, or to the right takes you back up to Rockpile.

From the loop completion to the trailhead is about 3 miles and is a backtracking of the way you came in so be sure and take the forks in the proper directions.

Hiking Tip — Blisters

The best way to prevent blisters is to purchase good quality boots that fit your feet and if necessary, a set of custom –made insoles as well. Applying moleskin to the heel and/or other places that have potential to rub or irritate before your hike even begins is also a smart preventative measure, however, if you do get blisters while trail-bound, here are a few helpful hints on what to do next:

- Clean the blistered area and rinse with water.
- Cut a "donut" out of mole skin so that the moleskin can be placed around the blistered area, rather than on the blister.

46. Rocky Top Trail

LOCATION: Rocky Top Trail is located in Lake of the Ozarks State Park at Osage Beach, Mo. The State Park is accessible from Highway 54, 1.2 miles north of the stoplight and turn off for Tan Tara, or 1.2 miles south of Grand Glaize Bridge.

LENGTH: Rocky Top Trail is 3 miles in length, and in the form of a loop.

COMMENTS: Rocky Top is one of the many trails offered within the boundaries of Lake of the Ozarks State Park. The park's immense size and extensive acreage has separated Rocky Top from the other hiking trails offered due to its Osage Beach Area location. The remaining trails wind through the acreage reserved at the lake's Grand Glaize Arm, and is covered elsewhere in this guide. The Rocky Top Trail is a very scenic and pleasant hike through hardwood forest that edges alongside the waterfront, and up to a nice vista overlooking the lake's main channel. The terrain is slightly rocky but can be hiked with ease, making it ideal for family hikes or an afternoon stroll.

TOPOGRAPHICAL MAPS: Camdenton

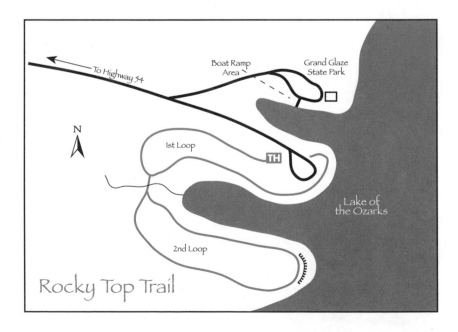

The trailhead begins at the sign and proceeds west. Immediately you will notice the trail's namesake as rocks and glades provide a rugged terrain characteristic of the Ozarks. The trail starts off through the trees and then quickly opens up into a meadow on top of the hill that gives one the sense of being on top of a mountain out west. Wildflowers are prevalent here, and mixed with large rocks scattered throughout the field, this area creates a BTV. At the opposite side of the clearing, the trail re-enters into the woods and moves slightly downhill until reaching a sign at ¾ of a mile that designates the beginning of the second loop. The trail to the right takes you to the second loop while left will complete loop 1 and bring you back to the parking lot. Head right and across the creek where you will reach a second fork, the official beginning of loop 2. You can of course do the loop in either direction but we will go left. The trail heads straight into a fairly dense hardwood forest and slowly merges closer to the lake. There are many huge gorgeous ferns hear, scattered throughout the forest and lining the trail. As you continue, the back end of "fern cove" comes into view on your left, and from here the trail will run parallel to the water for about ½ a mile. As the cove opens up into the lake's main channel, the trail curves right, leading slightly uphill and opens up on top of the bluff overlooking the lake's Grand Glaize Arm. It is a beautiful view; a BTV worthy of a few photographs and ideal for a quick break. From here the trail curves around the bluff and heads back into the woods. At 2 ¾ miles you will reach the fork designating completion of the second loop. Take a left, cross back over the creek and stay right at the next fork which will be the homestretch. This remaining ¾ of a mile leads along the opposite side of "fern cove", only this time the trail leads right alongside the water's edge. If you're lucky you might see turtles sunbathing on a log or shorebirds hiding in the quiet, tail end of the cove. From the main trail are several little off-chutes that head up and to your left, all of which take you back to the car. I would recommend though, following the trail alongside the water for the entire length of the cove. When you reach the end you will again have a perfect view of the lake's channel, but this time from the water's edge rather than the bluff. A left up the hill from the point will take you directly up to the pavilion and parking lot, thus completing the trail.

Hiking Tip — Staying Warm

Remember when mom wouldn't go let you play in the snow without a hat on? We'll there is a bit of truth to keeping warmer with a hat on. You will find this out for yourself when sleeping outside on a cold winter night. A stocking hat, fleece cap or balaclava will make your evening under the stars a bit more comfortable as body heat will be conserved. Also key to keeping warmer at night is not to breathe into your sleeping bag too heavily. The less moisture collected inside your bag, the warmer you will sleep.

47. St. Francois State Park

LOCATION: St. Francois State Park is located just off Highway 67 north of Bonne Terre and Deslodge. Travel west on Highway W .3 miles to Bray Road. Take a right on Bray, go .2 miles and turn left on Pimville Road. St. Francois State Park is 1.8 miles down Pimville.

LENGTH: The area holds four trails:
- Pike Run Trail — 11 miles
- Mooner's Hollow Trail — 2.7 miles
- Swimming Deer Trail — 2.7 miles
- Missouri Trail — ½ mile

COMMENTS: The entire St. Francois park area is fabulous in scenery and landscape, providing an excellent home for many wildlife species. Deer and turkey are commonly seen, adding the final touches to a woodland area beautifully dressed with dogwoods, azaleas and redbuds. The four trails are all color coded and very well marked so that hiking is made easy. The longer Pike Run Trail, outlined here, can be backpacked but water is scarce on the east side and should be brought in if doing an overnight.

TOPOGRAPHICAL MAPS: Bonne Terre

PIKE RUN TRAIL

The trailhead for Pike Run begins just north of the picnic area and heads in a northeasterly direction. The trail consists of two loops, north and south (6.7 miles), and you can hike around both to create one large loop of 11 miles. Begin with the south loop which is marked with yellow markers. From the trailhead, the trail is wide and winds up a ridge decorated with several dogwood trees pretty to view in the spring. Not long after starting the trail you will approach your first intersection which is the official beginning of the loop. Take a right and hike in a counterclockwise direction. From the fork, the trail climbs its first ascent and then returns back down to the creek bottom and back up again. Watch for views on your right, while on the ridge, especially during leaf-off, when the opened up window creates a BTV view. At 2.5, the trail moves off the ridge and there is a camping area to your right. It is off the trail about 1000 feet and has hitching posts for horses—a primitive camping site. The trail continues on past this site until at 3.0 you reach the intersection of north and south loops. Take a right to continue on around the north loop and take a left if you wish to return via south loop only (another 3.5 miles). Proceed right, and the trail winds through hardwood forest mixed with dogwoods, azaleas and redbuds—perfect setting for a springtime stroll. For a small stretch across the ridge, the trail becomes part of an old logging road. At 4.0 you veer off the logging road and to your left, with the trail taking you across a creek and past a small bluff containing the origins of a beautiful and welcoming spring exiting out from the rock. This is not only a pleasant BTV, but also the first place water is available on the trail since the beginning. The spring area, surrounded by vegetation encompassed in a mini rock formation, is an excellent spot for a rest or overnight stay. After crossing the spring area, the trail begins to climb straight up and at 7.3 you come around to meet the intersection again of the two loops; stay to your right and downhill. At 7.7 after hiking downhill, you'll cross another creek and then back up another large hill. At 8.0 the trail extends down to yet another water area, this one with some nice cascading waterfalls during wetter seasons. The trail follows this creek bottom for a while and then goes up again. At 10.6 you will reach the final intersection that when taken to the right, takes you back to the car.

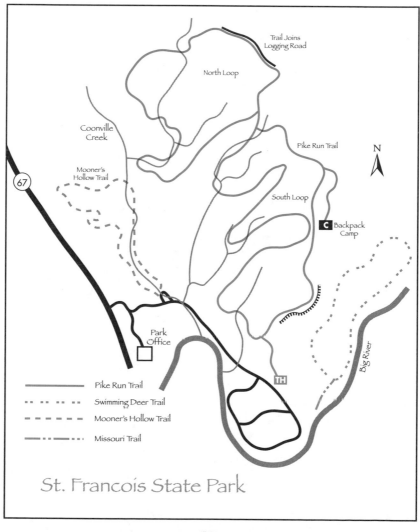

St. Francois State Park

48. Silver Mines Trail

LOCATION: Silver Mines Trail is located nine miles west Fredricktown on Highway 72, and 3 miles south down Highway D.

LENGTH: Silver Mines offers options in trail length, all remaining in the 1 to 3 mile range.

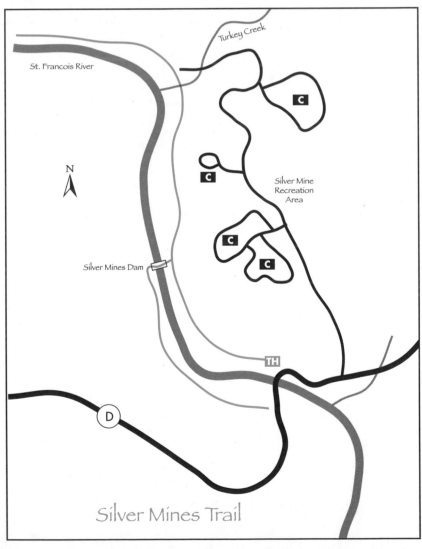

Silver Mines Trail

COMMENTS: This trail, modest in length but grand in scenery, pleasantly follows along the bluffs of the St. Francois River overlooking the shut-ins and rapids below. The area is extensively formed from granite and felsite rock masses lining the river's banks, and creating rapid water chutes, popular as a kayaker's playground, as well as excellent for a hiker's panorama. The trail is ideal for day hiking and picnicking with campgrounds available for those wishing to stay overnight.

TOPOGRAPHICAL MAPS: Fredricktown

From the trailhead and parking on the north side of the bridge, the trail begins up the river, taking on a northwesterly direction. The path is pleasant, accented by the large pines scattered throughout the woodland landscape. The river, to your left, can be seen from many different vantage points, as the huge rock formations allow access to the edge with views of the rapids, shut-ins, and sometimes kayakers below. The trail leads ½ mile upstream before reaching the remains of the historic Silver Mines Dam (down the sidetrail on your left), built in 1879 by large natural stones. The trail continues upstream past the dam with the continuation of outstanding views to the river. Eventually the trail reaches private property with an accompanied "No Trespassing" sign, and the trail must be taken back the same way to reach the trailhead origination. If the water is low, the river can be crossed at the dam, with the option to trek over the dam to continue the trail on the river's west side, looping back to the parking area. At higher water, the river is not crossable however, and the trail should be backtracked to enable a return to the trailhead.

Camp Recipe — Camp Creamsicle

Remember those creamsicles that the ice-cream man delivered on a hot summer day? Although not totally frozen, a camping alternative creates a similar treat.

> 1 t. flavored drink mix. (orange, raspberry etc.)
> 1 t. dry milk
> 2 t. instant vanilla pudding

Dump all ingredients into your camp mug, add cold water and stir. Camp creamsicle is ready to eat!

---

49. Taum Sauk Trail

LOCATION: The Taum Sauk Trail originates at Taum Sauk Mountain State Park south of Ironton Mo., and runs to Johnson's Shut-Ins State Park.

> **Taum Sauk Mountain Trailhead:** From the junction of Highway 72 and Highway 21, take 21 south to CC. CC ends at Taum Sauk State Park and the trailhead begins from the northwest corner of the park. This is the same trailhead location as the Mina Sauk Falls Trail.

> **Johnson's Shut-Ins Trailhead:** Johnson's Shut-Ins is located off Highway N, which can be reached from either 72 or 21.

LENGTH: Taum Sauk Trail is 12.8 miles in length and is not a loop so shuttle arrangements must be made.

COMMENTS: Taum Sauk Mountain, at 1,772 feet above sea level, is located at Missouri's highest point. The Taum Sauk trail, beginning at this point and stretching all the way to Johnson's Shut-Ins State Park, passes through the beautiful St. Francois mountains. With some outstanding geologic features and spectacular views, the trail provides an excellent backpacking, or extended day hiking excursion. The front half of Taum Sauk Trail is shared with the Mina Sauk Falls Trail, and thus features the highlight of Mina Sauk Falls, a 132 foot waterfall cascading down a series of volcanic ledges, to create Missouri's tallest water drop. Devil's Tollgate is also located on the trail and represents another geologic feature outstanding to the trail.

Water is plentiful on either end of the trail, although it might be a bit scarce in the middle. With most of the trail being encompassed as part of the Ozark Trail, it is well marked and easy to follow.

TOPOGRAPHICAL MAPS: Ironton and Johnson's Shut-Ins

The Taum Sauk Trail encompasses some of the Mina Sauk Falls Trail as well as a little of the Ozark Trail.

The beginning of the Taum Sauk Trail is actually the trailhead for Mina Sauk too. From the restroom facilities at Taum Sauk Mountain, proceed west down a paved path. You will reach a sign at the fork not far down that points left for the Ozark Trail trailhead and right for the Mina Sauk Falls. Go right. This little 1.2 mile section to the falls has a couple of very scenic spots and the Mina Sauk Falls themselves are gorgeous. Identified as the highest waterfall in the state, it cascades 132 feet down into a clear blue rock bottom pool—a definite BTV and well worth a few photographs.

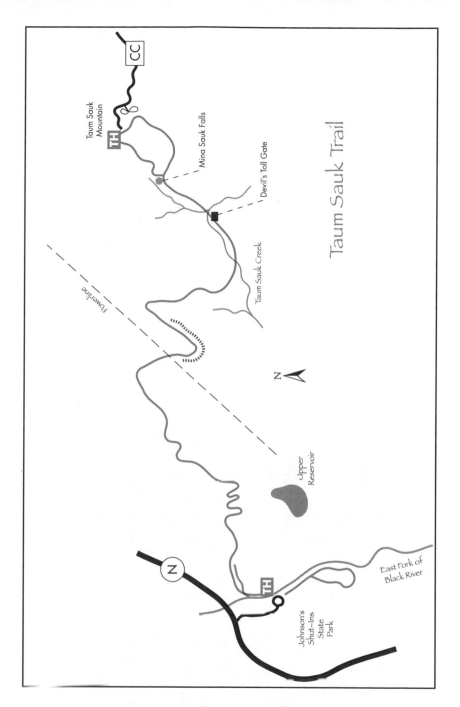

When you arrive at the falls, there will be another sign and fork in the trail. To the left, continues the Mina Sauk Falls Trail which loops back to the parking lot for a total of three miles. Right heads down to the bottom of the falls, as well as onward in the hike. From this point to Johnson's Shut-Ins State Park (JSISP) is 11.5 miles (Mileage for the rest of the trail will be given from this point. Remember though, that the hike to the falls was an additional 1.2 miles, creating a total mileage of almost 13.).

Down at the base of the falls the trail gets a little foggy. You need to cross the creek and look for the white OT markers. At the "T", take a right and head southwest alongside the creek. The trail is nice and flat here, and in wet season, the creek displays some scenic little cascading falls and water pools. Just over a mile from the falls you will cross the creek, and soon after, the trail goes right through Devil's Tollgate. The Tollgate is an 8 to 10 foot wide gap in a massive igneous boulder that holds the appearance of having been split down the middle and separated to either side of the trail. This makes for a very interesting geologic feature and is another BTV. At 2.0 you reach another sign indicating JSISP is 9.5 miles to your right. Head right across the creek. A campsite is on your right and the trail stays flat winding through a small pine forest area and then just slightly uphill, until at 3.0 you're hiking somewhat along a ridge. You will remain hiking along this ridge for approximately 1 mile and at 4.0 the trail will bring you down to a small creek crossing. From this creek, you will ascend very gradually for about ¾ of a mile and enter into a rocky field type area that sets on top of the hillside.

Taum Sauk Trail

Up on top here the trail winds around passing through a few separate clearings, each one giving you the feel of sitting in a field on top of a mountain. Keep your eyes out for markers as you hike through the open spaces because the trail can appear to lead back into the woods at a couple of misleading spots. The correct route will be clearly marked however so you should be able to find your way. The fourth fielded area, at 5.5, is a BTV, holding a spectacular view and providing a perfect halfway stopping point. The trail continues on from here to the right of the clearing and takes you through the woods for another ½ mile, until at 6.0 you arrive at the powerline. Look to the southwest and you will see the dam of the Upper Reservoir.

Past the powerline, the trail follows along the ridge in a northerly direction, and then curves back to the southwest so that you follow the ridge directly across from the powerline as well. It then switchbacks down and back up through a rocky glade area at 8.5. At this point you are following the trail across Proffit Mountain. One half mile later, at the 9 mile mark, you will find a sign designating the Upper Reservoir to be to your left, and JSISP to be 2.5 miles further to your right, or straight. Shortly after this sign is another one identifying a side trail left that leads to an overlook area. JSISP is again straight ahead and the trail remains mostly flat cutting through hardwood forest scattered with a few large pines. You will come to your final sign with 1.5 miles left, and at this point the trail criss-crosses back and forth across, and follows alongside a creek that is a tributary to the East Fork of the Black River, which flows through JSISP. This is a very pretty area, but might make for some wet crossings during springtime rains. Eventually the trail sweeps south, following alongside the East Fork of the Black River, and actually crossing at one point, over a foot bridge. Upon crossing, take a left on the opposite side and follow the gravel path that leads straight to the parking lot of the state park.

Camp Recipe — Pita Rice Pockets

Tired of just plain rice for the trail? Try this simple twist.

> Rice-A-Roni
> Parmesan Cheese
> Dehydrated Green Peppers
> Dehydrated Mushrooms
> Pita Bread

Cook the rice along with the mushrooms and green peppers. Stir in the parmesan last and then scoop servings into the pita bread. Very tasty!

---

50. Three Creeks State Forest

Northern Loop

LOCATION: Three Creeks State Forest is located south of Columbia off CR AB. AB is located off HWY 63, 10 miles south from Columbia or 5.5 miles north of the little town of Ashland. At the junction of CR AB and HWY 63 is the Deer Park Store located on the HWY 63's east side. Take AB west, and you are actually on Deer Park Road. Travel 1.7 miles down Deer Park road to a fork and sign indicating Three Creeks to your left. Turn left and the parking area is one-half mile down.

LENGTH: The trails here are in network form and therefore hiking length varies depending on route. Although the forest area contains over 10 miles of trails, this northern loop section runs just over 2 miles in length.

COMMENTS: As far as hiking and wilderness is concerned, Three Creeks is a hidden jewel within Central Missouri. Encompassing many of the same spectacular features as the neighboring Rockbridge State Park, Three Creeks displays massive bluffs and rock formations, caves and carved out creeks all situated within a much more remote setting. This Northern Loop Trail is fairly short but packed full of such tremendous scenery and fabulous sights that you will not want to rush through it, but rather spend some time exploring and enjoying the trail's highlights and features.

Three Creeks was simply named after the trio of creeks running through it. Catch this area in springtime when the creeks are each running and you will undoubtedly see some spectacular displays of water rushing through rocks and out from cave openings. You are also likely to get wet! The trail crosses Turkey Creek many times, so that during the spring, crossings will be wet. During times of high water and/or heavy rains, creek crossings, and thus hiking this trail could be impossible so watch your weather carefully when planning this trip. Trails are easy to follow but not marked. With the many trail junctions resulting from the network, it is easy to get confused so bring a map at least, and perhaps even a compass.

TOPOGRAPHICAL MAPS: Millersburg SW

The Northern Loop Trail described here begins at the end of the parking lot past the gate that keeps motorized vehicles out. The beginning is a nice flat double track trail that adopts an old roadbed for its path. Follow this across a meadow to the first trail junction and stay left. Shortly after this, upon entering the woods, the trail forks once more, and again you will want to proceed left. As it curves around to head more south, you immediately realize that the trail

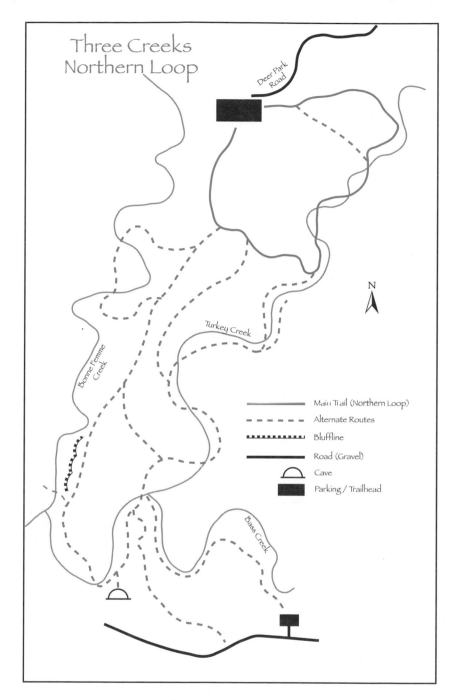

Three Creeks
Northern Loop

Deer Park Road

N

Turkey Creek

Bonne Femme Creek

Bass Creek

Main Trail (Northern Loop)
Alternate Routes
Bluffline
Road (Gravel)
Cave
Parking / Trailhead

is following along the top of a ridge. During fall and winter, when leaves aren't as thick, views of Turkey Creek lie below and to the left, while a shallow hollow dips down to the right. Slowly the trail eases down off this ridge, and as it does, intersects once more. The route right will take you around the longer southern route, and the left trail keeps you on track for this northern loop section. Continue left here and continue with the trail as it loops around to the northeast. Its not long before Turkey Creek and a definite BTV comes into view below and on the right. Also in plain view are the massive bluffs that rise up out of the creek's opposite bank, accenting the already fabulous surrounding scenery. Bushwhack off the trail a few feet and stand below these bluffs at the bank of Turkey Creek—it is quite the amazing sight!

Staying on the trail, it continues to follow alongside the creek until around the turn is a trail passage between a large bluff presiding on the left, and a house-sized boulder on the right. Another BTV, this area is gorgeous, and brings about the feeling of being within a mini canyon. Directly after this passage, comes the first crossing of Turkey Creek, and it is a wide crossing. If the water is running fast, don't try it; if its just there, plan on wet feet! The trail connects on the opposite side so that Turkey Creek is now on the left, accompanied once again by the BTV bluffline following just alongside it. If you took your shoes off to cross the creek, don't tie them too tight, because its not too much further before the trail crosses Turkey Creek again! Trading sides with the creek once more, the trail now travels along with the bluffline and running water on the right. A quarter of a mile or so further down, the trail crosses Turkey Creek two more times—one right after the other, and its after this final crossing that the trail reaches a fork. Left proceeds uphill via another old type roadbed, while right continues flat alongside Turkey Creek. Stay to the right. Following the creek on a long flat stretch, this section of the hike is like a pleasant stroll through the woods. The creek and bluffs are still in view to the right, but are less commanding in presence so that the opportunity comes to recognize and appreciate the beautiful hardwood and cedar mix of timber through which the trail now passes. Eventually winding left and away from the creek just a bit, the trail begins a short descent uphill until it reaches a ridge where Turkey Creek again comes into view, but from a higher vantage point. The towering trees rising up from the creek bottom are as amazing as the creek and bluffs themselves, and again the beauty of this little forest can be appreciated.

At the top of this ridge, the trail intersects with the roadbed that comes up from the last intersection. It crosses the trail and continues up, out into the field and back to the trailhead. Stay straight on the trail, crossing the double-track path and continue on into the woods. With fairly deep hollows on the left, the walk through this section is absent of the creek but nevertheless, beautiful in typical Ozark topography. Fall colors mixed within the trees are fabulous through this area, should you be fortunate enough to visit this place in October. Enjoy the homestretch through the woods here as soon the trail exits from the woods, opening up into a fielded area that leads back to the parking area.

Hiking Tip — Ridgerest Pads

A ridgerest pad can not only be used as a lightweight sleeping bag pad, but can also serve as an emergency item if necessary. Rolled and combined with some duct tape, the ridgerest can be used to immobilize a broken leg or arm.

51. Three Creeks State Forest

LOCATION: Three Creeks State Forest is located south of Columbia off CR AB. AB is located off HWY 63, 10 miles south from Columbia or 5.5 miles north of the little town of Ashland. At the junction of CR AB and HWY 63 is the Deer Park Store located on the HWY 63's east side. Take AB west, and you are actually on Deer Park Road. Travel 1.7 miles down Deer Park road to a fork and sign indicating Three Creeks to your left. Turn left and the parking area is one-half mile down.

LENGTH: The trails here are in network form and therefore hiking length varies depending on route. This route is the longer of the two described in this book and runs about 7 miles in length.

COMMENTS: Three Creeks, indicated by its name, is home to the three running creeks of Turkey, Bass and Bonne Femme. As if an area wasn't beautiful enough with presence of these three outstanding streams winding through a canyon like forest valley, Three Creeks State Forest also boasts of a tremendous collection of caves, rock formations, and towering blufflines. Combine all of these features together, add a stunning mixture of cedars and hardwoods, place them in a remote wilderness like setting and you have an absolutely fantastic spot for outdoor play. Three Creeks is definitely ideal for outdoor escapes, not just for hikers, but also for equestrians and mountain bikers. Don't panic with thoughts of trail sharing though, as the area is not heavily used to begin with, and some sections prohibit horses and bikes, reserving space for hiking only. The shorter section of trail is also recommended, however, if an overnight is desired, or simply a longer hike, try this outer loop, leaving plenty of time to explore and play within the heart of the hidden, enchanted-like forest of Three Creeks.

Definitely take a topographic map along, and compass as well, as trails are unmarked and fork in several varying directions along the way. In addition, the area houses many caves, sinkholes and other hidden treasures that are off the trail and require some map reading skills and adventurous instinct to find. The USGS topo is the Ashland quadrangle, and can be purchased at most area outdoor stores or through the Missouri Department of Conservation. Camping is allowed along the trail, although PLEASE use all available "no trace" backpacking skills as the trail and surrounding area is so pristine that not even a fire ring is visible. Take care to keep this forest looking "wildernessy"! Caution should also be noted here, concerning the potential water level that these three creeks can hold. During any wet month expect wet crossings, and during high water,

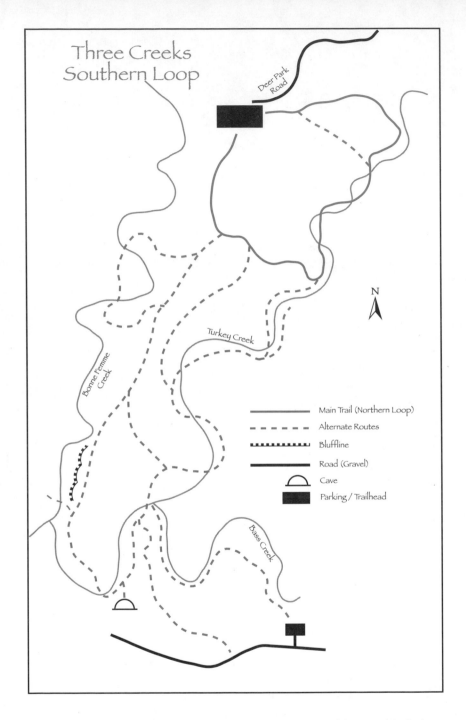

Three Creeks
Southern Loop

Deer Park Road

N

Turkey Creek

Bonne Femme Creek

Bass Creek

———————	Main Trail (Northern Loop)
– – – – –	Alternate Routes
▪▪▪▪▪▪▪▪	Bluffline
▬▬▬▬▬	Road (Gravel)
⌂	Cave
■	Parking / Trailhead

don't expect to complete this trail, as some crossings could most likely become dangerous and/or impassable.

TOPOGRAPHICAL MAPS: Millersburg SW

The Southern Loop Trail begins at the same place as the shorter Northern Loop, which is at the end of the parking lot past the gate that keeps motorized vehicles out. The two trails share a beginning of a nice flat double track created by the presence of an old roadbed. Follow this across a meadow to the first trail junction and stay left. Shortly after this, upon entering the woods, the trail forks, and again you will want to proceed left. As it curves around to head more south, you immediately realize that the trail is following along the top of a ridge. During fall and winter, when leaves aren't as thick, views of Turkey Creek lie below and to the left, while a shallow hollow dips down to the right. Slowly the trail eases down off this ridge, and as it does, intersects once more. It is at this intersection that the two trails divide.

The shorter route (Northern Loop) proceeds left, while the longer Southern Loop, described here, takes off to the right. Take a right and follow the trail as it moves alongside Turkey Creek, a clear water, flat, rockbottom stream carving its way through the valley floor just below you. At this point the trail is borrowing the top of a small bluff that runs the bank of the creek to which it slowly moves down off of proceeding less than half a mile to the first crossing. A trail intersection waits on the other side. You have already hiked about 1.5 miles so far, and you will want to proceed right. The stretch here is flat, with Turkey Creek on the right, following the path given by its respective bluffline. It's not long before the trail crosses Turkey Creek again, swapping the scenic waterway and bluffs for the trail's other side. This area is a definite BTV as the immensity of the protruding bluffline across the creek towers over and out from the hillside, providing a canyon like atmosphere and mountain like serenity. Continue down this stretch keeping an eye on the rock and cave formations hidden within this bluffline. Not much further down this fabulous stretch lies another creek crossing—this one a little faint and not quite so easy to find. Head diagonally across and down stream just a bit, bushwhacking through some overgrowth. The other side remains flat and continues with the creek.

At about 3 miles in the trail crosses yet another time moving along the other side to a roadbed intersection that leads up and to the right. Stay left and immediately the trail junctions with the joining of Bass and Turkey Creeks. This is one of the areas that appears to hold big water potential during river flood stage as the merged crossing is wide. If you look across and to the left up towards Bass Creek, you will notice a bluffline along with a trail beginning at the base of that bluff and following alongside it. This trail leads back to a cave located in the bluffline along Bass Creek. If time permits, this is some fun exploration. The main trail however, connects directly across the Turkey Creek side and immediately comes to another fork. Right continues the southern loop route, while left leads uphill, across a field and through the woods to a gravel road representing the south entrance. It's a pleasant hike, but a bit out of the way, so stick with the loop and continuing right. Right meanders around, remaining flat and crossing a few tributaries flowing into Turkey Creek. The next intersection, at approximately 4.2 miles, is actually a merging with a short side trail that leads to a huge cave opening setting just off the main trail. The shear size of this massive cave opening makes it a BTV, and an excellent place for an exploration stop. Continuing down the trail towards the right, the trail crosses over a few more tributaries and eventually across Turkey Creek one last time. Across the creek, the trail continues down a flat river bottom stretch lined with trees, eventually opening up into a large meadow which is the site and area of an old homestead. Midway through this field the trail divides again. Left veers off towards, and across Bonne Femme Creek, whereas right is the actual correct route for the trail's continuation. Follow it uphill to the ridge and as it levels off watch for an opening through the trees that yields a splendid over-looking BTV of the Bonne Femme Creek valley below. Some small paths lead-ing off to the left lead to the edge of the bluff where the panoramic view comes into full bloom. Through the trees, this view continues with the trail until at the top, a prairie area replaces the wooded timber of the past half mile. Another half mile and the trail meets the intersection of a shortcut trail coming up from the creek below. Stay straight heading across the field and passing by yet another fork on your left a bit farther down. The loop is almost complete as the next trail intersection marks the very first one encountered when begin-ning the trail. Stay left here, and the parking lot marking your return from an awesome day in the woods is not far off.

Hiking Tip — Weight Reducing Ideas

1. Take fewer clothes! You're backpacking, not making a fashion statement! Leave cotton and wool at home. Pack fleece (fleece doubles nicely for a pillow as well!), nylon and polyester clothing. Always pack in an extra pair of socks, but one of everything else is usually sufficient!

2. Take the smaller headlamps that work off double AA batteries rather than the larger, heavier versions that have bulky battery packs or utilize C and D sized batteries.

3. Drink lots of water when stopped and carry less! It's easier to carry in your belly, than on your back. Water filters can allow you to carry less water as well. Just filter out a drink at each stream crossing, rather than packing in extra water bottles.

4. Resist gadgets! This is tough when you're always trying to "one-up" your backpacking buddies on the newest latest and greatest, but gadgets can be heavy, and remember that the best policy is KISS—Keep it Small and Simple!

5. Carry a windscreen! In cold-weather especially, this lightweight addition will save you on having to carry extra fuel—especially on MSR stoves!

52. Chubb Trail

LOCATION: The Chubb Trail runs from Lone Elk Park to West Tyson, and thus has 2 different access points. Lone Elk is located off the North Outer Road of 1-44 in west St. Louis County. Hop on the North Outer Road at 141 and 1-44 going west and it will take you straight to the park entrance. For the Chubb Trail trailhead, park just outside the park's entrance, and the trailhead is on your right. West Tyson is also accessible from 1-44 and the Lewis Road exit. At the top of Lewis Road exit ramp turn right, proceed about 100 yards and the West Tyson park entrance is on your right.

LENGTH: The Chubb Trail can be anywhere from 7 to 9 miles long depending on which loop options are taken.

COMMENTS: This trail is unique in that it connects three of St. Louis County's park and reservation areas. Starting from the Chubb Shelter in West Tyson County Park, the trail covers a pleasant river valley bottomlands alongside the Mcramcc River, up through a gorgeous scenic section in Castlewood State Park, and settles into the homestretch through the area's lesser known but beautiful, Lone Elk Park. The combination of all three areas creates a perfect balance of varied terrain and scenery, an almost ideal length for a good day's hike and perfect sites on either end for picnicking, relaxing or wildlife watching.

Open to bikers as well as those wishing to hike, this trail is fairly popular, which may be its only drawback. The openness and length provide plenty of space for sharing however, and with the all there is to enjoy, wildlife included, you are guaranteed to delight in your day. Two different loops are encompassed within the trail, both of which allow for minor length adjustments to this hike, and alternate route options should you hike it twice or double back.

TOPOGRAPHICAL MAPS: Manchester

Most people hike this trail starting at the Chubb Shelter in West Tyson, but you can do it backwards, beginning your journey from the Lone Elk side. Either route direction is fine. Keep in mind that each of the trail's two end points have the more rocky, rugged terrain (the West Tyson side is probably the roughest terrain), with the mid-section of river bottoms being flat, easy and sometimes muddy during wetter months. From Lone Elk to the first trail loop junction it is only about. 5 miles. The right fork takes you under the railroad tracks via a small tunnel and alongside the Meramec River through a half-wooded, half-open, grassy bottomlands. This route is a almost a mile longer but provides you with some beautiful grassland and river scenes, particularly in the spring when

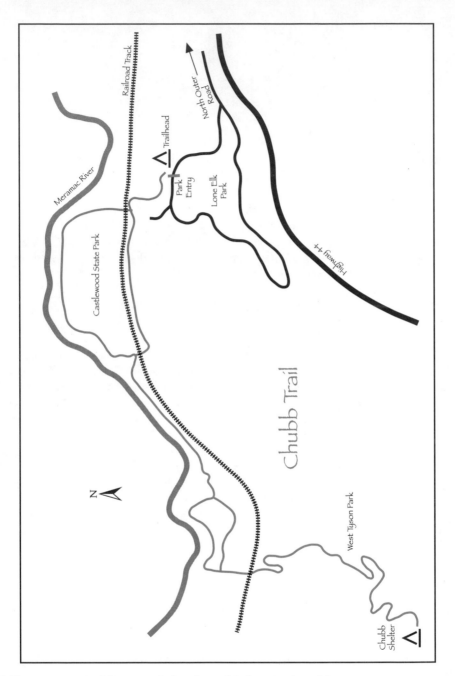

wildflowers are in bloom and the shore birds are viewable.

The fork in the trail at the end of your loop lies pretty close to the 3 mile mark and you will need to proceed right to continue the trail along the river. Appreciate your level ground for just a bit longer, because the climbing portion of your hike lies ahead. As you begin to ascend, the second loop option emerges, dividing low and high water options. As to be expected, the low water route proves to be a bit more gentle, but the high water option rewards your climbing efforts with some beautiful views of the Meramec River Valley. As the two route options join on the opposite side and remerge into the main trail, the rocky and more challenging terrain follows you upward, entering into West Tyson County Park. If you find the trail to be a bit rough for you, stop, take a look at some of the rock ledges you've been stepping up onto as you walk, and consider the increase in difficulty level should you be a mountain biker! In either case, West Tyson and the Chubb Shelter lie in wait not too far ahead. When finished you will have completed almost 9 miles.

Camp Recipe — Camp Cookies

These Biscotti Cookies are excellent for backpacking. Make them at home and take them with you. They are light-weight, stay fresh easily and are great to dip in hot chocolate or coffee for breakfast or desert!

> 4 oz. salted butter
> ¾ c. sugar
> 3 eggs
> 2 T brandy
> 1T grated lemon rind
> 1 ½ c. all-purpose flour
> ¾ c. self-rising flour
> ½ t. salt
> 4 oz slivered almonds
> 1 T aniseed
> * Optional ingredients: choc. chips, butterscotch chips,
>   dried cranberries, raisins Etc.

1. Cream butter and sugar. Add eggs one at a time, beating well.
    Add brandy and lemon-rind. Sift together all dry ingredients and
    add to butter mixture. Stir in almonds, aniseed and any other
    optional ingredients.
2. Refrigerate dough for 1 hour.
3. Halve the dough and shape into two "logs" on a cookie sheet. Bake at
    300 degrees for 20 minutes.
4. Remove, cool and cut logs into slices, separating and arranging slices
    on cookie sheet. Bake another 25 minutes or until dry and crisp.
5. Let cool, and pack 'em up for the trail!

53. Cuivre River Trail

Cuivre River State Park

LOCATION: The Cuivre River Trail is located in Cuivre River State Park just east of Troy, Missouri. From St. Louis, take I-70 west to Wentzville and HWY 61 north. Travel 61 north for 15 miles to the Troy exit and take a right on HWY 47. Follow HWY 47 for 3 miles, taking a left onto 147. Cuivre River is 2 miles down 147.

LENGTH: Cuivre River Trail is an 8 mile loop but can be shortened or lengthened via connector links between other park trails.

COMMENTS: Hidden within, and representative of northeastern Missouri's Lincoln Hills, Cuivre River State Park contains a diversity of rugged terrain and beautiful landscape that is both striking and unique for this area of the state. Resembling a bit more of the southern Ozarks section of Missouri, the Cuivre River Trail provides hikers with a sweeping view of the gently rolling northeastern farmland from amidst the top of a rugged 200 foot bluffline of Mississippi Limestone. The towering rockwall on which the trail resides formulates the bank and border for the river below that also claims this park's name: Cuivre River. Known more commonly as Frenchman's Bluff, this stretch of rock wall accounts for at least one-third of the Cuivre River Trail's path, creating an ongoing BTV for much of the first 3 miles. Beyond that, the trail graduates into a pleasant stroll through a more typical hardwoods setting, dipping down to run along the fabulous Big Sugar Creek. Fairly rugged but not overwhelming, this trail can be a very enjoyable day hike or can also be backpacked, particularly if linked with the neighboring Big Sugar Trail, for a longer length. The Cuivre Trail is marked all in red, with Big Sugar and Frenchman's Bluff, 2 trails adjoining to Cuivre River at points, marked in blue. Connector trails linking short-cuts or alternate routes are identified with white markers.

    Cuivre River State Park as a whole contains more amenities and unique features than just about any other Missouri park. With over 6,200 acres of wilderness like terrain, Cuivre River houses three state wild areas, an 18 acre lake, 30 miles of trails and 3 full fledged group camps. Competitive runs, scouting and orienteering championships have all been a regular part of Cuivre River, along with routine visits from hikers, backpackers and equestrians. Upon completion of the trademarked Cuivre River Trail, spend some time exploring this wonderfully remote tract of wooded acreage, discovering all it's little extras.

TOPOGRAPHICAL MAPS: Okete

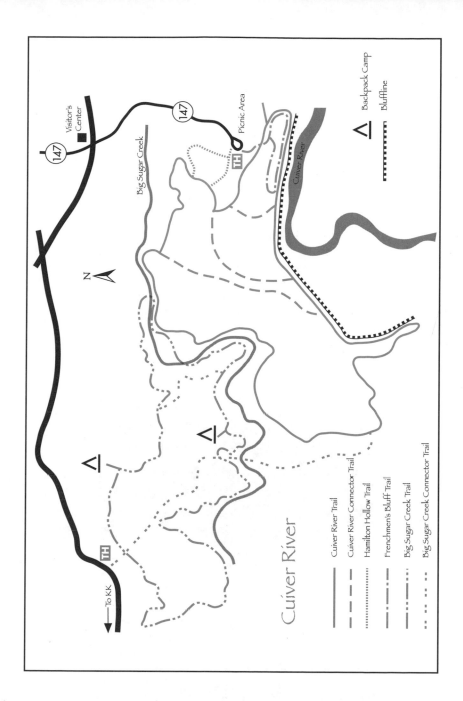

The Cuivre River Trail, sharing the same initial path for Frenchman's Bluff, starts at the back of the picnic area located at the end of 147, on the park's southwest side. Upon beginning, moving down slightly into the woods, the trail "T"s" off providing directional options either way. Take a left, which moves to another trail intersection where you will want to turn right. The third fork requires that you stay left, merging officially with the blue Frenchman's Trail and crossing a gravel road. Upon crossing the gravel road, the trail wastes no time climbing up to Frenchman's Bluff beginning the extended BTV and outstanding views afforded by the famed bluffline. The contrast of flat alluvial farmland below, against the stately, immense wall of limestone upon which the trail lies, is amazing!

For the next half mile or so the trail follows along the edge of this bluff with an intimidating 200 foot drop off into Cuivre River on the left, and a gravel road on the right. If you wish to hike just the Frenchman's Bluff Trail (a loop that totals just 2 miles), look for the cleared area on the roadside that appears to pass for a small parking area. Across this cleared type area is the trail leading back to the picnic area, thus completing Frenchman's Bluff.

To continue the Cuivre River Trail stay along the bluffline which will lead to the white connector trail option leading right. Stay to the left unless the shortcut route is desired. At this point, although still tied to the bluffline, the trail backs off the edge a bit and moves through a rocky ravine area packed with cedars. This is another BTV area in itself. As the second connector trail intersection is passed, the trail's setting actually intensifies in beauty as use from this point on is a bit less. Continue hiking along this "scenic trail highway" until, at about 2.5 miles, the trail hooks rather sharply to the right heading east

The view from the Cuivre River Trail

to northeast. Across the way, but in the distance, an active lime quarry can be heard, but not for long as the trail carves a nice straight and flat path deeper into the woodland area.

A gravel road crossing marks entrance into the Big Sugar Creek Wild Area—a beautiful pristine timber plot with lots of cedars, rolling hills and nice views. Moving down to the creek and bottomlands, notice a sinkhole or two along the trail. Representative of karst topography, these sinkholes are scattered throughout places in Cuivre River. A small tributary stream will be crossed followed by the larger and possibly wet crossing of Big Sugar Creek. Up a rocky slope immediately upon crossing, the trail continues on toward the ridge, moving up and over a small waterfall ledge that feeds into Big Sugar. The trek up is an increasing BTV, opening up gorgeous views to the left. Up on top, the trail empties onto what appears to be an old abandon house. Passing by, continue to the left along the ridge, enjoying the BTV for another fourth of a mile.

The ridgetop view ends as the trail curves right focusing on a downward scale to the Big Sugar Creek bottomland area once again. At the bottom, the trail "T's", merging with the blue Big Sugar Creek Trail. A left here will lengthen the hike, and if an overnight is in your hiking agenda, a couple backpack camps reside along this trail (see map). To stay with the Cuivre River Trail, take a right, keeping in mind that for a short jaunt here the trail will be marked blue and red. A bit further down the blue veers off to the left, so stay straight, or right and continue alongside the creek. Tall pines and rock shelves at certain points along this stretch accent this pretty little bottomland area, and as the trail moves away from Big Sugar, a white connector trail is met. Stay left, crossing a smaller creek tributary and you eventually come to a neat little circular mini rock wall area.

Passing this, the trail continues up another rocky stretch and flattens out just in time to meet up with the green trail connector on the left. This green connection left will take you back to the picnic area as well, and without much added length, so it is an option. Known as the Hamilton Hollow Trail, it moves through an area containing some of Cuivre Rivers oldest and most prized large trees. The Cuivre Trail stays straight and as it passes two more connectors on the right, it too moves through an area with some towering and large sized trees. At this point a creek is residing along the trail's right side and will continue to follow until the trail intersection marking your trailhead return appears on the left. Take the left option and it will return to the parking area. Now you can explore the rest of the park!

Hiking Tip — Tangy Water

If you're using iodine tablets to treat water, then you're familiar with the stale after-taste that those little tablets seem to create. A water filter leaves no such taste, and is the ideal choice for water purification. However, if iodine tablets are your method, then bring some Kool-Aid mix, Crystal Light, or Gatorade and pour a small amount of the granulated powder into the water to take the edge off that iodine flavor.

54. Graham Cave

LOCATION: Graham Cave is located 2 miles west of Danville, in Montgomery County. From Danville, travel 2 miles down I-70 to HWY TT.

LENGTH: The park offers 3 main trails; the Scenic Trail and Indian Glade Trail, which form a one mile figure-eight loop around Graham Cave, and the Loutre River Trail, a 1 ½ mile trail leading down to the river. Small connector trails links these three together, creating about a 3 mile network.

COMMENTS: The uniqueness of this historic landmark cave is largely due to its sandstone, rather than limestone make-up. The unusual construction of Graham Cave occurred from the dissolving of a dolomite rock which was stratified underneath a bed of sandstone. As the dolomite slowly dissipated, an empty cavity remained beneath the giant umbrella of sandstone, thus forming Graham Cave. 120 feet wide and 16 feet high, this rare structure is noteworthy enough in and of itself, yet it possesses a bit of history as well. Hidden within the depths of its earthen floor, lies thousands of years artifacts that researches and archeologists have discovered and used to piece together generations of this land's past.

The 357 acre park is small, but holds a beautiful collection of glades, savannahs, ledges and bluffs that assist in formulating gorgeous displays of springtime waterfalls. Short in length, yet packed with plenty to see, the trails here are perfect for family hiking or a relaxing day outdoors. All three trails interconnect with one another at points, but are all well marked and easy to follow. Picnic areas and campgrounds are available as well, making this an ideal daytime escape or overnight stay.

TOPOGRAPHICAL MAPS: Montgomery City

The trail leading to the park's main attraction, Graham Cave, leaves from the Scenic Trail trailhead at the interpretive shelter. There are two options to get to the cave from here, a 600 foot option as well as a thousand foot route. Since both are short, go for the longer route, as it leads uphill enough to offer some nice surrounding views. From the shelter, this longer option heads east and loops around to Graham Cave. Watch for the scenic bonus just before the cave, as the trail passes by a surprise BTV waterfall display created by one of the park's many little ledge outcroppings.

Stopping at the cave to catch readings on its history and to view the ongoing archeological research occurring is a must. Once you've thoroughly absorbed this highlight, the Indian Glade Trail leads to the left initiating another

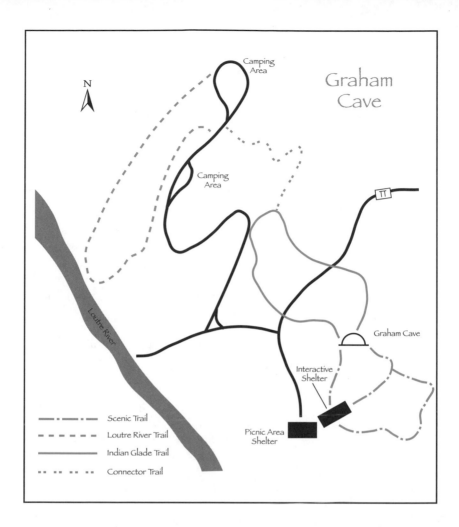

loop that returns to the cave after passing by the picnic area, or joins in with the connector trail. You can also take the Scenic Trail left from the cave to immediately return to the interpretive shelter. The connector trail, splitting at the picnic area, holds a couple of easy inclines and holds a few more waterfall sightings. This trail will exit around the park's camping area, where across the road lies the trailhead for the Loutre River Trail.

Loutre River Trail is an easy mile and half loop that resides largely along an old logging road. The ease of hike however, does not lessen its offering as many bluffs and waterfalls are located along its route and are worth viewing. The Loutre River follows the western flank of this short loop for a small bit, and it is here that you want to be careful to veer left off the roadbed, as the trail leads into the hardwood forest and back towards the camp area.

55. Green Rock Trail

LOCATION: Green Rock Trail begins at the trailhead located off Fox Creek Road, 1.3 miles west of the Allenton, I-44 Exit. The concluding trailhead lies in Rockwoods Reservation at the Visitor's Center, located off Highway 109, 4 miles from the Eureka I-44 exit.

LENGTH: The trail is non-circular, and 10 miles in length, although a short-cut through Greensfelder could shorten the trail down to 8.5 miles.

COMMENTS: This trail passes through two of St. Louis's most beautiful wildlife areas, Greensfelder State Park and Rockwoods Reservation. Both maintain a natural, preserved environment, richly decorated with large standing oak, and flowering dogwood that create an ideal setting for the numerous deer and turkey common to the area. In spring, this trail boasts of a generous collection of gorgeous dogwoods lining the woodland trail, as well as rock bottom creek beds forming water displays that accent the area's beauty. Fall reveals the gorgeous colors displayed in the trees as they change, and winter brings leaf-off periods, opening up the views and vistas visible from the ridge. In places, the trail holds some steady, steep climbs, but overall hiking is only moderately difficult with slightly rocky, rough terrain. Water during dry season should be packed in, as many of the creeks disappear during the hot summer months. With wetter weather, creeks will be running, and water availability should not be a problem.

TOPOGRAPHICAL MAPS: Eureka

From the Fox Creek Trailhead, the trail starts across the road and slowly proceeds uphill in a northerly direction. Alongside and to the right, runs a seasonal creek that cascades slightly down the flat lying bedrocks adding to the attraction of this thickly vegetated forest. The trail will continue proceeding north and uphill for ¾ of a mile before topping out along the ridge temporarily, and turning west to follow the contour of the hillside. In maintaining position along the ridge, the trail curves back around to the east and then repositions course northeast until coming to the first junction at 1.5 miles. Blazes marking the trail direct you straight ahead and back into the woods, still leading northeast for another mile, and exiting onto a widened gravel path in Greensfelder Park, to which you turn left. It is at this point, as you hike down the gravel path, that the option to shorten the trail approaches. About ¼ of a mile down, the trail will hold a double blazed tree on your right, with an accompanying side trail leading off the path and to your right, which is the offi-

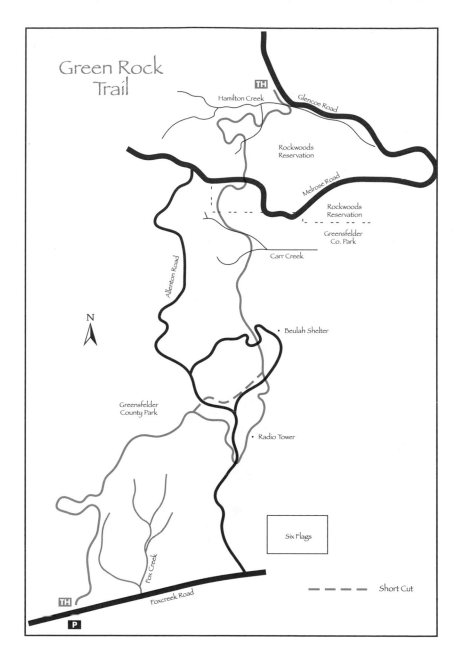

Green Rock Trail

TH — Hamilton Creek — Glencoe Road

Rockwoods Reservation

Melrose Road

Rockwoods Reservation

Greensfelder Co. Park

Carr Creek

Allenton Road

N

• Beulah Shelter

Greensfelder County Park

• Radio Tower

Six Flags

TH — Foxcreek Road

Fox Creek

P

– – – – – Short Cut

cial Green-Rock Trail. If taken, this trail leads south and then east, crossing Allenton Road on the southern outskirts of Greensfelder, and turning back north to lead past the radio tower and join back up with a more central part of the park. If you continue straight down the gravel path rather than turning right, the trail cuts directly across Allenton Road to Deer Run Trail, which, if taken right, meets back up with the official Green Rock trail just past the restrooms. This short cut eliminates the jog further south, thus reducing the trail's overall length by approximately 1.5 miles.

In either case, Green Rock Trail turns downhill from the flat Deer Run path just past the restrooms, and proceeds north down a steep and often times, muddy, equestrian use trail. At the base of this slide, turn right, and follow the trail as it cuts through the base of the hollow in the form of a widened cart path used by equestrians as evidenced by the cross-country fences placed periodically along the path's edge. At 4.0 the trail crosses a black-top road, continuing along the lower-lying, flat equestrian trail. As the trail narrows from its widened path, you enter back into the dense forest, thick with vegetation. You will pass a sign on your right designating a 2 mile trail (named the Ozark Trail, not to be confused with the OT trail), that leads up to one of the park's higher elevation areas bearing a scenic view of the surrounding area. To continue Green Rock, stay straight, and at the next fork, bear left, following the blazes to aid you in direction. This section, just after the fork, gives appropriateness to the "rock" part of Green Rock Trail, as the trail becomes almost glade like and the terrain rougher due to large rocks that make up the path. It is about ¼ of a mile past this fork that the trail crosses Carr Creek, and the rocky trail bed leads steeply uphill, climbing 200 feet in elevation to the top where it flattens out and enters into Rockwoods Reservation. The view up here would be fabulous during periods of leaf-off, creating a BTV. After the demanding and steep climb, the trail flattens out into a welcomed restful walk on top of the ridge that subtly leads up and across Melrose Road at 6.5.

After crossing Melrose, the trail loses all the elevation gained on the previous climb as it drops down into the hollow and across Hamilton Creek. Moving up on the opposite side, the trail climbs again, and as it flattens back out again, forks to the left. Another small creek crossing and one more short but steep, rocky climb, the trail comes alongside a ridge at 7.5, revealing vistas to your left during fall and winter leaf-off periods. Easing into a more leisurely hike, the trail maintains course on top of the ridge for a bit, where surrounding scenery is thick with dogwoods and holds many oak and ash trees towering in stature and huge in diameter. Gradually the trail works its way down into the hollow and across a small creek bottom, where it moves slightly up what was probably an old logging road at one time, although sufficient regrowth is evident now. You will cross Hamilton Creek one final time over a wooden footbridge, and the trail turns to the northwest exiting out into the field just before the Rockwoods Reservation Visitor's Center.

Hiking Tip — Wet Wood

When out on the trail during a cool fall or winter night, a nice warm fire can be excellent for atmosphere, relaxation and warmth. But what do you do if everything around you is wet? Surprisingly, firepaste gels have proved reliable in situations such as this. Build a teepee of small twigs and apply the firepaste to these. Place any dry paper you have in the middle and light. Slowly build around the teepee with larger wood and soon your wet wood will be burning.

56. Lewis and Clark Trail

Weldon Springs Conservation Area

LOCATION: Weldon Springs Conservation Area is located in St. Charles County off HWY 94 and HWY D. From the junction of I-40 and 94 near the town of Weldon Springs, go west down 94 and the parking lot for the Lewis and Clark Trail is on your left, just past Francis Howell High School.

LENGTH: Lewis and Clark are actually 2 separate trails. Lewis Trail is 8.2 miles and Clark is 5.3.

COMMENTS: The 7,356 acres of Weldon Springs contains a variety of natural features, wildlife and recreation activities. In addition to the two trails of Lewis and Clark, the conservation area also has an 8 mile Lost Valley Trail, and 5.3 miles of the Katy Trail to its credit. Flowing along the Weldon Spring's southern border, is the Missouri River, hemming in the area with its towering and immense limestone bluffs. No camping is allowed, due to the title of "conservation area", but between three hiking trails, the biking opportunities along The Katy Trail, and fishing in the Missouri, Weldon Springs provides plenty of outdoor entertainment for the day.

Hiking through the area is gorgeous, and although the trails aren't overly challenging in ascents and descents, terrain can be rugged and rocky in spots. The serenity and solitude is wonderful for this small area though, and the trails can be defined as most enjoyable. Lewis and Clark trails are both hiking trails only, while the equally scenic Lost Valley Trail is open to both hikers and bicyclists. The Katy Trail is of course open to hiking and walking as well as biking too. In addition to the marked and identified trails, there are some miscellaneous footpaths that intermingle throughout the conservation area allowing for some exploration and impromptu hiking if desired.

TOPOGRAPHICAL MAPS: Weldon Springs

Probably the best place to begin your hike on either of these two trails is at the parking lot off HWY 94 about 2 miles west past the junction of 94 and HWY D. Both trailheads are located here, and for a bit Lewis and Clark are one trail as they overlap for much of the western section. Hiking in a counter-clockwise direction, the trail begins in a bit of a southerly direction heading down towards the Katy Trail and Missouri River. You will love the forested scenery and rugged nature of this area. The trail makes a rather sharp change in direction to head more east while simultaneously taking up residence alongside the Katy Trail. Across the famed biking path lies the Missouri River with the limestone bluffs now in full view. Zig-zagging a little but still heading east for the

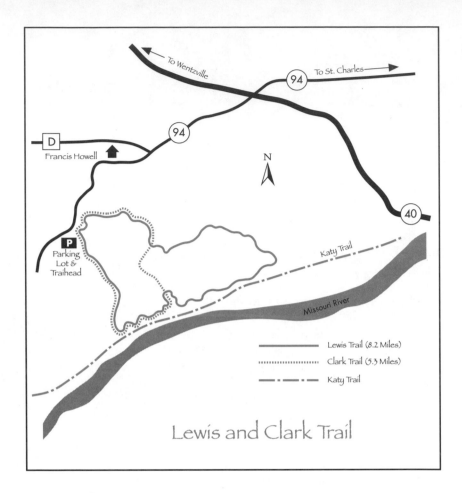

Lewis and Clark Trail

Lewis Trail (8.2 Miles)

Clark Trail (5.3 Miles)

Katy Trail

next mile, Lewis and Clark both start to curve around north again before splitting at about the 2.5 mile mark. The Clark Trail continues north, beginning to loop back, while the Lewis Trail proceeds to regain course east alongside the river again for another mile and three quarters or so. It won't start its rebound to loop back around until almost reaching the conservation area's eastern border, but a connector footpath found less than a mile from where Lewis and Clark split can be found leading north and across to Lewis's other side if a shorter route is desired. Otherwise, the two trails don't merge again until the last mile and a half of the Lewis Trail.

Hiking Tip — Waterproof Matches

To have a more reliable striking force on rainy weekend hikes, coat the length of wooden matches with nail polish to increase their waterproofness.

57. Lone Spring Trail

Cuivre River State Park

LOCATION: The Lone Spring Trail is located in Cuivre River State Park just east of Troy, Missouri. From St. Louis, take I-70 west to Wentzville and HWY 61 north. Travel 61 north 15 miles to the Troy exit, and take a right on HWY 47. Follow HWY 47 for 3 miles, taking a left onto 147. Cuivre River is 2 miles down 147.

LENGTH: Lone Spring consists of two 3 mile loops allowing for either a 3, or 6 mile hike.

COMMENTS: Lone Spring Trail is one of the more remote and least used trails in the already remote and beautiful Cuivre River State Park. Located on the park's extreme north end and extending throughout the North Woods Wild Area, Lone Spring possesses a rugged wilderness setting that is unique for trails located within a state park. The wild area through which this trail runs is pristine and untouched, claiming a beautiful stretch of Big Sugar Creek, as well as the park's largest natural spring, Lone Spring. Tall standing white oak, sturdy in stature through age, are also scattered among the wooded acreage and interwoven along parts of the trail.

Split into two 3 mile loops, Lone Spring is easily hiked in a short afternoon, but its serenity creates potential as a pleasant overnight trail as well. A scenic backpack camp is located along the northern loop end, situated upon the prong of a slightly rolling ridge. It is a nice site, but far from water, so be sure to pack in plenty, or be prepared to carry up from Big Sugar if the creek is running. Although this is a very lovely trail, Lone Spring represents only a small sample of Cuivre River's immense diversity and nature oriented offerings, so after hiking Lone Spring plan to spend time exploring more of the park's trails and highlights.

TOPOGRAPHICAL MAPS: Okete

A couple different trailheads mark optional starting points for this trail, but for now, use the parking area and starting point at the junction of the north end of the park road and HWY KK. From here the south, north or both loops of Lone Spring can be hiked. Description here will be on the north loop, although addition of the south section is not difficult at all. Begin across KK, just diagonally left from the parking area. There is a sign here identifying the north end trail loop length of 3.1 miles. Straight north through the woods for a short distance, the trail comes to a "T" that begins the loop. Take a left, following through the wooded area with a shallow hollow on the left. Leading to another trailhead

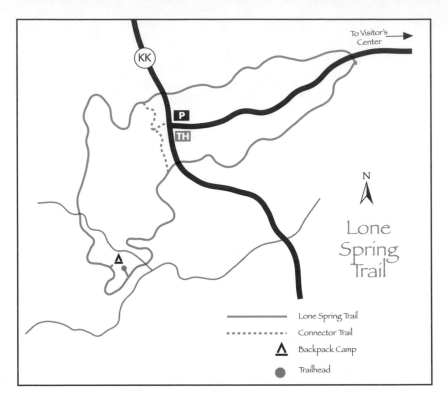

just off KK, the trail continues right for the north loop or left for the south. Take a right, hiking level for about a half mile before dipping down towards Big Sugar Creek. The trail will wind through the bottomlands briefly before crossing Big Sugar. Rather wide, this crossing could be a wet one if spring rains are at work! Shortly after crossing Big Sugar, a small footpath off the left side of the main trail leads to the trail's namesake, Lone Spring. Flowing from out of a rock-like ledge built within the hillside, this spring is beautiful when running and empties into Big Sugar Creek.

The trail begins to exhibit its best from this point on. Leading slowly and gently uphill, it narrows into some ridgeside hiking, opening up some nice views at points, of the river valley below. Once on top, another optional path to the right appears. This is the side trail turn-off that leads to the designated backpack camp, located 50 yards back or so. Moving past this turn-off, the main trail starts its way back down, crossing a small tributary at the bottom, and meeting up with an awesome looking triple-trunk tree just on the right. The bottomlands here are pleasant, with some mini bluffs along portions of Big Sugar. You will encounter another wide creek crossing close to one of these small bluffs, moving back up to the ridge afterwards. Along this ridge that skirts and contours the rolling wooded acreage, views of the hollow and creekbed below follow the trail, eventually meeting upon the crossing of a small tributary. One more short climb and the trail merges with a fork that if taken left crosses KK to continue the south loop. Stay right for the north loop, and wind with the trail to the next intersection where a left will return back to the original trailhead!

58. Rockwoods Reservation

LOCATION: Rockwoods is located on the west side of Highway 109 approximately 4 miles north of the I-44, Eureka Exit.

LENGTH: Rockwoods offers 5 trails:
  Lime Kiln Loop Trail—3.25 miles
  Rock Quarry Trail—2.25 miles
  Turkey Ridge—2 miles
  Trail Among the Trees—1.5 miles
  Wildlife Habitat Trail—300 yards

COMMENTS: Rockwoods Reservation is a wildlife refuge and state forest established in 1938 through endowments from a group of St. Louis businessmen, and is now managed by Mo. Dept. of Conservation as an area for conservation education. The rugged land topography, abundant wildlife and remote serenity create a sense of wilderness somewhat surprising in relation to this reserve's St. Louis location. The trails wind through gorgeous woodland hollows, giving display of the seasonal creeks nestled within the bottomland ravines, and then ascend to the ridgetops that overlook the area with rounds of outstanding scenery. Camping, horseback riding and mountain biking are all prohibited, making Rockwoods ideal for families or anyone wishing to dayhike and enjoy this protected wilderness area. If you're a dog owner, however, taking your four legged friend with you on occasional hiking excursions, you might make a note that Rockwoods prohibits all pets, even when kept on a leash.

TOPOGRAPHICAL MAPS: Eureka

LIME KILN LOOP TRAIL
As you enter Rockwoods from Highway 109, the trailhead for Lime Kiln is the first parking area and trailhead on the right. Located here is the remnants of an old "lime kiln" formally used to fire bricks quarried from the areas abundant rock. The trail begins here, and if hiked in a counter-clockwise position starts off to the east and eventually scales the hillside, climbing for about ¾ of a mile before leveling off on top the ridge. It remains on this ridgetop, yielding glimpses of scenery in leaf-off periods, before descending down the alternate side to join the creek bottom, thus following it back to the trailhead.

ROCK QUARRY TRAIL
Rock Quarry Trail officially begins on the northwest side of the visitor's center, following alongside the road in a northwest direction for the first stretch. As it

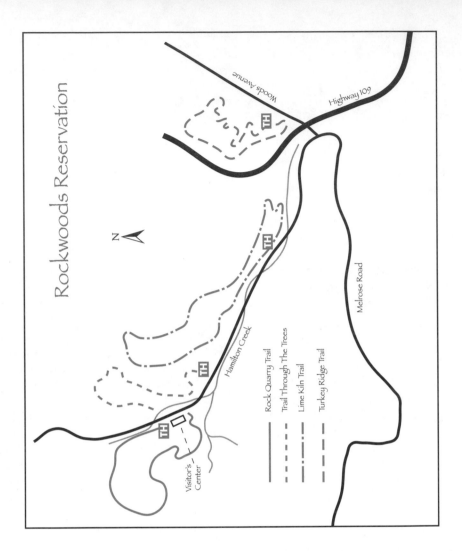

Rockwoods Reservation

Woods Avenue

Highway 109

N

Melrose Road

Hamilton Creek

Rock Quarry Trail

Trail Through The Trees

Lime Kiln Trail

Turkey Ridge Trail

Visitor's Center

veers away from the road and begins turning more directly west, it passes by sidetrails leading to Cobb Cavern on your right. Winding through hardwood forest, it follows alongside a ravine in places that has water cutting through it in spring creating some rushing cascades accenting the areas beauty. The trail ascends up to the ridge with built in stairsteps in places that cut down on erosion. The ridgetop stretch is beautiful, creating an ideal setting for the sighting of wildlife, and affording views through the trees to your right. A fork in the trail on the ridge offers a short-cut route to the left, leading down to the back of the visitor's center, while straight continues the trail with a bit more length, descending down to exit behind the center's south side.

TURKEY RIDGE TRAIL

This is currently the only trailhead that has its origin on the opposite, or east side of Highway 109, at the junction of 109 and Woods Ave. The trail starts off underneath a gorgeous stand of fairly young pines, complete with a bed of fresh smelling pine needles directly underfoot. Retaining the area's character of rocky glades and thick woodlands, this trail, when hiked in a counter clockwise direction, cuts a path through the dense vegetation and heads up a steady climb for the first half mile. During fall and winter when leaves are absent, views open up to the south from on top of the ridge. The trail switchbacks up the ridge, winds around on top, and then makes a slow descent down on the opposite side in completion of the loop.

TRAIL AMONG THE TREES

Trail Among the Trees starts out on the opposite side of the road from the visitor's center and immediately takes residence alongside a tributary to Hamilton Creek, leading into a beautiful forested hollow. This trail is unique because the majority of it is either well graded with cinders, or paved, making hiking easy and accessible, yet the terrain through which it cuts a path is rugged, isolated and untouched. The area is gorgeous, and the trail is ideal for a short hike that seemingly travels deep into woods. There is a booklet at the trailhead walking you through the trail and defining each highlight marked with a numbered post. It is easy to follow, but can contain some hefty uphill climbs in places. The trails ending point lies ³⁄₁₀ of a mile southeast of where it began, requiring one to walk back up the road to return to the starting point.

WILDLIFE HABITAT TRAIL

This little, paved, circular path serves as an interpretive trail for some of the areas trees and plant vegetation. Short in length, it is very easy to walk, and it contains a booklet obtainable at the trailhead, leading you through the various features.

Hiking Tip — Pole Position — And no I don't mean the video game!

Ever thought poles were reserved for the ski slopes only? Well, poles for the trail are becoming a hot thing. When used properly, trekking poles can improve your balance, save your knees, and increase your walking efficiency. In application of the cross-country ski method of pole usage, plant each pole in rhythm with each stride, actually pushing off a bit at the finish of each step. The pole that plants should be opposite of the leg that's moving forward, and the tip of the pole just slightly ahead of that boot. Trekking poles with adjustable heights are most ideal as they allow you to alter pole length according to the variance in terrain. Shorter poles aid in the uphill climbs, while longer lengths stabilize your descent back down. Whatever the terrain, trekking poles are an excellent tool to help ease the load of a heavy pack or smooth the journey down a challenging trail.

---

59. Washington State Park

LOCATION: Washington State Park is located on Highway 104, located off Highway 21, 15 miles west of De Soto, and 14 miles east of Potosi.

LENGTH: The park offers 3 trails:
  1,000 Steps — 1.5 miles
  Opossum Track — 3 miles
  Rockywood — 10 miles

COMMENTS: Located in the rugged hills and rocky glades of this beautiful area in Missouri, Washington State Park offers extraordinary natural features, as well as fabulous vistas overlooking the Big River. Adding to the area's scenic attraction, are Indian rock carvings located near the park's southern boundary, believed to be remnants from the inhabitants that lived in the area between 1000 and 1600 AD.

The three different trails offer variety in length for those wishing to explore the area. Due to the fact that the 1,000 Steps and Opossum Track trails each overlap with the Rockywood Trail, this guide will provide a general overview of the Rockywood Trail and how it connects with the other two.

TOPOGRAPHICAL MAPS: Tiff

ROCKYWOOD TRAIL
The trailhead for Rockywood is located behind the dining lodge and starts out in a northwesterly direction. The trail, marked with orange (sometimes red) markers, is easy to follow, although it typifies the rugged nature of Ozark terrain with footing being uneven and rocky in places. The first section of this trail leads you alongside the bluffs, opening up scenic views of the Big River winding beneath in the valley below. This beginning section is also shared by part of the Opossum Track Trail which veers off to the south, away from Rockywood, about ¾ of a mile from the trailhead. Rockywood trail continues straight past the junction with Opossum Track and heads uphill and then back down to a pleasant creek area which feeds into Big River. A short distance past this creek, on your right, is a designated campsite for backpackers, with an area just behind it recently destroyed by a small fire. The trail curves around south covering areas of hardwood forest mixed with scattered limestone glades. As the trail leads back to the east and begins to track through the lower portion of the park, it crosses the road and enters into a beautiful valley strung with unique and interesting rock formations. From this valley, the trail leads right through the Petroglyph area displaying the ancient Indian rock carvings, sketched in

dolomite rocks centuries ago. Out of the Petroglyph area, the trail crosses the pavement once again and runs parallel with the park road for ½ a mile before crossing it once more to join up with a section of the 1,000 Steps Trail. As you slowly descend from the road crossing towards the completion of the trail, there is an overlook on your right allowing view to the Big River and woodlands below. From this point to the trail's end it is less than ½ mile.

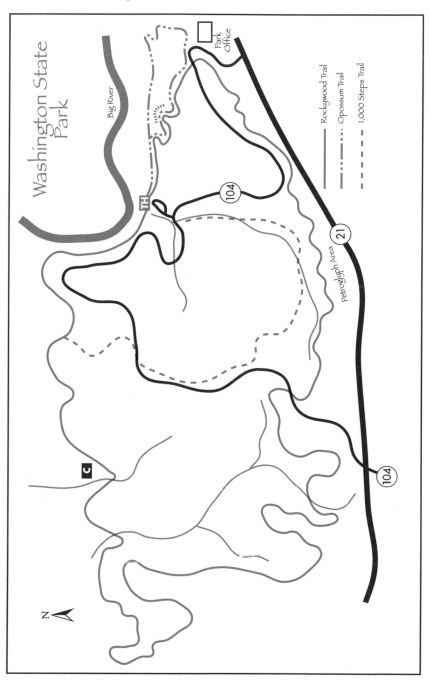

60. Weston Bend State Park

LOCATION: Weston Bend is located 1 mile south of the town of Weston on HWY 45 in Platte Co.

LENGTH: Weston Bend offers a variety of trails ranging in length from .5 to 3 miles long. The park also offers a paved 3 mile loop ideal for walking, hiking and bicycling.

COMMENTS: Just south of the quaint antebellum town of Weston, this 1,024 acre park holds history, recreation and natural beauty. With the area's rich loose soil combined with river access, Weston once thrived on the production and transportation of tobacco and hemp. Weston flourished as enterprising citizens took advantage of the fortunes to be built from the town's most valuable asset—the Missouri River. In 1858 however, this asset was lost as the Missouri suddenly changed course, leaving Weston absent of its port and growth attraction. With such preserved antebellum architecture, plenty of history, a winery and some quaint bed and breakfasts, the town of Weston itself is worth a visit and stay.

The park's historic side centers around Weston's story, preserving some of the old tobacco barn structures and creating plots of mini tobacco crops that display its growth and maturing process. From a recreational viewpoint, Weston Bend claims ownership to a beautiful setting of wilderness terrain, and ridgetop overlooks that formulate a collection of BTV's for any hiker. The discovery of multiple panorama views accessible from short trails outlined within a relatively small park will surprise most, and credits Weston with possession of a jewel state park. With five trails spread throughout the park, varying in length from .5 to 3 miles in length, this park provides ample opportunity to spend the day exploring on foot. Opting to ride, rather than walk? Bring two wheels and take advantage of the 3 mile paved bike path that loops around the east side of the park. Camping and modern facilities allow overnight accessibility as well.

TOPOGRAPHICAL MAPS: Weston

The park offers five different trails, most of which posses their own trailheads and begin from different sections in the park. Each are well marked and are identified separately by their individual color assignments. The first trail encountered upon entering the park is the 3 mile bicycle loop located on the left hand side. Continue on down from that, about ¾ of a mile and a trailhead designated by a "sink overlook" sign leads to one of the most scenic hiking sections of the park, Harpst Trail. The Harpst Trail leads first to the sink overlook via a blacktop paved path, but then veers off from the pavement onto a sod footpath that leads into the hardwoods. The overlook is spectacular. Views of the river below are easily captured up here, as well as a glimpse of the trains that once complimented the river traffic flow. The ridgetop trail and high overlook is beautiful, especially when considering its ease of access. The hike is ideal for families with kids, and even handicap accessible.

Past the overlook, the trail moves on to the left continuing along through hardwoods bringing yet more views and BTV's that capture attention and create anticipation for what might be ahead. The trail's western pass provides views overlooking the Missouri River, and slowly inclines down to parallel the mighty Missouri for a short bit. As it pulls away from the river and narrows, the trail intersects with the paved bike path. The bike path is a one lane paved trail that is designed for hikers as well. Take advantage of this, and proceed left along the paved path for a while, until reaching the sod trail intersection that takes you back to the overlook. The completed loop equals approximately 2.5 miles.

Weston Bend offers many other trails, each of which is simple to follow. Bear Creek and the Missouri River Trail are short hikes of .5 miles each. For those seeking a little greater length, the North Ridge Trail, at the park's northwest edge, is a pleasant one-way hike totaling 2 miles. Be sure to take a quick look at the old wooden tobacco barn by way of another short hike as well.

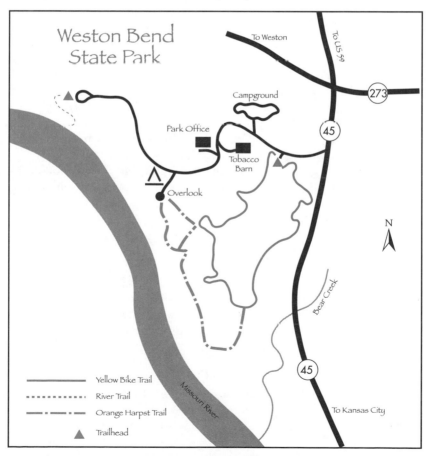

61. White Bison Trail

Lone Elk Park

LOCATION: Lone Elk Park is located in West St. Louis County off the North Outer Road of I-44. From I-270, travel west to the HWY 141 exit. Pick up the North Outer Road there heading west, and it will take you straight to the park entrance.

LENGTH: The White Bison Trail is a 4 mile loop.

COMMENTS: Lone Elk Park is probably recognized most in the outdoor crowd as one of the access points for the well known Chubb Trail, but the uniqueness and beauty of the park itself is often overlooked. Acting almost as more of a reservation area than a park, Lone Elk is home to herds of bison, wild elk and rare species of birds. The destiny that this area would house such a unique offering of wildlife began immediately when the land was territory to one single "lone elk", thus trademarking this park's name. Soon after Lone Elk became a park in 1964, children at Rockwoods School District put together a plan that eventually brought in a small herd of wild elk from Yellowstone National Park, to join the lonely bull who had founded the land. In 1973 the St. Louis Zoo got involved with the introduction of bison into the park, and shortly thereafter the Raptor Rehabilitation and Propagation Project joined in with the preservation of bird species in the area. With such a congregation of organizations and programs involved within this park, Lone Elk has a lot to offer. The mostly wooded acreage is gorgeous and the opportunity to see elk and buffalo alongside the more common Missouri wildlife species is an awesome experience.

TOPOGRAPHICAL MAPS: Manchester

The White Bison Trail begins at the visitor center and makes a loop through most of the park's center. To actually view the bison however, you will want to drive through the bison area located more towards the park's southwest section. The trail loops past picnic areas and shelters, and on the park's north side, comes along the shore of the little lake centered within Lone Elk. Hike in the spring or fall and you're almost sure to see the Canada geese, and maybe even a blue heron along the water's edge. As the trail passes by the park's entrance gate, there is a lookout tower that can be utilized to view wildlife or simply the surrounding wooded area. This is also the location of Lone Elk's other trailhead, the Chubb Trail. If you wish to explore the entire Chubb Trail, check out the details on it elsewhere in this book, however, if you want just a small sample of it, you could do a small section called Castlewood Loop. From the trailhead here to the beginning of Castlewood Loop is about .5 miles. The loop itself runs approximately 3 miles, thus making it about a 4 mile round trip hike. If you stick simply to the White Bison Trail then you will loop back to the visitor center. Leave yourself some time to pass through the center and educate yourself on some of the birds of prey and wildlife preservation information provided by the Raptor Rehabilitation and Propagation Project.

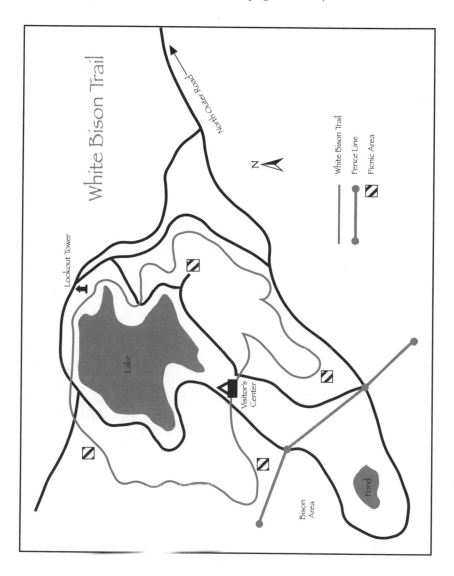

Over the Border...

If you've enjoyed the serenity and natural beauties hidden within trails of Missouri, then you will greatly appreciate the backcountry terrain that lies over the border in Arkansas. I am a mountain wilderness, "out west" fanatic, and long time fan of the state of Montana, and I once ran across a book of that great state entitled: "Montana, The Last Great Place". As much as I love Montana, I had to adjust that title in my mind a bit as I first read it, adding "Next to Arkansas". Arkansas is one of those "last great places", possessing virgin scenery, hidden geologic wonders and pristine untamed rivers all within a gorgeous wilderness setting to be enjoyed by any die-hard outdoor enthusiast.

I write about a handful of Arkansas trails in this section (not really even a handful, as so much is out there) because I continually stand amazed at the beauty of the area, double checking my whereabouts at times to be sure that I'm still in the midwest! If you get a chance to visit "The Natural State" use this guide to get you started as the trails here are a few of the more common, "must see" attractions located in Arkansas's northern section, many of them focused around the Buffalo River. (Another sight to behold!) If you like what you see and you're up for more, than I highly recommend the Arkansas hiking expert Tim Ernst and his series of guides on hiking Arkansas, the Ozark Highlands Trail and other hidden highlights held within the borders of our southern neighbor. The trails of Arkansas are his backyard, and it was one of his books that first got me interested in the area. So once you venture "over the border", find it hard to drag yourself home, and hunger for a bit more of this area's "last great place", contact Tim at 1-800-838-4453 and he will guide you deeper through the woods and trails of Arkansas.

I also write about these trails with great caution and warning. As with any "last great place", it is the last because others have been ruined. Don't ruin what we have! All wilderness areas, in Missouri, Arkansas or wherever, need to be treated with respect, making every effort to enjoy the works of God within nature, without destroying them. Trails and backcountry areas that are abused leave scars upon them that are sometimes irreversible. So, hike, backpack and explore responsibly, taking care to leave any ground upon which you hike, in as good of shape, if not better, than when you entered!

Trail Locator — Arkansas

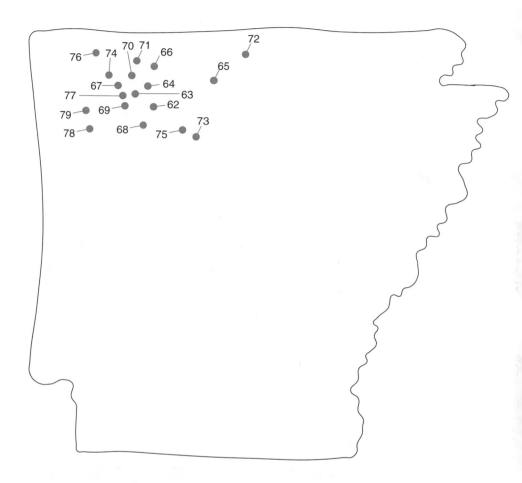

62. Alum Cove Trail
63. Buffalo River Trail
    (Boxley to Ponca)
64. Buffalo River Trail
65. Cow Creek Trail
66. Cecil Creek Loop
67. Centerpoint Trail
68. Glory Hole
69. Hawksbill Crag
70. Hemmed-In Hollow

71. Hide-Out Hollow
72. Indian Rockhouse
73. Kings Bluff
74. Lost Valley
75. Pedestal Rocks
76. Pigeon Roost Trail
77. Round Top Mountain
78. Shores Lake Trail
79. White Rock Mountain

62. Alum Cove Trail

LOCATION: Alum-Cove is located off HWY 16, 1.2 miles south from the junction of HWY 16 and HWY 7, or 1 mile north from the community of Deer Arkansas. The turn-off from HWY 16 onto Forest Road 1206 is marked, and should be easy to find. Follow 1206 for 3 miles and the turn for the trailhead is down the road to your right.

LENGTH: This is a short loop, just over one mile in length.

COMMENTS: For only being one mile in length, this trail has a lot to offer! Possessing one of the largest natural rock bridges in the Midwest, along with a bluffline full of dazzling rock formations and small caves, Alum Cove is a hiking highlight worth the trip. The boldness and sheer size of the bridge itself will amaze you, and the waterfall spilling over the bluff situated just behind the bridge accents this natural phenomenon even more.

On the trail's opposite side lies a tremendous bluffline packed with jumbled rock combinations that create openings, tunnels and small caves waiting for exploration. With a small creek running across the lower portion of the loop, this area is a fabulous little hike and an excellent place for an afternoon stay. No camping is allowed in this area, so make plans to picnic and spend the day.

TOPOGRAPHIC MAPS: Deer

The natural bridge on Alum Cove Trail

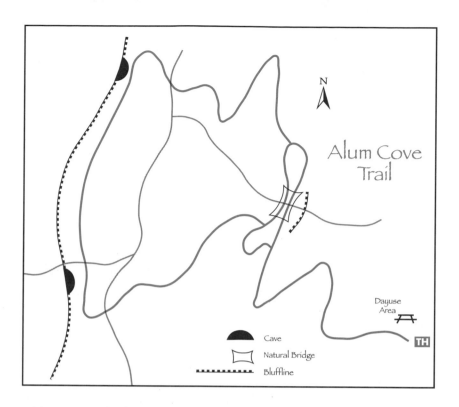

The trail begins on the backside of the picnic area located just beside the parking lot. A widened and smooth path, the trail begins to head downhill, switchbacking across the hillside to bring you straight to the Alum Cove Natural Bridge. An incredible sight and definite BTV, this natural rock bridge arches across the creek to span 130 feet in length with a thickness of 12 feet. The trail leads over the top, where a stone railing resides along the bridge's edge. If you catch the trail to the left, just before walking over the top, it will lead you down to the natural bridge's base where its magnificence truly shines. Directly behind the natural arch is a solid piece of sandstone rock, creating a bluffline backdrop that displays a nice sized waterfall spilling over its edge during springtime. A BTV from down below as well, this massive rock formation is an impressive sight and a true creation masterpiece.

From the base of the bridge proceed on across, beneath the mammoth sized rock structure, and head back into the woods. Descending downhill, the trail brings you to a stream crossing featuring some nice pools and small water pour-overs when rain has been present. From here, the trail edges uphill slightly to curve left and come alongside the beginning portion of extended bluffline. Housing many little cracks, openings and creative rock features, this entire bluff is worth some exploration. The trail follows along much of this rockwall's length before curving back left to re-cross the opposite end of the same stream and head back uphill. An easy trek up, the trail winds around shortly to return to the base of the natural bridge. Trails on either side will take you up to the bridge's top side and then lead you back uphill to the trailhead via the same switchbacks you came down on.

63. Buffalo River Trail

Boxley to Ponca

LOCATION: The trailhead for this Buffalo River Trail beginning starts at Boxley. From Ponca (the trail's termination point), take HWY 43 southwest to its junction with HWY 21. Turn left onto HWY 21, following it one mile past the crossing of the Buffalo River to the trailhead parking lot located on the right.

LENGTH: This section from Boxley to Ponca is 11 miles long, but if you wish to continue down the entire Buffalo River Trail, your trip can be extended all the way up to 36.5 miles!

COMMENTS: As you will quickly discover, hiking in Arkansas is more than just a stroll through the woods. This trail, complete with rocky terrain and challenging climbs, exemplifies much of the gorgeous topography and splendid scenery found in this "Natural State". With creative rock formations, water winding through twisted creeks, and views overlooking Boxley Valley, this starting section of the Buffalo River Trail sets the tone for some excellent Arkansas hiking.

Established in 1972 as America's first river to be designated and protected as a national park, the Buffalo boasts of some spectacular features, many of which can be accessed via the Buffalo River Trail. One of the more recent additions to this riverside trail, Boxley to Ponca, is now the beginning portion of the 36.5 mile route that follows the twists and turns of the mighty Buffalo all the way through to Pruitt. It is also a portion of the trail least used, but the views along its course and the creeks crossing its path, make it a beautiful hike and one well worth pursuing. Plan however, for a definite full day, as the eleven miles covered along this upper Buffalo stretch is long and a bit challenging!

TOPOGRAPHIC MAPS: Boxley and Ponca

To begin this trail, cross HWY 21 to a gravel road that leads across Smith Creek and into a field. You will think that you are entering onto someone's property, and in fact you are, so be considerate. Skirt the left side of this long field, and the trail will merge up and into the woods towards the back. The initial climb from the field and through the woods is pretty steep, leveling off about half a mile up and crossing through another field. Start your trek across this field to the right as it moves slightly uphill, but steer more to the left as it levels off, and you will pass by a pond and some nice views of the Upper Buffalo Wilderness area. At 1.5 this intermittent view opens up into a full fledged BTV, exposing the landscape and wilderness of the Boxley area. Take in the scenery, as from this vantage point the trail drops down to meet up with a gravel road at about 1.75. Turn right and hike along this road for less than half a mile, keep-

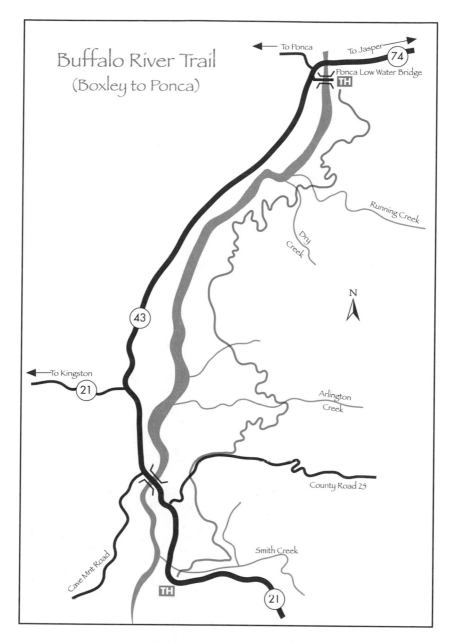

Buffalo River Trail
(Boxley to Ponca)

To Ponca
To Jasper
74
Ponca Low Water Bridge
TH
Running Creek
Dry Creek
N
43
To Kingston
21
Arlington Creek
County Road 25
Cave Mnt Road
Smith Creek
TH
21

ing your eyes peeled for a sign indicating the turn-off back onto trail turf, which is to the left, back into the timber.

Off the road, and trail-bound once again, the trail winds downhill to cross a couple of streams that carry a collection of small waterfalls pouring over typical Arkansas, moss covered rocks—a beautiful scene when the water is running! Continue through this area of streams and water creations (an entire area of BTV's), and soon the trail begins to drop a bit more drastically, crossing Arlington Creek at a little over 3 miles. As you can guess, the former trek down rebounds with a steady uphill climb next. Steep at times, but with some nice view breaks, the upcoming hill climbs for about three quarters of a mile before leveling off and merging with an old roadbed. Turn left here and follow this roadbed, which is thankfully level for the next 1.5 miles. This roadbed-trail takes you by an old homesite, and then past a cool little spring emerging from a rock on the right, before turning off to the left and heading downhill. (Don't miss the turn-off !!)

Going down, the trail passes by some spectacular springtime waterfalls, as well as fabulous leaf-off views. This stretch of moss-covered rocks and cedar-treed bluffs is a beautifully pleasant section, and continues rather nonchalantly as it eases down to cross Dry Creek at 7.5 miles. Up from Dry Creek, you will cross a dirt road, continuing straight across. Remaining level for a short bit, the trail then drops down slightly for a possible wet crossing at Running Creek. Across a field on this creek's opposite side lies the last long incline, taking you up to some BTV's of Boxley Valley. The tail end of this uphill stretch moves through some neat areas that wind around portions of rock that look like pieces of a bluff scattered across the wooded terrain. In between the abstract art of fragmented boulders, lie a few small stream crossings, each with a unique water formation when springtime rains permit. A very eye-catching section, this portion of the trail eventually levels off, moves around Big Hollow and even begins a slight downhill.

The homestretch starts at mile 10 where the trail borrows an old roadbed for the final mile into Ponca, remaining mostly level or downhill. The trail here winds its way down, passing through some grand finale views during leaf-off, which reveal glimpses of Ponca and the low-water bridge. As the trail drops you down to this destination, be aware that you are hiking somewhat within elk territory! One of Ponca's unique attributes is the presence of wild elk herds that reside quite a bit in the valley that lies below where you just hiked. The elk can sometimes be seen early in the morning grazing around the low-water bridge area, and have on occasion, been seen along this portion of the trail. So keep a look out, you never know what you might see! The trail ends at the Ponca low-water bridge where you can either pick up your vehicle, hitch a ride back to Boxley, or continue the Buffalo River Trail on to Steel Creek.

Elk relaxing in the field below the Buffalo River Trail

64. Buffalo River Trail

Ponca to Kyles

LOCATION: The Buffalo River Trail has many different access points. The section described here begins at the low water bridge in Ponca Arkansas and ends at Kyles Landing. Ponca is a small Arkansas town situated along the Buffalo River, right off HWY 43 south of Harrison about 23 miles. The low water bridge at Ponca is the first turn-off to the left (east) after the junction of 43 and 74. Kyles Landing is accessed via a turn-off to the left (north), 14 miles from Ponca, up HWY 74 going towards Jasper.

LENGTH: This trail has length options ranging from 2 to 36.5 miles. The section described here is 8 miles long, running from Ponca to Kyles.

COMMENTS: If you're a Missouri resident and never been to the Buffalo River, then you'd be surprised that one of this country's most fabulous wilderness areas is located right at your back door. The Buffalo National River was established in 1972 as America's first river protected as a national park, and very few places across our nation can match the serenity and beauty of the Buffalo and it's surrounding wilderness. Ponca itself, the small town near the upper Buffalo, resembles a mini version of a small mountain town, complete with a canyon like atmosphere, plenty of boaters and backpackers, and even a small herd of wild elk. With a healthy dosage of available trails, coupled with one of the country's most spectacular rivers, the Buffalo Wilderness Area needs to be visited at least once!

TOPOGRAPHIC MAPS: Ponca and Jasper

The Buffalo River Trail is still under construction, although a large portion of it has been around for a while and is open to the public for hiking. Eventually this trail will connect with Arkansas's Ozark Highland's Trail which will someday also connect with Missouri's Ozark Trail—imagine the network available if that ever completes! The small portion described here provides just a taste of the Buffalo, and is an 8 mile section that runs from the low water bridge in Ponca, to Kyle's Landing, a popular access point for the Buffalo during boating season. Another fabulous and newly added section that could easily be added to this portion, is an 8 mile hike starting upstream at Boxley, exiting out at Ponca.

   The trail is not overly difficult but does involve a few climbs up to some spectacular vantage and view points for the Buffalo. Since a vehicle shuttle is required, if you are without, contact the Buffalo Outdoor Center (BOC) at 1-800-221-5514 and they can probably provide shuttle service for a small fee.

Rustic cabins and canoe rentals are also available through the BOC and serve as an excellent way to combine a weekend getaway of floating and hiking.

From the parking area at the low water bridge, walk across the bridge and a little to the left up a rocky path that may be cabled off. Walk around the cable and you will find the trail to begin to the left, cross under the HWY 74 bridge and begin following alongside the Buffalo River. Edging along the top of a bluff, this first half mile or so opens up some splendid views, both up and down stream, of the Buffalo River. Climbing gradually the trail shares the path of a roadbed for a bit before veering off right, away from the river's side and towards a few creek crossings. Hiking during the springtime here is a real treat as the Buffalo is not only running full force in all its splendor, but seasonal waterfalls crop up within the feeder streams as well, crossing paths with parts of this trail. Regardless of water level, the views along this trail are always present, and you're first glimpse of Roark Bluff (the huge "painted" bluff along Steel Creek) is forth coming. Continue down the trail as the BTV and splendid views continue as well. Bee Bluff, just downstream but on the river's opposite side also emerges along with other glimpses of the mighty Buffalo. At about 1.5 the trail passes through a mini corridor opening created by a splitting of the bluffline on either side, and winds its way through a maze of rocks and trees—this area is fabulous, and a definite BTV.

Beginning to ease down somewhat without easing off any scenery bonus's, the trail makes its way down to Steel Creek. You will encounter a fork that if

The view from the Buffalo River Trail

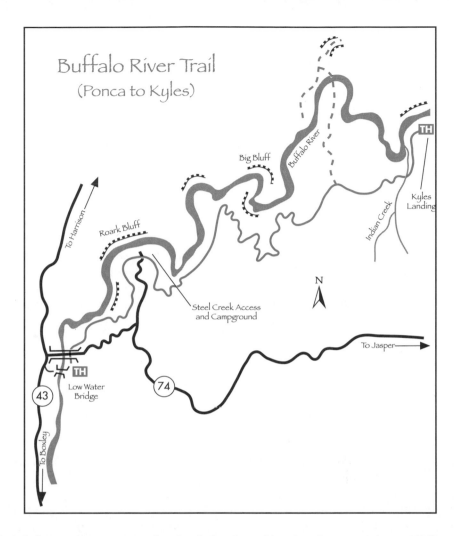

Buffalo River Trail
(Ponca to Kyles)

taken left empties out onto the Steel Creek parking lot. Stay straight and follow the trail that parallels the open field and campground. The striking white, black and gray features of Roark's Bluff are now even more intense as its presence is just across the river now. At 2.0 the trail crosses the road leading into Steel Creek and continues through the woods on the opposite side, uphill via some steps and covers ground behind all the ranger facilities here. Passing through the hardwoods, the trail skirts around the entire ranger station property, and crosses Steel Creek at 2.5. Steel Creek feeds into the Buffalo, so be prepared for a possible wet crossing if the river is up.

For the next mile the trail climbs, crossing some small streams with excellent waterfall potential during spring and offering a few stopping points to rest while catching an awesome view. The ultimate BTV is at 3.5 however, where all of Steel Creek, the Buffalo and the Ponca Wilderness Area are below and in full magnificent view. The view continues for about the next half mile or so, and good thing, because it serves as your motivation to continue the somewhat steep uphill trek. Leveling off a bit and even heading slightly downhill, watch for sinkholes around the four mile mark, as the trail moves slowly away from any sight of the Buffalo. Don't panic though, the river, its sound and its scenery become a part your hike once again at just over the 4.5 mile mark where Big Bluff enters the picture. Follow the trail uphill as it levels and then descends, crossing streams two or three times that each have excellent potential for "water art" if the season lends itself to such.

At 5.5 the trail intersects with an old roadbed. Stay straight, following the trail as it follows a small stream, crossing it shortly before heading uphill. At just over the 6 mile mark, watch as the trail passes by a section of bluff that creates a wet weather waterfall—a definite BTV if you're lucky enough to catch it at the right time. Climbing still further, the trail continues on past this small scenic spot and as it levels off at 7.0, it also intersects with another old road. Take a left and use this old road as the trail for the next half mile. The next intersection, located about 7.5, offers a couple options. The main trail continues by turning right here, but the option a bit further down that goes left, heads down to the river at Horseshoe Bend where Hemmed-In Hollow can be accessed, as well as other points along the Centerpoint and Compton Trails. This direction gives you an option of getting to Hemmed-In Hollow, but the 2 mile side-trip is very steep—a noticeable factor going down, but even more noticeable when coming back up!!

Taking a right to head towards Kyles is definitely the easy route as the uphill climbing of the past few miles pays off with some downhill from here on out. Following a path along a hillside, the trail offers a few distant glimpses of your destination as it carries on through the forest. Passing a bench at 8.5, the trail begins a descent that intensifies as the trail goes. Views open up occasionally and a vista point is available via a small spur trail extending out about 8.8. Just beyond this point, where the trail curves sharply right, a view opens up that allows you a peak at Indian Creek—an absolutely fantastic and amazing area to explore and hike through on another Arkansas journey. Just a bit further down, at 9.5, the trail will cross Indian Creek itself, giving you a small opportunity to see just some of what this area has to offer. (A small trail leading right at this point heads up the Indian Creek direction.) Across the creek, a turn to your left leads to an intersection with a sign indicating the direction to Grey Rock. Follow this sign as it leads past Grey Rock and directly to Kyles Landing. You have finished this section of the Buffalo River Trail.

Hiking Tip — Dehydration

Drinking plenty of water while on the trail is essential. Make an effort to take in fluids at regular intervals. Once you feel thirsty, it is likely that your body is already dehydrated by one-third of its needs.

65. Cow Creek Trail

LOCATION: From Yellville Arkansas, take HWY 62 east, through Flippin, to HWY 101. Turn south on 101, cross Crooked Creek via a one-lane bridge, and drive through Rea Valley. Continue down the gravel road when the pavement ends (it might be rough!) and it will lead into the Buffalo National River Park boundary. Just past the park boundary lies Hathaway Hollow trailhead, located on your left. Cow Creek Trail is located on the northeast end of this parking lot.

LENGTH: The Cow Creek-Cook Hollow loop is 12 miles in length with optional added side-trips available as well as alternate shorter hikes.

COMMENTS: Prepare for some drastic elevation changes as this trail possesses a couple steep ascents and challenging climbs. The trail tends to rise to the ridge quickly, descend down much more subtly, and then trek towards the top again with an almost sudden burst. Views from the ridges are excellent however, especially during late fall and winter when leaves are absent from the trees. The 12 mile length coupled with the challenging terrain and extra side-trips, advise that you attack this loop over a two day period rather than one, which unless shortened for a more ideal day hiking length, makes this a nice backpacking trail. A gravel bar along the Buffalo River, located on the trail's eastern border, serves as an excellent campsite, providing you with water, a big open sky, and an awesome view of one of the river's famed landmarks, Elephant Head Rock. Cow Creek is one of the lesser used Buffalo River Trails, which also gives it some added bonus points for those seeking out a more remote and wilderness setting.

TOPOGRAPHIC MAPS: Buffalo City

You will begin your journey from the trailhead located on the parking lot's northeastern edge. Don't expect much of a "warm-up" because the trail initiates an ascent almost immediately that challenges you with a half-mile climb right off the bat. Moving up to an area that is part of Hathaway Mountain, the trail rises almost 500 feet over a relatively short distance, creating one heck of a hill to start you off! An intersection towards the top of this first trek requires that you stay to the right as the trail first moves across a short gladed area, and then thankfully heads downhill to cross Cook Creek. Upon crossing, another intersection arises to which you will want to turn right. Making its way up to Granite Mountain, the trail leads another formidable ascent across contour lines that gives new definition to the term "straight up"! Topping out at over 1100 feet,

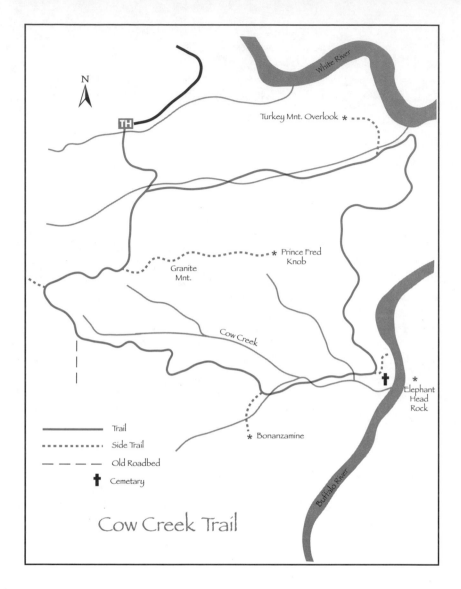

N

TH

White River

Turkey Mnt. Overlook *

* Prince Fred
  Knob

Granite
Mnt.

Cow Creek

†

*
Elephant
Head
Rock

——————— Trail

·············· Side Trail

— — — Old Roadbed

† Cemetary

* Bonanzamine

Buffalo River

Cow Creek Trail

this three-quarter mile climb ends at Granite Mountain and another trail inter-section.

The trail option left remains on top for a bit as it leads across the mountain's ridgetop to a highpoint edge known as Prince Fred Knob. The side-trip here adds about another mile (half a mile each way) and might be a good destination and turn-around point for those wishing only to explore this area for a day. The main Cow Creek loop however, continues to the right and also remains flat, giving views to your left of the Cow Creek valley and drainage area. At this point the trail has taken residence along an old jeep road, and about a half mile down, it comes to a fork. The trail right leads to another access point somewhere further down the old road you drove in on. Stay left here though, as you want to continue around the main route. Left continues along the old roadbed and begins a nice welcomed descent down towards Cow Creek. Shortly after this downward trek begins, the trail merges with another road that takes off to the right and heads up. Stay left and continue down as the trail is now paralleling Cow Creek, which is down and to your left. Straight ahead and in the distance, glimpses of the Buffalo River's Elephant Head Rock are possible during times of leaf-off. Keep following the old jeep road and as you approach the 4 mile mark you will come to the crossing of Cow Creek. A faint trail intersection that offers an option to the right is located here, leading to an old abandon mine.

For the main trail, stay on the road to the left and cross the creek, following alongside it for a short bit before merging with another little intersection. Stay to your right, and the trail will lead past a small spring known as Fox Den Spring. With Cow Creek still on your left, follow the trail another mile before reaching yet another fork. Stay left, crossing the creek once more to arrive at a "T" intersection. Turn left at this junction, crossing Cow Creek one final time and passing by an old cemetery on your right. Shortly after this, a fork to the right leading to the Buffalo River offers you a stopping point and campsite location should you wish to stay overnight. The trek down to the river can be a bit of a challenge, as you will fight a bit through the surprisingly large sized cane that is grown up along this trail. The gravel bar available for camping here is excellent though, and a welcomed stopping point after covering the last 5 miles.

From the intersection and turn-off for the Buffalo River, the main trail proceeds left and still remains tied to the old jeep road which leads over a more mild terrain for the next 3 miles. Up and to your left is a clear view of Prince Fred Knob, the taller mountain that you were on top of earlier if you chose the short side-trip. On your right are locations for some old homesites that once stood in this area. In fact, as the trail forks about 3 miles down from the Buffalo River intersection, a side-trail right leads to the "Old Hudson Place" which is a short side-trip and exploration site. The main trail remains to the left and crosses Cook Creek to begin its homeward bound trek along this creek valley hollow.

Another intersection shortly after the crossing of Cook Creek offers a final side-trip option to the right leading to Turkey Mountain Overlook. This giant fragment of granite rock jutting out over the valley qualifies as a BTV, and is part of the magnificent Stair Bluff that offers views of the surrounding White River basin area, as well as glimpses of Buffalo City. The main trail continues along Cook Creek to the left however, and crosses it several times in attempts to lead you back towards the original trailhead. This final stretch is about 3 miles in length, and intersects with your return route at a "T" located at the base of a steep incline. Left leads up to Granite Mountain and is the direction you hiked at this loop's beginning. Heading home now, you will want to turn right and head back up to Hathaway Mountain. The steep trek upward leads back across an intersection that you want to stay to the left of, and heads down hill to return to the trailhead in less than half a mile.

66. Cecil Creek Loop

LOCATION: Cecil Creek is located in the Compton Arkansas area, 8 miles north of Ponca and 18 miles south of Harrison. From Ponca, take HWY 43 north for 8 miles and turn right onto the gravel road just across from the Compton One-Stop. This gravel road veers right at an old stone building and continues straight, passing the turn-off for Hemmed-In Hollow as well as the parking area for Hide-Out Hollow. Continue on this road for about 6 miles, and be prepared as it can get rough and rutted in spots, as well as quite muddy after a good rain. The trailhead starts right across from the old Erbie church.

LENGTH: The entire loop is 7.4 miles, but shorter options are available.

COMMENTS: Especially after a good rain, this trail can be spectacular. Cecil Creek and its tributaries join forces with the bluffs, boulders and rugged terrain to bring you a stunning display of gorgeous waterfalls and other fabulous water formations. In addition, much of the southern portion of Cecil Creek Trail runs along the Cecil Cove Bench, which is a flat trek across the top of the ridge offering tremendous views of what truly are the Ozark "mountains". It is also along this section that many old homesteads can be discovered, as well as some wonderful little springs. The lower portion of this loop leads down towards the Buffalo River where the most well preserved homestead resides; the J.W. Farmer place.

The loop can be easily completed in one day, but plenty is present in the way of side-trip explorations if you wish to take your time and make this a backpacking overnight. Be careful during weekends of extremely high water as Cecil Creek during flood stage is a raging whitewater rush that is pretty much impassable. Usually however, the creek disappears underground in places so that you have completely dry crossings, so for the most part it shouldn't be a problem.

TOPOGRAPHIC MAPS: Ponca and Jasper

The trailhead for Cecil Creek starts just across the way from the church, moving past the restrooms and on into the woods. Moving down slightly along a rocky path, the trail leads rather quickly to a beautiful little stream crossing and beaver pond. With a large rock bluff to your left outlining the backside of a pool of beautiful blue-green water, this pond area is gorgeous, and an excellent BTV introducing you to what will be a fabulous hike. After crossing the small stream feeding this pond via Van Dyke Spring, the trail loops around to the left providing a better view of the bluffline and water pool. Water is now to your

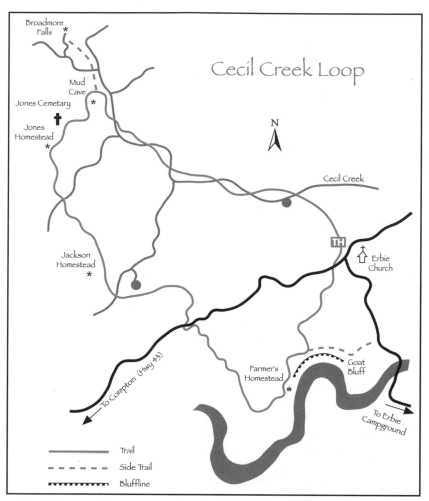

Cecil Creek Loop

Broadmore Falls *

Mud Cave *

Jones Cemetary †

Jones Homestead *

Cecil Creek

N

TH

Erbie Church

Jackson Homestead *

Farmer's Homestead *

Goat Bluff

To Compton (Hwy 43)

To Erbie Campground

——— Trail
– – – Side Trail
▪▪▪▪▪▪ Bluffline

left and right as the trail winds through the woods to empty out into a clearing at half a mile in. Across this clearing and back into the forested area, the trail is following Cecil Creek moving to and from it in proximity at different points. At one mile in, the trail crosses Cecil for the first time. If wet weather has been the norm for a period before your hike, this crossing might require removing your boots, or at least some creative rock hopping! Moving in and away from the creek once again, the trail moves through the bottomlands area to cross with Cecil for a second time at about 1.5. The crossing here is interesting, as much of the time this part of Cecil Creek is dry. Look to the left while walking over the dry bed of smooth stones, and you will see where water feeding the former portion of the creek is coming out from beneath the ground. This is because water from this creek actually disappears, running underground for a good portion most of the time. If rains have been heavy enough to cause a run-off of water above ground for this portion, then crossing might be a bit challenging to say the least!

After this hopefully dry crossing, the trail wanders around to the right and comes alongside the dry creekbed that now has a gorgeous rock wall bluff lin-

Jones Homestead Remains

ing its opposite side. This stretch of trail, highlighted by the creek lined bluffs and cedar thick forest is a beautiful little stroll along an easy level terrain. At just under two miles, you will cross the creek one more time, following it further as it winds around along your left now. Not too far after crossing, the trail comes upon a man-made rock wall that extends for a short length on your left. Neatly and carefully stacked with smooth stones, this rock wall dating back to pioneer days, is in amazingly intact condition and adds a nice highlight to this trail stretch. Pass this wall and the trail will dip down to cross Cecil for the final time before heading up into the woods. At 2.2 miles, you will encounter a trail intersection. To the left will be the continuation of this Cecil Creek Loop. To the right however, is an awesome little side trail that leads about a mile further down to Broadmore Falls. If water is running, and you have the time, then take this side trip that leads to a fabulous display of boulders, rock formations and waterfalls. Also down this side-trail, not too far from the intersection is an awesome little campsite located right by a clear blue pool of water residing at the base of a mini bluff. Flat, with trees and a fire-ring, this is an ideal overnight location.

Back to the intersection. Take a left here for the continuation of the main trail, and gear up for a rather hefty climb. The trail moves up and as it switchbacks to the right, passes by a bluffline located off into the woods that houses Mud Cave—another side-trip if desired. Curving to the right from this area and staking out its uphill course, the trail winds up the hillside for the next half mile. Some nice views begin to open up on both sides when leaves are absent, and you can sense the elevation gain as you look across to opposite ridges. At 2.8 the bulk of the climbing ends, bringing you to the site of an old family cemetery: Jones Cemetery. A very remote place that sets on the top of the mountain, this quaint and very interesting cemetery is a pleasant spot and one that seems almost ideal as a final resting place for those who lived out in these woods generations ago.

As you continue past this cemetery, the trail will climb just a tiny bit more, bringing you by the remains of some old homesteads that were once places of residence for families of the pioneer times. At 3.0 portions of an old log structure lie close to a small intersection that leads to the right. A remaining stone chimney here represents what was once the Jones place. It is amazing that people lived and survived way up here! Just past he Jones place, a stone wall on the right outlines what was once home to the family of Faddis-Keaton. There is at least a spring-fed stream here which was probably an excellent source of water for this family.

Moving on past the homesteads, the trail winds around on top of this "bench" area, remaining mostly level and offering fabulous views across the way to your left during leaf-off times. The trail is wide, sharing paths with an old roadbed that was most likely the transportation route used by the families living in the area way back. Crossing several spring-fed streams, these next two miles are easy and pleasant walking.

At 5.2 the trail exits out onto the gravel road that you drove in on to reach the trailhead. Take a left here and two options are available. The first option is to simply follow the road all the way down to the trailhead, a distance of 1.4 miles. The second option, which is better, is to follow this road for a short distance (800 feet), picking up the ending portion of this loop trail on the right. This continuation on the road's opposite side is on your right as you're walking down the road, and is blocked by large boulders in front. The trail leads from between these rocks slightly uphill and curves around to begin a long downhill trek. Rocky and rutted, this old roadbed that leads down for the next mile, ends with a "T" intersection at 7.4 miles. The trail running perpendicular with the one just hiked in on is the Buffalo River Trail. The house and homestead area just in front of you is the old J. W. Farmer's place—a super cool homestead location with three or four fairly well preserved buildings that you can explore around. Please respect the area and the old weathered structures, as they are so unique, standing as remnants of this area's history.

From the trail intersection, take a left, passing by what remains of an old wooden spring house, and to a place where the road and trail divide. Moving off the roadbed that has been a part of this trail for quite some time now, take a left into the woods winding through a maze of timber and boulders. As the trail meanders away from the field area located to your right, it climbs rather sharply uphill, twisting through an awesome BTV area of rock ledges and cedar trees. When it begins to level off at about 6.7, the trail comes alongside the bluff's edge to open up some outstanding views of the Buffalo River lying quite the distance below. You are now hiking upon a portion of the tall bluffline known as Goat Bluff, whose base originates from the waters of the mighty Buffalo. Following the rocky edge for a short distance, the trail arrives at another intersection. To the right is an extension of the Goat Bluff Trail, and leads down to another old homestead site. To the left is the continuation and homestretch of this Cecil Creek Loop Trail.

Take a left here and you will pass through some cedar grove areas as the trail initially follows alongside an open field. Moving along level ground, as it graduates more directly into the woods, the trail will pass by an old man made stone wall similar to the one seen earlier back at this trail's beginning. At 7.3 the trail empties out onto the old gravel road taken to get to the trailhead. Take a right here and follow the road for one-tenth of a mile to arrive at the church and parking area.

67. Centerpoint Trail

LOCATION: The Centerpoint Trailhead is located off HWY 43, just 3.5 miles north from Ponca Arkansas, near the Buffalo River.

LENGTH: The complete trail length described here will be 8 miles—4 miles to the Buffalo River, and 4 miles back; however, Centerpoint has other length options as well. Connecting to the Compton Trailhead, length is about 6.5 miles, or shorter routes are available too. (Directions to Compton Trailhead are in the Hemmed-In Hollow Trail section of this book.)

COMMENTS: With so many route options and different highlights available via this trail, Centerpoint serves as the hub for a perfect afternoon, day, or weekend of hiking. Be prepared though, wherever your destination is from this trailhead, it is sure to be down, which means an uphill trek upon return. Much like the Hemmed-In Hollow Trail, although not quite as steep, Centerpoint drops down more than 1000 feet to the Buffalo River, creating a strenuous hike out on the backswing. Sights along this trail make the uphill climb returning well worth it though!

Highlights along this trail include Granny Henderson's Cabin, Big Bluff and Jim's Bluff, the Buffalo River itself and many scenic overlooks all captured within the Ponca Wilderness Area. From Centerpoint you can also connect with the Compton Trail if you have the ability to shuttle vehicles. Hemmed-In Hollow is also accessible from here, and is a bit easier route than Compton, although longer.

TOPOGRAPHIC MAPS: Ponca

Beginning from the trailhead, your path is an old road bed that is smooth at first, heads downhill pretty quick, and aside from a few rutted areas, is generally pleasant walking. Views and glimpses of possible BTV's pop up along the way, as the trail begins to steepen past the one mile mark. About a mile and a half in, a fork offering a footpath off the road and to the left should be taken. After turning left here, watch for another trail fork left, which you will also take, and continue on. As you follow the trail down, take notice of the views that provided glimpses of the Buffalo River below as well as evidences of karst topography in the form of sinkholes and such. At just over 2.5 miles, the trail levels off at a intersection that looks like an area used before as a campsite. The main trail continues straight. However, if you take a short side trip to the right, you will experience one of this trail's highlights.

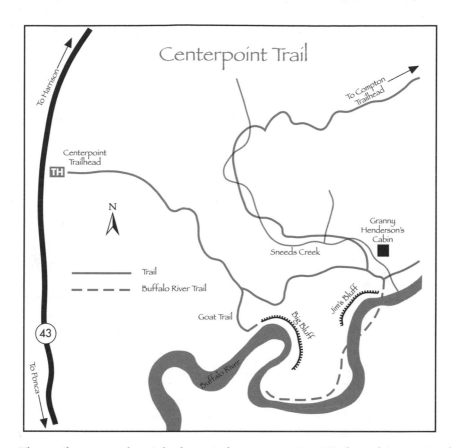

Centerpoint Trail

To Harrison →

To Compton Trailhead →

Centerpoint Trailhead
TH

N

Granny Henderson's Cabin

Sneeds Creek

—————— Trail
— — — — Buffalo River Trail

Jim's Bluff

Goat Trail

Big Bluff

43

To Ponca →

Buffalo River

The trail spur to the right here is known as Goat Trail, and it won't take long before you catch the idea behind the name. Looking somewhat like it was created for a pack mule or yak, this trail is narrow with a steep and dangerous drop-off along its edge. Be very careful here as people have fatally fallen off this trail! The destination point of Goat Trail is Big Bluff, a fabulously tall bluffline that towers over the river and extends across the ridge. Although up high, you're not on top, because as you walk along the ledges of this bluff, huge amounts of rock still rise and overhang above you. The whole setting sort of makes you think of this spot as an Indian dwelling or outlaw hideout—cool spot and definite BTV!

Back to the main trail. Heading straight at the campsite intersection carries you down just a bit further, till at 3.0 a crumbled rock wall along the road follows you. Just after this the trail hangs a left, continuing down. At 3.5 an intersection provides another spur trail and highlight. Take a quick left and arrive at Granny Henderson's Cabin. This is a splendid little cabin that has been somewhat restored and is definitely worth a few moments of exploration. What an awesome place to have a cabin! If you stay left and continue on past the cabin, the trail leads up Sneeds Creek to exit via the Compton Trailhead. If you're not planning to exit out at Compton though, take a right and continue down the main trail to the next small spur trail right, which will lead to an awesome bluff and BTV known as Jim's Bluff. This overhanging bluff that is so striking that it

Sneeds Creek on the Centerpoint Trail

almost appears painted, is a Buffalo River highlight, as well as a scenic stopping point for this trail.

Returning back to the main trail; instead of a short right that took you to Jim's Bluff, you could stay straight. This option leads along the flat valley floor that follows the Buffalo, heads across Sneed's Creek and provides access to Hemmed-In Hollow as well. You can continue on this route if you desire to hike all the way to the Compton Trailhead, or you can return to Centerpoint by retracing your steps back.

Camp Recipe — Camp Chicken

Tired of the same ole freeze dried, add water entrees? Be creative and try your own lightweight version.

At home combine these ingredients together in a ziploc bag:

    1 c. instant brown rice
    ¼ c. slivered almonds
    ¼ c. dried mushrooms
    2 T. onion flakes
    1 T. green or red pepper flakes
    ½ t. salt

At camp, combine the above ingredients with the following and cook for about 15 minutes:

    1 ½ c. water
    1 large can of chicken (or two smaller cans)
    2 packages of instant cream of chicken soup mix

68. Glory Hole

LOCATION: Glory Hole has a trailhead that is a bit of a challenge to find. Located 6.2 miles east from Fallsville, on HWY 16/21, the trailhead is found on the road's right-hand side, and is more of a pull-in off the road than it is a parking area and trailhead. As you come from Fallsville, look for a large red barn with a big white "E" on the front of it, situated on the left, 5.7 miles down. Half a mile from the barn is a gravel road on the left. Pass this, and as the road curves uphill, there is a house on the left with a gate at its entrance posting a "no parking" sign. Directly across the road from this house is an old jeep road pull-off that drops down over the shoulder. This is your trailhead.

LENGTH: This trail is two miles round-trip.

COMMENTS: As you can tell by the above directions, this trail is a bit remote and visited too frequently! Possessing a subtle beginning and an unknown title, this trail will absolutely astound you with its amazing display of rocks and water. Centered around a huge opening carved within the middle of a giant rock-slab shelf, Glory Hole is this trail's feature presentation, yet not the only highlight worthy of noting when describing this enchanted little area. An absolute must to hike when water is running, the hollow area for Glory Hole's setting is a magical display of creation's natural "waterpark" with running streams, spill-overs and waterfalls intermingled everywhere all perfectly land-scaped to create a fantastic setting. Catch this area after a good rain, bring a camera and a picnic lunch, and plan to explore and appreciate this hidden yet spectacular spot.

TOPOGRAPHIC MAPS: Fallsville

The old jeep road that begins from the shoulder of HWY 16/21 is the trail's initial path curving around into the woods and moving slightly downhill. There is no trailhead and no markers so don't feel lost from the lack of these. The jeep road that paves the trail's course will lead about .3 miles down into the woods to a small area where a trailhead sign does exist. You could even drive down to this point if your vehicle is of the four-wheelin' type; however the walk is easy and pleasant so starting from the road is fine. When you arrive at this trailhead point be sure to veer to the right, off the old road and follow the trail deeper into the woods as it moves downhill.

With a gradual descent, the trail curves around to the right and moves down into the hollow where it crosses a very pleasant little creek at about the .6 mile mark. This creek, known as Dismal Creek is the one that will flow

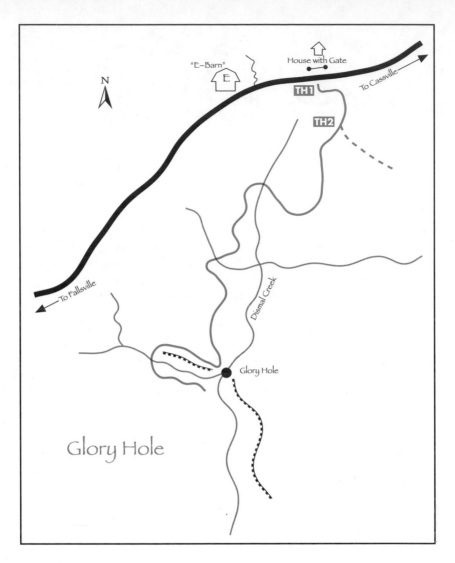

Glory Hole

down into the Glory Hole where you are headed, so the more water here, the better! Crossing the creek, the trail winds around paralleling the streambed for a bit, although not immediately beside it. You will come to another crossing which is a stream tributary to Dismal Creek, and then the trail winds a bit more narrowly down through an area of young pine trees. Twisting between trees in the canyon of this wooded hollow, the trail introduces you to the pristine and remote nature of this hidden area. The sound of running water is everywhere, and glimpses of the creek to your left, combine with multiple hillside stream run-offs ahead, to create a picture perfect scene. The trail empties out onto a gladed area that serves as a platform for the large boulders and tremendous rock slabs that are now in front of you. The Glory Hole is part of this rock conglomeration and is located in the streambed to your left. Wander over to the edge and watch as the water disappears through the almost perfectly round hole seemingly carved out of the rock. A BTV and awesome sight! Standing on the bluff at this point you can look out and see the incredible beauty of this tiny hollow. The bluffline extends to the left while steep creeks creating waterfalls while carving their way down the hillside are located to the right. Follow the bluff's edge to your right and the trail will make its way down to the base of the rock upon which you are now standing. It is down underneath this giant rock slab that Glory Hole empties out, gushing gallons of water down through the rock roof and into a pool below.

When you've taken in all there is to see and enjoy here, you can return to the trailhead via a re-tracing of steps down the same trail. If the water is running steadily however, and you're up for some minor trail-blazing, then follow the creek all the way up to where it meets the trail. Mini waterfalls and cool rock formations are all along this steep Arkansas creek, and the trek back stream-side is well worth it!

Glory Hole

69. Hawksbill Crag

LOCATION: To find this trailhead, drive south down HWY 43 from Ponca to HWY 21 south. Travel one mile down HWY 21 and just before the road crosses the Buffalo River, take a right onto a gravel road, known as Cave Mountain Road. About 6 miles up, (and it is definitely up!) the trailhead can be found on the road's right-hand side.

LENGTH: This trail is 3 miles, round trip.

COMMENTS: The drive to the trailhead for Hawksbill Crag more challenging then the hike itself! Short in length, and in "out and back" form, this trail is an easy afternoon hike that holds an unmatched BTV that is a splendid scenery flick of the Whitaker Creek Valley, and surrounding Arkansas wilderness. Hawksbill Crag, also known as Whitaker's Point, is a giant rock outcrop that

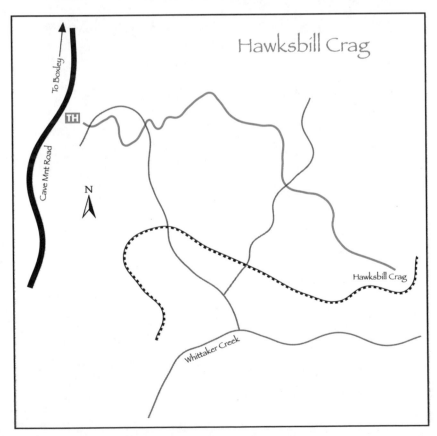

extends over the side of a huge bluffline affording views of Arkansas terrain that reaches for miles. The trail is not particularly tough although the uphill trek back notifies you that it was a steady downhill for most of the hike in. With the bluffline running along both sides of the crag, and Whitaker Creek running below, the area has tons of exploration potential in addition to the actual trail.

TOPOGRAPHIC MAPS: Boxley

Across from the trailhead parking lies the start of the Hawksbill Trail, as it leads slowly down into the woods. Most of the hike to the crag is through this hardwood forest type scene and is fairly easy hiking as it switchbacks down to a more level terrain. Crossing a few creeks that hold some bonus waterfall scenes in spring, the trail eventually shares the path of a widened roadbed at about one mile in. The final creek crossing just before joining path's with this road holds a trail spur to the right that holds some BTV waterfalls in spring and some excellent exploration potential.

Continuing down the main trail, sneak previews of the bluffline emerge through the woods on your right. The trail is still back a bit from the edge, but eventually it veers closer to the bluff, hiking just along side it. Once the trail and bluffline connect, look ahead and to the right; Hawksbill Crag is right there protruding boldly from the rock face and looking out over the valley below. One of the smaller outcroppings just before reaching the crag offer some awesome photo shoots of Hawksbill, capturing the giant rock's outline and shape as it hovers out over the edge. Spend some time exploring, relaxing and awing for a bit and when you are ready to return, head back the way you came in.

Hawksbill Crag

70. Hemmed-In Hollow

LOCATION: Located off HWY 43, 8 miles north of Ponca, lies the tiny community of Compton (Don't blink, or you'll miss it!). Turn east (left if coming from Harrison) onto a small dirt road located just across from the Compton One Stop. Veering to the right at the fork located by the old stone store, follow this road approximately one mile. Take a right at the sign and upcoming intersection, the trailhead will be on the left.

LENGTH: The hike to Hemmed-In is about 2.5 miles from the trailhead (5 miles round-trip). Continuing on from the falls, a loop can be hiked that totals 8.5 miles.

COMMENTS: Yet another famed area and highlight of Arkansas and the Buffalo River, Hemmed-In Hollow stands as the tallest waterfall between the Rockies and the Appalachians. Nearly 200 feet in height and nestled deep into what looks like the end of a rock walled canyon, Hemmed-In Hollow is immense, amazing and unmatched in Ozark's splendor. The hike can be done in an afternoon, but bring plenty of water, and prepare for quite the challenge as the hike out is especially steep, providing you with a good work-out to say the least! If you opt to loop this trail rather than simply hiking to the falls and back, then the rough trek back up will occur on the tail end of the loop. Either way, a 1000 foot change in elevation occurs, so be prepared.

The falls at Hemmed-In Hollow are a definite highlight and well worth the "out and back" trek if 5 miles is all you care to do, but if you get a chance to spend a day on the entire loop, do so, as many other cool features surround this area as well. The Buffalo River lies just below the falls, and overlook spots along the bluffline give some nice views of this Northern Arkansas treasure. Low-impact backpack camping is permitted, but pets are not.

TOPOGRAPHIC MAPS: Ponca

Start at the trailhead on the left, as it leads more directly to the falls (the one on right is where you return if doing the loop) and head off into the woods. As the trail begins its downward trek with small switchbacks, views along the trail's edge open up, offering a few nice BTV's and overlooks of the Buffalo River basin below. Just before the mark of the first mile, the trail arrives at a four way intersection. Stay straight and continue down the main trail leading to the falls. Views will continue to expand as you head down this steep and rocky path, making this trail slightly difficult, yet beautiful in terrain and topography. Catch this trail in late fall when the leaves have thinned out and you're up for a real scenic treat. BTV's pop up all along this trail and especially at switchback

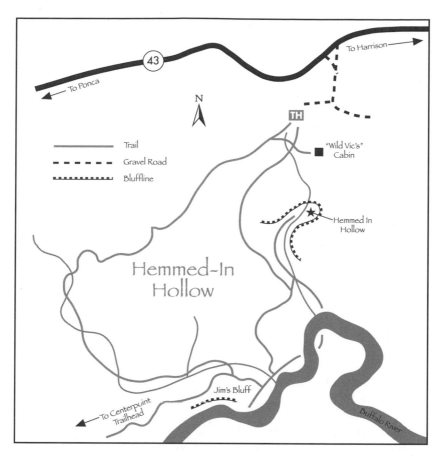

junctions. One in particular that is worth noting lies about a mile and a half in, where a giant rock slab provides a stopping point for you to take in the awesome beauty of surrounding trees, bluffs, and even a glimpse of Hemmed-In itself.

Continuing on past this most excellent photo shoot, the trail heads down still further, crossing two small creeks before reaching a trail intersection at just under 2 miles. Getting closer now, a left at this junction leads to the falls, and is where you want to go. Right leads down to the Buffalo River and is a continuation of the loop, should you wish to hike all 8.5 miles. As you proceed left, evidences of your entrance into a rock walled hollow begin. Rock formations emerge, along with large boulders and eventually a small little rocky stream. A trail intersection leading right is a path to the Buffalo used by canoeists that hike up to the falls from the river, as well as an extension of the Buffalo River Trail. Stay straight at this junction (A sign here prohibits camping beyond this point) and the trail crosses another rock-bottomed creek housing a few neat water formations of its own during wet months. The trail continues alongside this creek as the water escorts you to Hemmed-In Hollow. You will have no doubt of your whereabouts upon arrival, as the towering 180 foot walls of the hollow stand unmatched to almost any other Ozark area hiking destination! Enjoy this most splendid BTV and return either by way of the same route or proceeding around the entire loop if desired.

71. Hide-Out Hollow

LOCATION: The turn-off for Hide-Out Hollow is located just north of Ponca Arkansas off HWY 43 in the town of Compton. Coming from Ponca, take HWY 43 north 8 miles and turn right onto a gravel road located just across form the Compton One-Stop. This is the same gravel road that takes you to the Hemmed-In Hollow trailhead. Veering right at the old abandon stone store, drive down this road 3.5 miles, passing the turn-off at the one mile mark for Hemmed-In Hollow. The Hide-Out Hollow turn-off is on the left, just past the sign marking the park boundary.

LENGTH: This is a 2 mile round-trip trail.

COMMENTS: This short little hike leads to an absolutely fabulous setting that boasts of some panoramic views, beautiful waterfalls, and a winding bluffline. True to its title, the destination for this trail resembles what one might see in an old western movie if a few outlaws were present hovering beneath the rock shelf that encircles the hidden setting. During springtime, the rain accents this already spectacular area with a collection of waterfalls that run down the creek and over the many ledges and drops, created by the bluffline and fragmented rock pieces. The hike in is mostly level and leads to the top of the actual Hide-Out Hollow where there's plenty to see, but if the adventurous rock-climbing side of you is daring enough, then options leading down into the hollow allow for some added exploration as well.

TOPOGRAPHIC MAPS: Ponca

From the parking area, the trail takes off straight into the woods and is marked fairly well with white rectangular looking markers. Winding through a very pleasant timber and cedar area, the trail moves downhill slightly to cross a delightful little creek. Gradually moving back up the hillside upon crossing, the trail flattens again as it treks across a rocky terrain. The trail moves easily through some cedar and pine areas, and at about .6 miles, it arrives at an area of scattered boulders on the right. Their fragmented placement and collection of lichen green shades earn them a title of BTV, and exploring around them is much like a mouse winding through a giant maze in search of cheese. Find the path that leads straight down from this jumble of broken boulders, and you're in for another BTV – this one in the form of an awesome overlook. A portion of Hide-Out Hollow can be seen to your left, while the Cecil Creek Valley lies in the distance to your right. The platform on which you are standing at this point is part of the giant winding bluffline that creates the hollow and will follow you for most of the rest of the hike.

Make your way back up through the boulders and find the main trail again which leads down to another portion of this bluff holding an excellent view as well. A boulder the size of a rather large house sets straight across from this ridge and is quite intriguing as it has several cedar trees growing right out of it. The trail continues to the left and pretty much follows the edge of the bluffline, providing views across the hollow and winding through some rocky cedar glade areas. Listen closely and the sound of rushing water should begin to foreshadow what lies ahead. Make your way through the sort of faint trail options and you will arrive at a creek directing water across large flat slabs of rock to disappear over the edge. This is the head of Hide-Out Hollow and the creek is forming the largest of this area's waterfalls. Take a careful walk over to the edge and take in the fantastic scene lying below. The giant bluffline that encircles the area creates a continual edge for multiple waterfalls during really wet times, and the overhanging rock that creates a roof to walk under from below, definitely characterizes a "hide-out" setting. Enjoy the uniqueness and beauty of this little Arkansas highlight and then retrace you steps to return to the trailhead.

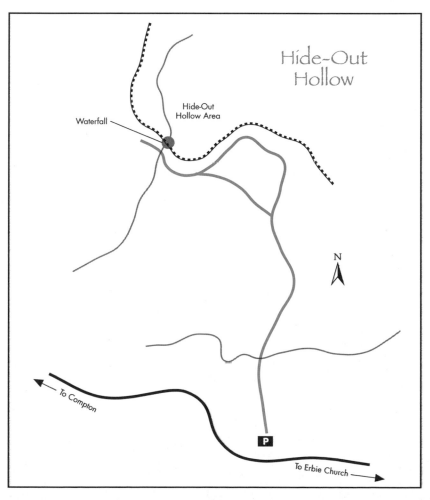

72. Indian Rockhouse Trail

LOCATION: Indian Rockhouse is located at Buffalo Point on the lower Buffalo. From Yellville Arkansas, take HWY 14 south, 14 miles to Caney Arkansas. HWY 14 jogs a bit here, so take HWY 26 towards Rush, turning back south on HWY 14 again shortly. Follow the signs, as the Indian Rockhouse turn-off is a couple miles down on your left.

LENGTH: This trail is 5 miles long round-trip, but can be shortened if desired.

COMMENTS: A bit less remote then most Arkansas trails, Indian Rockhouse might not sound too appealing to the hard-core or serious hiker, however, this trail is packed with many surprising features that pop up all along the trail in a sort of "scavenger hunt for the next treasure" fashion. In addition, this trail also caters to the aggressive hiker, as it provides an incline spur trail ranking on the edge of mountaineering that leads up to Bat Cave. Don't be intimidated if you're seeking something a bit more relaxing though, because aside from the challenging Bat Cave spur, this trail is ideal for most hikers, and even has a bit of a nature trail twist as certain points along the way label plant species and such.

   With Buffalo Point being such a popular river access, this area is also packed full of facilities, housing everything from camping and cabins, to a restaurant and visitor's center. The main attraction of course, being the Buffalo River, this would be a perfect trail to combine with a day of floating, and or a weekend of camping. Cabins ranging from rustic to more modern, are available April through November and reservations can be made by calling Buffalo Point Concessions at 501-449-6206.

TOPOGRAPHIC MAPS: Cozahome

Starting at the trailhead just past the visitor's center, the trail starts off on a nice easy widened path that descends a bit downhill. You will notice the nature trail side of this loop as signs labeling plants, flowers and trees appear periodically. The first real highlight however is the "Sinkhole Icebox" which lives up to its name most noticeably in the summertime when a nice blast of cool air contrasts the otherwise hot and muggy temperatures.

   From the Sinkhole Icebox the trail heads down a bit, veering left to descend more, and leading to a cool bluffline, creek and waterfall. This is a BTV, and just an awesome spot to hike through. Moving past the bluff, the trail grants you a first time glimpse of the beautiful little Panther Creek, as it creates a path that moves alongside it. Lining the creek are bluffs, hardwoods and

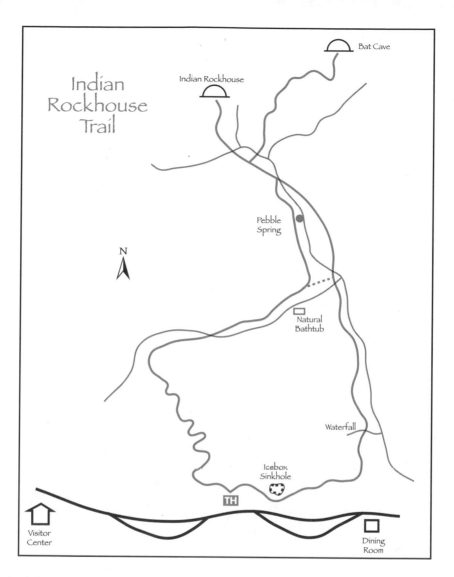

Indian
Rockhouse
Trail

Bat Cave

Indian Rockhouse

Pebble
Spring

N

Natural
Bathtub

Waterfall

Icebox
Sinkhole

TH

Visitor
Center

Dining
Room

rock slabs, making this Ozark mountain stream a mini BTV in and of itself. Follow this pleasant run of scenery as it takes you up to a small cave shooting off some of that "Sinkhole Icebox" air, and then to a road intersection. The main trail continues straight, but left gives the option of a shorter loop if desired.

Staying straight on the road, the trail takes you across the rock slab bottom of Panther Creek and then uphill to a flattened ridge where you can peer down at the fabulous water run to your left. There is another short-cut path on the left as well, offering another quick return home, if needed, otherwise continue on to the "Sculptured Bedrock", located on the trail's right. It is just after this that the trail crosses Panther Creek again and merges with the return route to your left. Don't take a left yet though, because the best is still yet to come.

As you continue straight, the trail is heading towards the actual "Indian Rockhouse" of this Indian Rockhouse Trail. Before arriving there however, it challenges you with the spur to the right, leading up (the key word here being, UP!) to Bat Cave. The hike up to the cave is definitely steep and rocky to say the least, and probably about a mile in length. If you're hiking during the summer, be prepared to appear is if swimming were the sport of the day when finished, not hiking! Bat Cave is pretty cool though; remote, nestled into the wooded hillside and huge. Walking up into it you will welcome the incredible blast of cool air that is like nature's own air conditioner housed within this rock mouth opening. Enjoy the break, and be careful coming back down as loose rock makes the return trip a bit difficult as well!

Back to the main trail to the Rockhouse. Stay straight at the Bat Cave turnoff (or turn right if coming down from Bat Cave), and you will cross Panther Creek once more before arrival. The Rockhouse is a sight to see! It is like a really cool cave, and then some—rock formations, cave formations, running water, and other geologic creations all wrapped up into one. Spend some time at this BTV, before heading back to the main loop.

The main loop and return trail is found by re-tracing steps back past the Bat Cave turn-off and turning right at the next intersection. (If you come to Panther Creek again, you went too far.) Turning right should put Panther Creek on the left as the trail follows alongside it to the next highlight of this giant trail scavenger hunt, Pebble Spring. A short path leading off to the left takes you directly to the spring which is another BTV and pleasant little area.

Moving on down, the trail will intersect and turn right as it proceeds to bring you back around the main loop. Watch the small stream on the trail's left as is contains the most unique feature of the "Natural Bathtub"—and yes, it really does look like an imbedded bathtub! A fabulous stream highlight for the scavenger hunt finale. After your bath, follow this little streambed to its crossing and the trail edges uphill just enough to prepare for the much steeper climb that lies ahead. Switchbacks assure you that the climb is now into full swing and a small spur trail left leads to an old quarry, if you're in for a side-trip. Continue right and uphill for trailhead destination, and soon things will level off again with the trail leading through two wooden gates on either side of a road crossing, and back to the trailhead.

Hiking Tip — Winter and Water

If you're extreme enough to find yourself out on the trail on one of those frigid cold nights, you might wake up to find water in your Nalgene bottle frozen. To eliminate this morning frustration try one of these tips:

- Purchase an insulated jacket for your bottle. You can usually find insulated covers made to fit the specific size bottle you have, and it might help keep water cooler during hotter summer hikes as well.
- Bring your water bottle in the tent with you and place it inside the bottom of your sleeping bag.
- Wrap your bottle in extra fleece or clothing and bury it in the middle of your pack.
- If the temperature isn't too awfully extreme, then simply turn your bottle upside down overnight so that any minor freezing occurs on the bottom end of you bottle, not the top.

73. Kings Bluff

LOCATION: Kings Bluff shares the trailhead with Pedestal Rocks and is located just east of Pelsor, off HWY 16. Take HWY 7 south from Jasper all the way to Hankins General Store where HWY 7, 16 and 123 all meet. Turn east down HWY 16 at this junction and travel 6 miles, looking for the sign (labeled for Pedestal Rocks) to the trailhead, which is located on the highway's right-hand side.

LENGTH: Kings Bluff is a two mile loop that possesses some side-trip exploration areas as well as a possible connection with Pedestal Rocks Trail to total almost five miles.

COMMENTS: Probably over shadowed a bit by the neighboring and more well known Pedestal Rocks, Kings Bluff is like a best kept secret or treasured find. A massive rock bluff that overlooks a deep hollow and winding creek bottom, Kings Bluff portrays a breathtaking view of the wilderness area beneath you. Highlighting this incredible sight even more is the presence of a 100 foot waterfall, residing on the bluff's western edge that spills over the rising rockwall into a shallow pool below. One of the tallest and most spectacular waterfalls in the area, this steep water drop adds the finishing touches in both sight and sound to the Kings Bluff area.

If you have the time while visiting this area, it is strongly suggested that you hike through Pedestal Rocks as well, a loop connection that can be added for another 2.6 miles. The trailhead shared between the two trails is designed for more day-use, possessing picnic tables and restrooms, but not campsites.

TOPOGRAPHIC MAPS: Mt. Judea and Parthenon

The trailhead for Kings Bluff starts at the signboard just past the restrooms. Sharing starting points with the Pedestal Rocks Loop, the trail heads off into the woods splitting immediately. The trail to the right is the option taken for this loop, and it leads slightly uphill along an older roadbed. Flattened out along this upper portion for a bit, the trail passes by a faint extension veering left, and then descends in the form of switchbacks, bringing you down to the hollow below. As you approach the creek running to your right, it appears that you have arrived at the bottom of a shallow wooded valley. It won't take long to discover your assumptive mistake however, as soon the trail exits out onto the rock platform of Kings Bluff. Opening up tremendous views directly in front of you, this bluffline is an awesome sight and very much a BTV! The creek that greeted you at the final switchback now spills over the edge to your

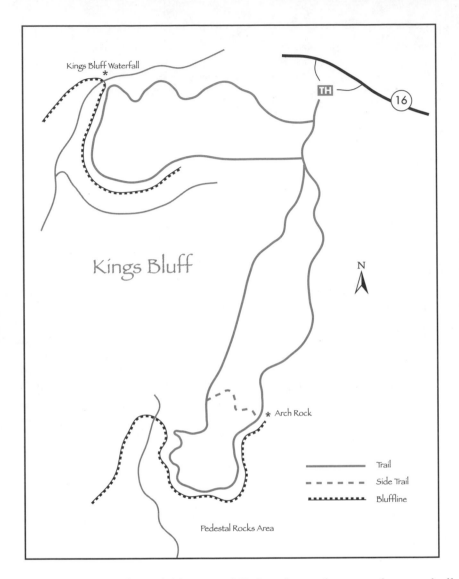

far right creating a formidable waterfall that drops down to the true hollow depths. Further right and back into the woods from the open rock platform, a faint trail leads all the way around the ridge that encircles part of this chasm. A delightful cascading creek moves down the steep ridge over here, and views of the waterfall drop from the opposite side are excellent as well.

Continuing on after much reflection and lots of camera shots, the main trail curves around this ridge to the left crossing a break in the bluffline. Just past this little curvature lies a path leading down off the main trail and into the hollow. Steep and rocky, this small side-trip is an exciting adventure as it leads to the base of the waterfall just viewed from above, other water creations, and a small little cave. In addition, the views from below back up are incredible, as Kings Bluff becomes even more impressive in scope and size.

Back to the main trail. Past the side path leading down into the hollow, the trail remains glued to the bluffline as it curves around away from the Kings Bluff area. Somewhat smaller in scale yet equally intriguing, this section of bluff is a small taste of Pedestal Rocks, possessing fragmented rock statues and twisted bases that appear to have a table perched on top. The extended views continue with the bluffline and the trail skirts around this edge until the mile and half mark. It is here that the trail winds with the curvature of a small ravine through a boulder-strewn area, and to an intersection with a sign at 1.9. To the left is the return route for the trailhead and parking lot. Options to the right and straight are the ones that begin and end the Pedestal Rocks Loop. Hiking this loop will add another 2.6 miles to your hike – a trip well worth taking if you have the time. For completion of the Kings Bluff Trail go left, and the trailhead area is one-tenth of a mile down.

Kings Bluff

74. Lost Valley

LOCATION: Lost Valley is found off HWY 43 in Arkansas just outside of Ponca, and before Boxley. HWY 43 can be accessed out of Harrison, Arkansas going south, and leads straight to Ponca.

LENGTH: Lost Valley is an out and back trail totaling 3.5 miles.

COMMENTS: If you've ever watched the old TV series way back entitled "Land of the Lost", that's what certain features of this truly enchanted trail will remind you of. With geologic treasures, rock formations, caves and natural arches all hidden within the corners of this short little hike, the Lost Valley Trail could not have been named more appropriately. Aside from the last steep trek that leads to a cave at the trail's end, this hike is relatively mild, and is ideal for just about anyone. Lost Valley also resides within the spectacular grounds of the beautiful Buffalo River, so hiking can be combined with some canoeing if desired.

The Lost Valley Campground, holding basic sites at the trailhead, is a perfect place for an overnight stay, making this an excellent trail and weekend choice for the family. Between boaters and hikers however, the campground fills up fast on spring and fall weekends, so claim your spot early should you wish to overnight it. Other campgrounds are available at nearby Kyles Landing and Steel Creek along the Buffalo, should you be SOL at Lost Valley.

TOPOGRAPHIC MAPS: Osage SW

The trail starts at the back of the campground where a bridge carries you over Clark Creek. Wide, flat and winding through a forest of large and old trees, the trail takes on an "afternoon stroll" type character that makes for a pleasant walk. The creek you just crossed now runs to your right and is a pleasant ripple of gently rolling water over smooth stones. Be prepared though, as its upper half holds some cool stuff! At approximately a half mile in or so, the trail will fork right and the action begins. Small side trails off to the right will lead to some spectacular sights: a natural bridge, giant bluffs, and the amazing Eden Falls. The first of these is the natural bridge. Off and to the right, this almost magical pool of clear blue water accompanied by a small pour over coming out from the rock, is like a mini version of some hidden tropical oasis, minus the palm trees. Further down and also to your right is a "doubly good" BTV, as a massive rock face and cave opening sets on one side, while a deep pool being filled by another tropical-looking waterfall sets on the other. The falls are actually a series of ledges that originate from the top where Eden Falls Cave resides.

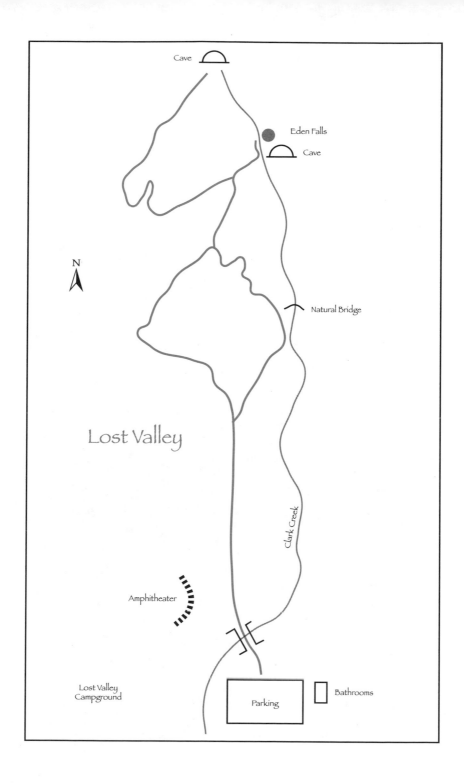

Cave

Eden Falls

Cave

N

Natural Bridge

Lost Valley

Clark Creek

Amphitheater

Lost Valley
Campground

Parking

Bathrooms

Following the trail up from the falls leads to Eden Falls Cave, as well as a splendid view of some of the deep valley below and towering rock walls across the way. The last part of the hike leading to the cave can be a bit steep and the trail rather narrow, so be careful and watch close if you're hiking with children. From inside this cave, housed high within the side of the bluff, Clark Creek originates. Gaining momentum from the elevation drops and rock formations situated below, it is from here that the creek graduates into the series of awesome water formations seen on your hike up. Take a breather, enjoy the view, and as you head back down from the cave, stay to the right and you will cover some new ground on your return hike.

Lost Valley

75. Pedestal Rocks

LOCATION: Pedestal Rocks is located just east of Pelsor, off HWY 16. Take HWY 7 south from Jasper all the way to Hankins General Store, where HWY 7, 16 and 123 all meet. Turn east down HWY 16 at this junction and travel 6 miles, looking for the sign to the trailhead, which is located on the highway's right-hand side.

LENGTH: The Pedestal Rocks Trail is a 2.6 mile loop that can be combined with the neighboring Kings Bluff Trail to total 4.6 miles.

COMMENTS: Nothing short of amazing, this little trail leading along a ridgetop of breathtaking views, offers panoramic scenery amidst the top of a most unusual bluffline. Pedestal Rocks is an incredible collection of creative rock formations, natural arches and broken bluff fragments that all combine to formulate a masterpiece of nature. The sandstone rock that this bluffline consists of twists and separates to create the most unique pattern of platform-like rocks, termed "pedestals" that are the theme and title for this trail. From the tops of these "pedestal rocks" the Arkansas floor drops, seemingly lost beneath you as a view of pristine wilderness extends out for miles. A BTV for the entire bluffline length, don't visit this place without your camera or without some time to appreciate the awesomeness of creation.

The 2 mile connecting loop of Kings Bluff can be added to this hike for a longer trek if desired. Fabulous in its own right, Kings River Bluff has a beauty all its own with outer portions of its extended bluffline resembling portions of Pedestal Rock. Both loops are fairly easy to hike, but require time to enjoy. The trailhead area is equipped with picnic tables and a restroom but is not an overnight camping place, so plan to spend the day.

TOPOGRAPHIC MAPS: Mt. Judea and Parthenon

A trailboard with a map and general information marks the starting point for either Kings Bluff or Pedestal Rocks. Heading almost due south, the Pedestal Rocks Trail will be the one taking off to the left or straight from this starting point. Nice and level, the trail moves through the woods for one-tenth of a mile, bringing you to a junction with three options. Right leads to Kings Bluff, while the options of straight ahead and left mark end points for the Pedestal Rocks Loop. We will proceed left, hiking this trail in a clockwise direction.

Turning left, the trail edges downhill slightly moving off the roadbed and into the woods. The trail is easy to follow and as it drops down to a leveled off point, it curves around with the ridge, crossing a couple of streams highlighted

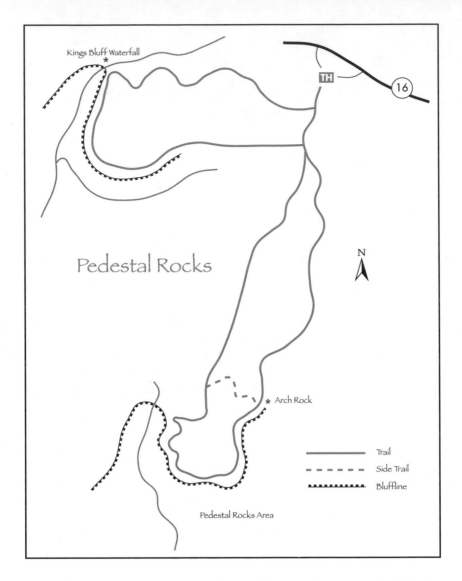

Kings Bluff Waterfall

TH

16

N

Pedestal Rocks

Arch Rock

Trail
Side Trail
Bluffline

Pedestal Rocks Area

with waterfalls during wetter months. Aside from these wonderful pleasant creeks and their accompanied water decor, the trail arrives at its first major highlight, Arch Rock. Looking much like boulders stacked together forming a tall tunnel through which you can easily walk through (maybe even drive through!), Arch Rock marks the beginning of the on-going and ever-increasing collection of prized rock formations typical of this trail. Just past the arch and through the woods, a trio of three isolated rock bluff pieces rise with the trees, and beyond these the bluffline commences. A continual BTV from this point on, every portion of the bluff holds a unique feature, and each rock possesses some sort of pedestal resemblance. A large rock slab resides at the portion where the trail curves around, and it is here that some spectacular views come into play. Stone steps beyond this flat rock platform lead down into the hollow and underneath the massive bluffs. The main trail however, stays on top, leading straight ahead past an old roadtrace and continuing along the ridge. The trademark pedestal of this trail sets at 1.5 miles in, rising out from one of the bluff extensions that lure you from the woods to the ridge's edge.

Take notice of the trail as you continue on from this point. Just beyond this main pedestal, the trail winds up the hillside to your right. A fainter trail continues around the ridge and ends shortly at a stream flowing down the hillside – a nice continuation of fabulous scenery, but the wrong route for trailhead return! The climb uphill from the bluffline intersects with a wider path that you will want to follow right. This old roadbed is the trail's path for the remainder of your hike. At 2.3 the loop is actually complete, as you are at the same four-way trail intersection that was encountered earlier. If you want, this is a good place to add a few more scenic miles of the Kings Bluff Trail, which would be the option to your left. The trailhead and return to the parking area, however, is one-tenth of a mile straight ahead.

Pedestal Rocks

76. Pigeon Roost Trail

LOCATION: The Pigeon Roost Trail is a part of Beaver Lake State Park and the Hobbs Management Area. From Eureka Springs Arkansas, take HWY 23 south for 12 miles, turning back west onto HWY 127. Look for HWY 12 almost immediately, taking it to the left towards Rogers, Arkansas. The trailhead and parking lot are off the road to your right, just before War Eagle Mill.

LENGTH: This trail is an 8.4 mile loop with a connector trail in the middle allowing for a shorter hike.

COMMENTS: If you've spent time in the past at some of Missouri's area lakes, you will greatly appreciate the beauty of Beaver Lake to which this trail backs up to. The undeveloped, remote nature of Beaver's shoreline, coupled with the pristine clear blue water quality expected more from a rocky mountain stream, makes this lake a best kept secret for water bums, birdwatchers and fishermen. Pigeon Roost skirts this lake only on its north side; however, a few nice rocky ledges are positioned here for a few moments of enjoyment, or 5 primitive campsites are also located in the area for backpacking and overnights. (Reservations for campsites need to be made in advance. Call 510-789-2380.) The trail is fairly easy to hike, can be completed in a day, and holds shortcut options for a smaller loop if desired. Neighboring War Eagle Mill is an excellent place to stop and visit before or after your hike, and of course, Eureka Springs deserves some exploration as well if you've not yet been.

TOPOGRAPHIC MAPS: War Eagle

The trail begins at the parking area's backside and takes off to the north, turning left off the roadbed that it initially shares at just under .5 miles. The intersection marking the beginning and completion of the entire loop comes shortly after, to which you will want to take a left. The trail does a bit of a zig-zag here as it rises and falls from creekbed and ravine, to ridgetop and hillside. Follow its path, and at 2.0 the trail meets up with an old roadbed. This is the optional shortcut that if taken right, will lead you to the trail's other side and back around for about a 4.3 mile total.

For continuing around the entire loop, stay straight, crossing the road while the trail hugs the side of the hill before dipping down and crossing a streambed. As you move back up towards the ridge, the trail will cross one old roadbed, and then follow another one as it flattens out on top. Keep track of the white blazes directing your path, and the trail will arrive at a cool little overlook that gives you a first time peak at Beaver Lake. Curving around right

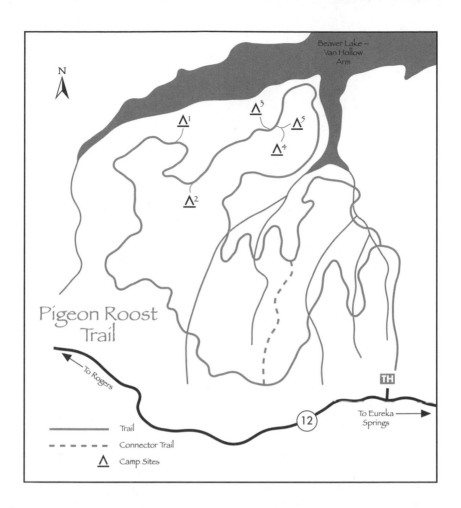

after this nice BTV, the trail then passes the first of the primitive campsite collection. Skirting by the other four as well, the trail then comes right to the lake's shoreline giving you a close up view of the gorgeous Beaver Lake water and its encircling shoreline. Back in a cove here, the water is still and the atmosphere quiet—an excellent stopping point.

Curving left and along another tiny finger of the lake, the trail moves upward along the side of and then into part of Pigeon Roost Hollow (hence the name if this trail). Look for a few sinkholes located on the trail's right-hand side as you are moving down from the ridge, heading for the streambed crossing below. Doing the "roller coaster" up and down again, the trail eventually arrives at the roadbed marking the shortcut trail at just around 6.5 miles. Stay to the left, actually on the old road for a bit, before dropping down again for another look at Beaver Lake. Take in what you can because the trail leaves the lake for good after this, following alongside, or rather along both sides, of a small stream feeding into the lake. The loop's completion is at just under 8 miles, where you will want to stay left and head uphill, back to the parking area.

77. Round Top Mountain

LOCATION: Round Top is located just outside of Jasper, Arkansas off Highway 7. From Jasper, which is 12 miles south of Harrison, take Highway 7 south 2 miles. Round Top is located on the west side of the road.

LENGTH: There are two trails here, a lower loop trail that extends around the mountain and then the ridge top trail that circles the mountain top's perimeter. These two loops together total about 4 miles in hiking length.

COMMENTS: A fairly recent hiking addition for the Arkansas area, Round Top trailhead and visitor's center was established in 1997. Although newly developed trail wise, Round Top has quite a historic background. The area was homesteaded in 1905 when a Polish immigrant who came to America to study medicine was accused of murdering a fellow physician. This accused immigrant, Mr. Iry Adles, fled to the safety and remoteness of this area where he practiced holistic medicine and apparently saved many lives. Found dead in 1920, it is supposed that Mr. Adles was bitten by a rattlesnake. Round Top was then returned back to property of the state and remained secluded and serene until 1948 when a B-52 Bomber crashed into the side of the mountain, killing all of its military passengers. A memorial marking the site still remains today, as does some of the debris and engine parts from the aircraft itself.

Currently owned and managed by the Newton County Resource Council, Round Top is a fabulous hiking area with a tremendous amount to offer in the way of widespread views, bluffs, cliffs, rock formations and interesting trees. Possessing the tranquility and remoteness of a backcountry setting as well as a powerful display of creation, this short hike carries you through an excellent piece of the Arkansas wilderness. The lower loop edges up against the stately bluffs forming the above trail, while the ridge top trail opens up a panoramic display of beauty allowing you gaze down at the vastness of remote countryside situated below. Aside from a hefty elevation changes between loops this trail is reasonable in terrain, length and difficulty for any level of hiking.

TOPOGRAPHIC MAPS: Jasper & Parthenon

The trail begins just to the back of the Visitor's Center and restrooms to head up in a northwesterly direction. Labeled as the Ray Crouse Trail, this first section of trekking takes you upwards and quickly passes by the first of many benches placed along portions of the trail for resting and relaxing purposes. Switchbacks and a natural rock staircase assist you in this initial trek upward. Take noticed of the prized Red Oak that stands situated between two benches

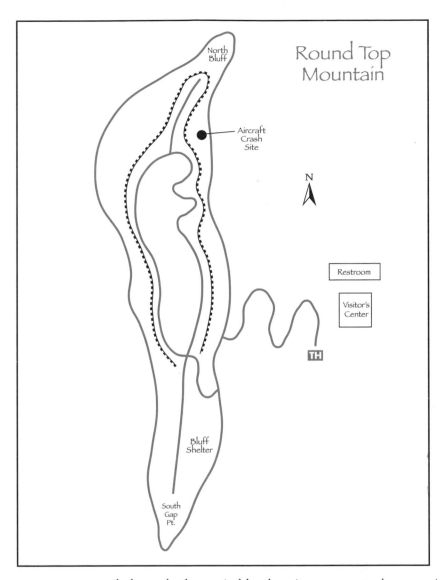

Round Top
Mountain

North
Bluff

Aircraft
Crash
Site

N

Restroom

Visitor's
Center

TH

Bluff
Shelter

South
Gap
Pt.

as you curve around through the switchbacks—it appears to be growing directly out of the rock! After passing this amazing Red Oak, you will have arrived at the trail's first fork. The crash site for the B-52 Bomber lies down the trail on to your right about a quarter of a mile. To your left is junction taking you up to Round Top Mountain. Either direction is fine as this is the lower loop beginning point. You haven't come very far at this point, but the picturesque nature of this area is already established as bluffs, views and rock outcroppings all join together in forming an unbelievable atmosphere.

Taking a right at this fork leads you towards the crash site and along the immense bluffline that accompanies you on your left. Some beautiful views open up in spots along this route that are especially breathtaking in late fall and winter when leaves from the thick stand of trees are absent. The crash site location is evident as a stone memorial commemorating the date and passengers killed lies just off the trail, as do a few remaining engine parts and various other debris. After a few moments of exploring and studying this historic spot along your hike, the trail moves on and brings you to a fabulous SOS overlooking miles of Arkansas territory in what is known as the "Grand Canyon of the Ozarks". Definitely a photography masterpiece, this open view is unbelievable. Follow the trail onward as it passes by several labeled trees, one of which is a large Sugar Maple—a popular tree for Arkansas, hence all the maple syrup for sale in the many little tourist shops situated along those twisty Arkansas roads.

Views that definitely qualify as SOS's continue all along this route with various spots providing benches to sit down on for a moment so that you can enjoy the awesome sights before you. Take in all you can as the hiking continues, marveling at the bluffs and overlooks that seem to be the norm for this trail. As you curve around the bend on the trail's south side and into the massive "bluff shelter" area, another interesting site comes into play—an Indian burial site. The caves within these bluffs alongside the trail were at one time homes for Indian cliff dwellers whose past are marked by this spot. Boulders and rocks immense in size and striking in setting scatter themselves within this area, definitely giving hint to an Indian dwelling place at one time.

Just past this point comes another trail fork. Left leads up another rock staircase to the actual Round Top Mountain, while right finishes out the lower loop and returns to your starting point. Take a left here and proceed up. At the top, several trail markers indicate your whereabouts. Left is an out and back route leading to an overlook and highpoint known as South Gap Point, while right is the loop and higher elevated site of North Bluff and Round Top. Straight across is the West Trail which also formulates part of the loop that encircles this upper ridge. Proceed left for the side trip to South Gap scenic point and you will be rewarded by another breathtaking SOS scene from atop a large rock outcropping hosting several trees growing from it, as well as a split rail fence guarding you from the edge. Return to the main upper ridge loop staying straight at the earlier described intersection so as to make your way towards Round Top. Located at the center on the ridge, Round Top is definitely a highpoint for the area elevation wise. With surrounding area vegetation so thick, views from this point are actually better during leaf-off, although the area is beautiful all year round. A series of switchbacks take you down from Round Top to an intersection where another side trip leading to the North Bluff sets. Again, the view is spectacular, and the small climb upon arrival well worth it! You are almost above the crash site from the trail below, and the entire Arkansas valley and canyon area are opened up below you—an absolutely awesome SOS! Heading back down the spur to the previous intersection, stay right for the West Trail which continues around the mountain's ridge carrying on this trail's character of fabulous views and striking scenery. You can see the Little Buffalo River below as the trail winds through pines and rocks carrying you across the ridge. Eventually this West Trail loops around to the four-way intersection that you came upon initially as you arrived at the top of this ridge. Continue straight and head back down turning left at the next intersection that leads back to the completion of lower loop. The end of the loop terminates and you will want to swing right taking you back to the trailhead and your vehicle.

78. Shores Lake Trail

LOCATION: Shores Lake starts at White Rock Mountain. From HWY 23 at the town of Cass near the Mulberry River, go west on FR #1501 which is gravel. (Be prepared for about 16 miles worth of gravel!) Follow 1501 (you'll have to decipher its direction as you come upon forks in the road) to Shores Lake where it will graduate into some pavement for a short bit. Turn right onto FR #1505 (also known as CR#75) and continue past the lake area, back to the gravel road and up to FR #1003. Turn left at FR #1003 and then right again back onto FR #1505. Staying right at the next intersection will lead you to the White Rock Mountain entrance.

LENGTH: Shores Lake is a 14.5 mile loop. If you have shuttle options however, you can hike just from White Rock Mountain down, reducing the length to 8 miles.

COMMENTS: Shores Lake is a popular recreation area for Arkansas residents and is a beautiful spot to spend time swimming, fishing, picnicking, and of course, hiking. The climb from Shores Lake covers some 1700 feet in elevation gain and therefore can be a tough hike. Starting from White Rock to end at Shores Lake however, is the easiest option and shuttle service can usually be found from Paula at White Rock for a small fee (501-369-4128). The most ideal option for a memorable weekend is to reserve one of the rustic cabins available at White Rock, stay for a couple nights and take time to enjoy two or three full days of White Rock, Shores Lake and the surrounding area.

The eight mile trail down to the lake is pleasant in both scenery and terrain. Not as strenuous as the upward trek, this hike travels along some ridges that afford some excellent views, crosses a few creeks that might display some waterfalls during wet months, and winds through miles of beautiful timber, housing some huge trees and a few nice sized boulders as well.

TOPOGRAPHIC MAPS: Bidville

Starting from White Rock Mountain to head down to Shores Lake, you will begin at the end of the road leading down past White Rock's lodge and cabins. Start this hike on the same path as the White Rock Mountain Rim Loop Trail, turning right at the second intersection of that trail's beginning. You are on a spur trail marked with blue blazes that is leading down to connect with the Ozark Highlands Trail. As the trail winds rather quickly down a rocky path, it hangs a left to level off, taking you alongside and almost underneath a portion of White Rock's huge bluffline. An Ozark Highlands Trail register box is situ-

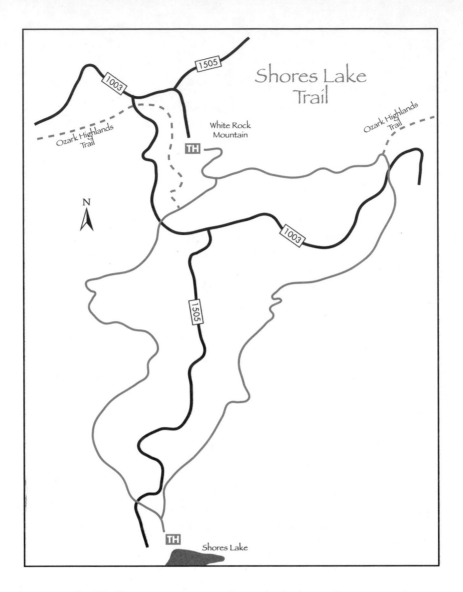

White Rock
Mountain

TH

Ozark Highlands
Trail

Ozark Highlands
Trail

1003

1505

1003

N

1505

TH

Shores Lake

ated just on the bluffline's opposite end to which the trail passes and continues downhill as you proceed to the left. (Turning right takes you down to Shores Lake as well, but is the western half of this loop.) Follow the white blazes now and as the downhill begins to flatten, the trail will widen, and an intersection indicating the splitting of the Shores Lake Trail from the Highlands Trail arises (about the 2 mile mark). Proceed right and you are officially on the eastern side of the Shores Lake loop.

Remaining somewhat level for a bit, the trail crosses FR #1003, continuing on straight across. Views of the surrounding area begin to open up here, creating some mini BTV's for the next 2 miles. To your left the terrain drops down into the hollow through which Salt Fork Creek runs and during leaf-off periods you might catch glimpses of the ridge rising back up on the hollow's opposite side. As the elevation drops just a bit, the trail dips down to cross a very pleasant little creek that feeds into Salt Fork and then joins an old roadbed to your left. Follow this road for about a half mile or less where the trail's continuation heads left again, off the road and alongside a bit of a ridge. For the next mile and a half, as the trail levels off, glimpses through trees reveal some awesome views, creating a few more BTV's and continued pleasant hiking. As you approach the Shores Lake end, just before dropping down, the trail passes through a few boulder strewn areas mixed within a setting of some veteran trees, noteworthy in size. The trail intersection at the base of the last small descent is the junction of the loop trail. Left will take you to the actual Shores Lake trailhead, while right continues back up to White Rock Mountain via the loop's western half.

White Rock Mountain — High point of the Shores Lake Loop

79. White Rock Mountain

LOCATION: This is not an easy place to get to, but that's what makes it so cool! From HWY 23 at the town of Cass near the Mulberry River, go west on FR #1501 which is gravel. (Be prepared for about 16 miles worth of gravel!) Follow 1501 (you'll have to decipher its direction as you come upon forks in the road) to Shores Lake where it will graduate into some pavement for a short bit. Turn right onto FR #1505 (also known as CR#75) and continue past the lake area, back to the gravel road and up to FR #1003. Turn left at FR #1003 and then right again back onto FR #1505. Staying right at the next intersection will lead you to the White Rock Mountain entrance.

LENGTH: The trail here is a two mile loop. White Rock also serves as a trailhead for a section of the Ozark Highlands Trail, as well as the Shores Lake Trail.

COMMENTS: White Rock can easily hold its own against any western mountain range scene, or eastern Appalachian Trail highlight. There is not a single spot along this two mile trail that boasts of anything less than an absolutely breathtaking scene. A trail that literally loops around the entire rim edge of this mountain, White Rock claims beautiful sunrises as well as spectacular sunsets, opens up views extending for miles, and outlines beautifully carved rock formations hidden within it's bluffs. Truly a hidden jewel of Arkansas, White Rock Mountain is unmatched in setting, and should be a definite vacation highlight should you ever venture down into this part of the country.

Containing three rustic cabins and a lodge built by the Corps in the 1930's, White Rock provides the perfect setting for a rugged, and totally relaxing weekend. The cabins run about $50 per night and can be reserved by calling Paula at (501) 369-4128. There are also places for primitive camping. This is a relatively flat and easy trail to hike, although open ledges are everywhere, so be super cautious, and keep a tight rein on any children that might be hiking with you. The journey down 16 miles of somewhat confusing gravel roads is a journey in itself, but for the hikers that seek true remoteness, this is it!

TOPOGRAPHIC MAPS: Bidville

The Rim Loop Trail begins at the end of the gravel road that leads past the lodge and three rustic cabins. Heading out to a point, stay straight as the trail merges with two others coming in from your right. First, the continuation of the loop, and second, the Ozark Highlands Trail. Stay on the main path, which is Rim Loop and you will soon come to a sort of point, which is the beginning of the ongoing, ever-increasing, amazing views that characterize this entire trail.

Curving left, the trail skirts right along the ledge, offering not only spectacular views through the trees but also remarkable peeks of giant sandstone rocks, forming bluffs as they rise to create the platform upon which you are walking. Continue following the trail around and you will arrive at one of the rock pavilions residing along this trail. Located almost at the one mile mark, and facing northeast, this is a beautiful place to watch and shoot photos of the sunrise. Past this shelter and looping around, the trail will cross the road that leads to White Rock's entrance to continue straight across. Residing along the west portion of White Rock now, the trail continues around the bluff, extending more excellent views, including a glimpse of the next pavilion that sets out upon the portion of the bluff extending out to a point. As you approach this pavilion you arrive at one of the most gorgeous places along this trail, and a fabulous spot to watch the sunset. This is also the spot most accessible from the White Rock parking area, and thus a popular area for those sightseeing and picnicking. Follow along past this pavilion and the trail loops around behind the old lodge, the cabins and back to the final pavilion and trail's end.

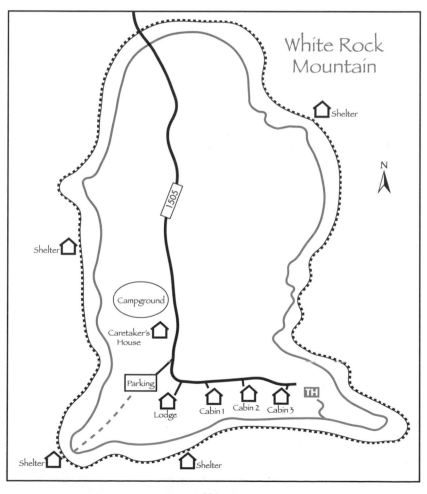

Hiking Tip — Leave No Trace

The best backpackers leave their locations of camp untouched so that future hikers passing through will not have noticed the fact that someone had stayed there. "Leaving no trace" means precisely that – leaving no trace of your stay. This theory is what preserves the wilderness, and maintains an areas natural pristine state. When practicing leave not trace camping, here are a few tips:

- Know the area you are visiting and any special concerns associated with it.
- When hiking, stay on the designated trail and don't shortcut on switch-backs.
- When choosing a campsite pick an established legal site that will not be damaged by your stay.
- Camp at least 200 feet from any water source.
- If you haven't eaten it, pack out everything you packed in.
- Where fires are permitted, use established fire rings and do not leave unburned trash in ring.
- If no fire ring exists and a fire is necessary, build a small fire without building a ring, blackening large stones and logs, or breaking branches off trees. Scatter ashes out over a large area after fire is completely cool.
- Latrine use should be at least 200 feet away for any water source, should be deposited into a 6 to 8 inch hole and covered in such a way as not to be noticed. If toilet paper is a must, then use sparingly and burn before burying.
- Upon leaving, inspect your campsite for trash and/or any evidence of your stay.